MW00333656

HOT GOALIES

Stan Fischler
with Chico Resch

Warwick Publishing
Toronto Los Angeles

© 1997 Stan Fischler, Glenn Resch

All rights reserved. No part of this book may be reproduced or transmitted in any form, including photocopying, recording in any audio/visual format, or by any information storage and retrieval system without the written permission of the publisher.

Published by Warwick Publishing Inc.
388 King Street, West, Suite 111, Toronto, Ontario M5V 1K2
1424 North Highland Avenue, Los Angeles, CA 90027

ISBN: 1-895629-96-9

Front cover photograph: Dan Hamilton, Vantage Point Studios
Photographs of Johnny Bower, Terry Sawchuk and Glenn Hall: The Harold Barkley Archives
Photographs of Ken Dryden, Jacques Plante and Roy Worters: The Fischler Archives
Photographs of Martin Brodeur, Patrick Roy, Dominik Hasek and Grant Fuhr: Dan Hamilton, Vantage Point Studios
Design: Kimberley Young, Mercer Digital Design
Editorial Services: Harry Endrulat

Distributed in the United States and Canada by Firefly Books Ltd.
3680 Victoria Park Avenue, Willowdale, Ontario M2H 3K1

Printed and bound in Canada.

To every goaltender who fueled the fires of our passion: Turk Broda, Al Rollins, Nick Pidsdony, Glenn Hall, Muzz Murray, Martin Brodeur, Bill Smith, Chico Resch, Kelly Hrudey, Sean Burke, Frankie Brimsek and Moe Roberts. Just to name a few. S.F.

One night on Long Island our six year old daughter, my wife, and I were walking into the rink for a game. As I was leaving them at the door to the wives' room, I bent down to give my daughter a kiss and tell her I'd see her after the game. I looked at her and told her that I'd win the game that night just for her. Her big, brown eyes stared back at me and she said, "maybe you will and maybe you won't, but I love you Daddy." I've never forgotten those words. I have the utmost regard for the women of hockey. It is to them for their steadfast support that I dedicate this book. G.R.

Table of Contents

Today's Stars

Patrick Roy

Dominik Hasek

Mike Richter

Martin Brodeur

John Vanbiesbrouck

Curtis Joseph

Grant Fuhr

Felix Potvin

Nikolai Khabibulin

Ed Belfour

Sean Burke

Andy Moog

Jim Carey

Guy Hebert

Bill Ranford

Mike Vernon

Ron Hextall

Kirk McLean

Daren Puppa

Ken Wregget

Jeff Hackett

Trevor Kidd

Jocelyn Thibault

Stephane Fiset

Ron Tugnutt

Tommy Salo

The authors' original aim was to cover every aspect of each goaltender who played in the NHL during the 1996-1997 season.

Ambitious though it was, our plan exceeded the limitations of space and ultimately was not possible to achieve within the confines of these pages.

Our more realistic goal, therefore, was to examine as many different types of netminders as possible — in terms of style, age and performance.

We determined that at least one starting goalie from each of the 26 teams would be covered and that target was reached.

Unfortunately, in the process we were compelled to omit competitors we otherwise would have wanted to include.

For example, we have unbound admiration for performers such as Glenn Healy who had been Mike Richter's understudy on the Rangers from 1993-1994 through 1996-1997.

We would have liked to profile "Heals" as well as the other worthies like Rick Tabaracci, Chris Osgood, Garth Snow, Olaf Kolzig, Damian Rhodes and Mark Fitzpatrick, just to name a few.

We enjoy watching each and every one of them for a number of reasons. And if their omission hurts any feelings, we apologize.

This was one "save" we could not make!

PATRICK ROY

"I have the love to win. I hate to lose.
Maybe it's more than the hate to lose than the love to win".

Is he the best goaltender of the past decade?

Patrick Roy certainly has compelling credentials. He has won two Stanley Cups with the Montreal Canadiens and one for the Colorado Avalanche.

He has won three Vezina Trophies as the National Hockey League's best goaltender and annexed the Jennings Trophy no less than four times.

There are some who insist that Roy is a team-maker or team-breaker, as the case may be. After all, he did orchestrate Les Canadiens' 1993 Stanley Cup triumph with no less than 10 sudden-death overtime triumphs. And after he exited Montreal under a hail of controversy, the Habs began a nosedive that culminated with a five-game playoff defeat in 1997 that was squarely the fault of inadequate goaltending.

Prior to Roy's ascent with the Avalanche, the franchise had never come remotely close to winning a championship. With Patrick in the crease, the 1996 march to Lord Stanley's mug seemed ridiculously simple. Add to that the two Conn Smythe Trophies which he collected as the playoffs' most valuable player, and it becomes apparent why the native of Quebec City has become a legend of the pipes.

"I have the love to win," Roy succinctly explains. "I hate to lose. Maybe it's more the hate to lose than the love to win."

Whatever it is, Roy is what he is in part because of Francois Allaire, who shaped his style and psyche as the goaltending coach in Montreal. Allaire, who has since moved on to teach goaltending for the Mighty Ducks asserts that Roy is to the playoffs what Reggie Jackson was to the World Series. The bigger the game, the better the performance.

"A guy can be the best quarterback, but if he never wins the Super Bowl, for the people it's not the same," says Allaire. "You have to win the ultimate. All the great athletes understand that out of instinct."

Instinctively or otherwise, Roy has been a compelling figure ever since his first major triumph in 1985 as a rookie wearing the *bleu, blanc et rouge*. Facing the favored New York Rangers in the playoffs, Roy suggested a nervous figure on the verge of a breakdown as the Broadway Blueshirts fired volley after volley at him.

Even more arresting was Patrick's habit of violently jerking his head back and forth in grotesque shakes while he awaited a face-off. It appeared to some that he was just one misstep away from a breakdown that would once and for all abort his career before it ever really got off the launching pad.

The shakes notwithstanding, he survived the Rangers series, not to mention the finals and became the youngest NHL player to win the Smythe. "It was the best goaltending we had since I came to Montreal," said veteran Habs defenseman Larry Robinson at the time.

Roy's most impressive performance was delivered in Game Three at Madison Square

Garden. The assaulting Rangers poured 47 shots at him over three periods and 13 more in overtime before Claude Lemieux scored the winner. Veteran Canadiens such as Bob Gainey couldn't help comparing Roy to Hall of Famer Ken Dryden, Montreal's goaltending ace of the 1970s.

"Dryden would keep us in a lot of games for the first period," said Gainey, "and that allowed us to regroup. But Roy was under a barrage from the opening face-off and it never let up. I've never seen a goalie play a game like he did against the Rangers in the playoffs."

Although it was too soon to forecast at the time, Montreal's — and, more specifically, Roy's — victory over Calgary in the 1986 Stanley Cup Finals was both symbolic for Patrick as well as a portent of things to come for the young goaltender. If nothing else, his *clutchability* demonstrated that when the playoff chips were on the line, his goaltending improved.

"Playoffs is not a matter of money," says Roy. "It's a matter of pride. I'm a person with a lot of pride. I love to do well. We play for money during the season but during the playoffs, we don't make a quarter of what we make during the season.

"Winning the Stanley Cup is something you never forget in your life. It is something you go to the Hall of Fame one day with your little boy and say, 'Hey, look, this is what happened in my career.' It's more a matter of pride than being a money guy."

Whatever it is — or was — Roy established himself as a competent first-string goalie after that first Stanley Cup win, although he would not drink champagne from the silver mug again until 1993 when the Habs appeared to be no more than a middle-of-the-road sextet with scant hopes of deposing Pittsburgh as champions.

By this time, a shadow of doubt had beclouded Roy's reputation. His play had been substandard during the 1992 playoffs, and his regular season mark wasn't any bargain either. Even the fans were turning against him. A poll conducted by one newspaper concluded that Roy should be traded. When the Habs — and Roy — dropped the first two games of their opening round challenge against the Quebec Nordiques, critics expected Coach Jacques Demers to replace Roy with young, inexperienced Andre Racicot.

Demers resisted the temptation and Roy justified the move by returning to form and knocking Quebec right out of the first round. "Demers always believed in me," says Roy. "I had a lot of critics. If we had lost to Quebec in the first round it would have been a long, bad summer, and probably Patrick Roy would have been part of some trade."

But fate intervened on Montreal's behalf as the Habs progressed through the playoffs. For starters, the Penguins were upset by the New York Islanders who then collided with Les Canadiens in the third playoff round. By this time the New Yorkers were battered with injuries and utterly fatigued.

Roy guided the Habs to a five-game win over the Islanders that was considerably more difficult than it appeared on paper. Two of the games were long-distance sudden-death affairs in which Saint Patrick was compelled to defuse both the explosive Benoit Hogue and Pierre Turgeon on breakaways.

"I didn't mind going into overtime," says Roy. "I knew my teammates were going to score if I gave them some time. My concentration was at such a high level. My mind was right there. I felt fresh, like I could stop everything."

The irony of ironies was that Islanders Hall of Famer — and Montreal native — Mike Bossy was the instructor who tipped off Roy on the secret of stopping a one-on-one.

"Mike told me that I had to protect the 'five-hole' because if a guy has to go top shelf he misses the net most of the time."

Remarkably, that playoff series was significant for Roy's record-tying 11 straight playoff victories of which seven came in overtime. For those who prefer Alfred Hitchcock scenarios, the Islanders series merely set the stage for a melodramatic Cup Final between Montreal and the Los Angeles Kings, whose captain just happened to be Wayne Gretzky.

The Habs lost Game One at Montreal's Forum and Roy pointedly accused his teammates of falling in love with their press clippings. "When everyone is telling you how great you are doing, you start to believe it," he warned.

Following the game, Roy drove his wife, Michele, to the hospital where she gave birth to the couple's third child, Jana. Patrick remained with Michele to coach her through the delivery.

Defeating Los Angeles was a bit more difficult. Down by a game, the Habs appeared on the verge of losing the second match, also at The Forum. Trailing by a goal as the third period wound down to its conclusion, the Habs pulled a desperate ploy. Coach Jacques Demers called for a measurement of Kings defenseman Marty McSorley's stick. Sure enough, it was illegal, and Montreal went on the power play.

Defenseman Eric Desjardins tied the score, sending the game into sudden-death overtime. While Roy held the fort, Desjardins delivered the winner, and the series was tied at one. Montreal then captured Game Three at the Great Western Forum in Inglewood, California, also in overtime.

In Game Four, Roy demonstrated a side of him that both enrages and engages fans, depending on how they view the goaltender. Late in the overtime, as the Kings desperately attempted to put the winner past Patrick and tie the series, Kings sharpshooter Luc Robitaille seemed to have the game-breaker on his stick but was thwarted by Roy, who then froze the puck and looked up at another enemy forward, Tomas Sandstrom. As the television cameras zeroed in on the goaltender, Roy winked as if to suggest that if the Kings thought they would penetrate him, they were just wasting their time.

Viewers throughout North America were repeatedly shown the Roy wink on replays and soon the switchboards were alight with both commendation and condemnation. Critics believed that Roy was being unnecessarily cocky, while supporters claimed it merely was the reflection of a confident man.

"The puck looked as big to him as a manhole cover," said *Sports Illustrated*.

Roy explained his actions: "Sandstrom was always in my crease, bothering me, hitting at me when I had the puck. When I made the save on Robitaille, Sandstrom hit at me again. So I winked. I wanted to show him I'd be tough; that I was in control."

It would be difficult for any goaltender to be in better control. Roy won that particular overtime game, finishing the playoffs with ten consecutive victories in the Canadiens' 1993 postseason run for their 24th Stanley Cup. Considering that Roy came close to being replaced by a no-name after the first-round losses to Quebec, his return to form was all the more amazing.

"Roy's struggles were new to him," recalls former teammate Kirk Muller. "Montreal fans expected a lot from him to the point where he couldn't really have a bad game — ever. As a result, the struggle he had made him a better goaltender and pushed him to a new level."

Roy's style, the butterfly, was honed to sharpness by his goaltending coach, Allaire. Originally conceived by Hall of Famer Glenn Hall in the late 1950s, the butterfly — or inverted V formation — became more popular in the 1980s and into the 1990s by which time it became the standard operating procedure for puckstoppers.

"It came about," says Allaire, "because nowadays players don't have two or three seconds to shoot, and to score up top. First you have to see a good spot, then you have to reach it. The shooters are under too much pressure most of the time to do that. That's why the bottom of the net is so important for the goalie."

Not only was Roy perfecting the butterfly he also was inspiring a legion of young Francophones who chose to ape their Montreal hero. "Patrick had become a superstar in the province of Quebec," Allaire recalls. "As a result, all of the good athletes decided that they wanted to be goaltenders. Because of that, there's going to be a big generation of them coming from the
province in the next few years."

Roy's popularity seemed assured in Montreal as long as two demands were satisfied: (1) He had to continue to maintain a high goaltending standard, and (2) he had to have a coach who both understood and tolerated Patrick's idiosyncrasies.

Like many goaltenders, Roy suffered through superstitions, periods of depression, and uncertainty. But he also developed enormous confidence over the years and attained a level of adulation in French Canada that won him the nickname Saint Patrick. Some in the media regarded the goaltender with something amounting to sainthood. Others in management felt likewise and rewarded Roy with a team-high $2.8 million salary.

However, Mario Tremblay was not among them.

Once a hard-nosed forward on Montreal's Cup-winning teams in the late 1970s, Tremblay actually was Roy's roommate when Patrick was a Canadiens rookie. Before becoming the Habs coach early in the 1995-96 season, Tremblay had been a sportscaster who was not averse to criticizing Roy.

When Tremblay moved behind the Canadiens bench, his treatment of Roy was significantly harsher than that of his predecessor Jacques Demers. Under Demers' reign, Roy was allowed to criticize teammates and act as a coach-without-portfolio. Under Tremblay, Roy was merely one of 20 hockey players. Take it or leave it.

Roy took it — under protest — until a game against the Detroit Red Wings at The Forum. To say the least, the Montreal goaltender looked awful. He allowed five goals in the first period and two more in the first five minutes of the middle period. By now, the Forum faithful had turned conspicuously unfaithful. When Roy made a relatively easy save, the crowd cheered sarcastically, prompting Patrick to return the insult by mockingly lifting his arms in the air.

If the embarrassed goaltender had expected his coach to relieve him from his misery, he was sadly mistaken. Tremblay compelled Roy to stay between the pipes until the score was 9-1 with eight minutes remaining. The coach finally signalled a change whereupon Roy skated to the bench, and removed his mask.

But the goalie was finished. As he walked past Tremblay, Roy glared at his coach, who promptly returned the favor. "If looks could kill," commented *Sports Illustrated*, "there would have been a double murder."

Roy knew that Canadiens president — and ardent fan — Ronald Corey was sitting directly behind the bench. Suddenly, the goaltender left his position on the backup goalie's wooden stool and walked past Tremblay again to Corey. Without hesitation, he told the president, "This is my last game for Montreal!"

He then passed Tremblay a third time and barked in their native French, "T'as compris, 'stie [Did'ya understand, dammit?]" After the period ended, they resumed their shouting in the clubhouse.

Long after the game the bitterness seemed to grow in its intensity. Canadiens rookie general manager Rejean Houle was confronted with an excruciating decision — should he favor his goalie over his coach? For Houle, it was a no-brainer. A day after the incident, Houle revealed that Roy not only had been suspended but would be dealt.

"I was brought up on the Montreal Canadiens with big stars like Jean Beliveau, Henri Richard, Bob Gainey, Guy Lafleur, and never once did I feel those guys asked for or got special treatment," said Houle. "Nobody is more important than the team." Houle underlined his point by dealing Roy to the Colorado Avalanche on December 6, 1995, with Canadiens captain Mike Keane for 20-year-old goalie Jocelyn Thibault and forwards Andrei Kovalenko and Martin Rucinsky.

Roy's debut in Denver hardly was auspicious. He lost, 5-3, to the Edmonton Oilers at McNichols Arena, which was 1,000 short of capacity. He knew he was off his game and apologized to Coach Marc Crawford after it was over. Some of his former mentors were sympathetic, among them Canadiens assistant coach Steve Shutt.

"For ten years Patrick not only had to carry a team but the province," said Shutt. "Now he goes to Colorado, and all he has to do is stop the puck. That's the best thing that's happened to him."

In a sense it was.

Once Roy acclimatized himself to life in the Rocky Mountains and his new team, Patrick and the Avalanche began a relentless march to the playoffs. Once there, they established themselves as solid contenders after easily defeating Vancouver in the first round.

By this time, Roy had regained the swagger that had been so much a part of his character when he was a winner in Montreal. During a second round verbal joust with then Blackhawks ace Jeremy Roenick, Roy delivered the perfect squelch, saying he couldn't understand Roenick's jibes because he had his two Stanley Cup rings filling his ears. (Roenick has never played on an NHL championship team.)

That Roy would even think about mouthing off with a swift-talker like Roenick speaks volumes about the goaltender's confidence. "Patrick is mentally strong," says Avalanche goalie coach Jacques Cloutier. "Playing 10 years for Montreal, you had better be mentally strong."

During the third-round bloodbath with the Detroit Red Wings, Roy was physically strong as well, occasionally swinging his stick like Paul Bunyan felling trees. In one nationally televised episode, he whacked Dino Ciccarelli so hard, the Red Wing disturber collapsed in front of the Colorado net. And Roy escaped without a penalty!

After disposing of Detroit, Colorado marched through Florida in four straight games and won the franchise's first Stanley Cup. Patrick allowed only four goals in four games. "When I get into the playoffs," Roy explains, "I'm facing one team for a whole series, and

it's a lot easier for me to concentrate, knowing the team. I play better knowing the players on the other team.

"It was important for me to show the people in Denver that I could do well in the playoffs, but also to show the people in Montreal who had given up on me and also the people around the league who believed that maybe the best was behind me."

Roy continued his stellar play in Denver during 1996-97, a season during which the Avalanche suffered an inordinate number of injuries. "He was our superstar," recalls coach Marc Crawford.

The 1997 playoffs would be yet another test for Roy. He out-played Chicago's Jeff Hackett in the first round, during which the champions won four games to two. He then bested Edmonton's Curtis Joseph in a five-game second round which was anti-climactic compared with the Conference Finals that pitted Colorado against Detroit.

More specifically, Patrick Roy vs. Mike Vernon.

"When I came to Colorado," said Roy, "I had two Stanley Cups. Then, I got a third in 1996 and began thinking about the fourth."

Detroit would be a formidable obstacle for Roy and his Avalanche.

DOMINIK HASEK

"When I was young, I didn't walk the right way. My back was bent. They recommended exercises and I exercised every day with my mother to keep my spine straight."

It was easier to say in January 1997 that Dominik Hasek was the best goalie in the world than it was six months later when the Buffalo Sabres he was awarded the Vezina Trophy for the third time.

Something happened to the Czech-born Hasek that remains a mystery and could remain a one long after Dominik retires from his anxiety-ridden profession. The "happening" evolved as deliberately and mysteriously as an Alfred Hitchcock thriller and eventually emerged as the detonator of explosions both in and out of the Sabres dressing room and front office.

When the smoke had cleared, this much was known: Hasek was still regarded by many as the National Hockey League's best at what he does, but a cloud of doubt had appeared that would shroud his reputation long after the controversial 1997 playoffs had ended.

Had Dominik quit on his teammates?

Why did he assault a distinguished member of the Buffalo media?

Did the goaltender and Coach Ted Nolan suffer an irreparable rift?

Could he return to the Sabres in 1997-98 and still be effective?

These were some of the questions raised in the wake of Buffalo's strangest postseason in the club's 27-year history.

There was, however, no question about Hasek's previous accomplishments which placed him — along with Mike Richter, John Vanbiesbrouck, et al. — in the top rung among major league goaltenders. The difference between Hasek and the others is that he was a late discovery. Very late.

He played for the Blackhawks under Mike Keenan but was relegated to second fiddle behind Ed Belfour. Keenan thought so little of his Czech stopper that Hasek was allowed to move on to Buffalo in August 1992.

Then Sabres GM John Muckler perceived the genius in Hasek that eluded the gaze of the Blackhawks brass. "Dominik is a great student of the game," says Muckler. "He's just as intense when he's not playing as when he is playing. Some goalies relax when they're on the bench, but he always looks at who's out there and how they do what they do. That's what helped him make the transition from European hockey, which is very different. "

Actually, Hasek's Buffalo debut in 1992 was less than awesome. Even he admits that. "I was too anxious. I was pushing too hard. Then, as I was coming into my own, I got hurt. I was out for 24 days. The night before I was due back, I turned on the radio and heard that the Sabres had traded for Grant Fuhr. Right away I knew that I was a backup goalie again."

But not for long. Fuhr suffered a knee injury that sidelined him in November 1992. Hasek seized the moment — and the opportunity. He literally dazzled Buffalo fans with his footwork and his élan. At times he seemed like a man possessed, sometimes wander-

ing far out of his net to field errant pucks. Occasionally, he would even comport himself as a "third defenseman," challenging the enemy as they skated over the blue line.

"I had noticed earlier that when there was a breakaway, the forward was usually sprung by a hard pass or a blocked shot. Either way, there was a couple of seconds when he was looking down at the bouncing puck, trying to get it under control. That's when I have to hit him. By the time he looks up, I'm on top of him.

"It would work nine out of 10 times. And when it did, the people would go crazy, and the whole team would get a lift. When the players see the goalie attack like that, the aggressiveness rubs off, and even if the other teams score, the whole team might still get a lift from it."

Hasek has been getting a lift out of goaltending ever since his childhood days in Pardubice which, under Communist rule, was an industrial center in Czechoslovakia. His father worked in the nearby uranium mines, coming home only on weekends.

On one such weekend the local team had a tryout for six-year-olds. Arm in arm with his dad, Dominik attended the audition, although he admittedly was ill-equipped. "One day, they held a tryout for six-year-old boys and Dad took me there," Hasek says. "I didn't even have real skates. I had those blades that you screwed onto the soles of your shoes. But I was tall, and the nine-year-olds didn't have a goalie, so they put me in with them. Ever since I can remember, I always made straight for the goal."

From the first, Hasek was good enough to compete with the older players. Like many other goalies, he had very good reflexes, but it was his flexibility that separated him from the goaltending mass. He was double-jointed and could do a kneeling split. "The doctors always used to shake their heads when I did it," Hasek says now.

Dominik's mother remained unimpressed. "I never believed in hockey being the whole life for Dominik," says Marie Hasek. "Hockey's just a game. Besides, Dominik always had the intellectual propensity to do well academically."

Czech-born novelist Jan Novak — now based in Chicago — closely followed his countryman's career from its earliest days in Pardubice. "Dominik was as much of a child prodigy in hockey as Mozart had been in music," says Novak. "There was the same sense of a precocious youth testing himself against the world, of trying to see where the limits lay."

As it happened, the sky was the limit, but it had to be approached slowly and steadily. One who helped Hasek's acceleration was Zdenek Uher, who had been head coach of the Tesla club in Pardubice. Uher remembers Dominik as an absent-minded goaltender who once forgot his goalie pads before a big game against Kladno.

"We had to ask Kladno to find us a pair of pads," Uher remembers. "You can imagine what kind of junk they loaned him. I told Dominik, 'If we lose tonight, they'll say that we threw the game. And I'll hold you responsible for it.' Kladno pulled out all stops, they outplayed us in all phases of the game, but Dominik was absolutely incredible. We won by a goal and kicked Kladno out of the first division."

Hasek was in orbit and continued to climb toward the Czech goaltending stratosphere. The Chicago Blackhawks radar picked him up and drafted his rights. If Dominik signed he would have had to defect and leave his family in Pardubice. He was a big fish in a little pond and loved it. Besides, he wanted to complete a degree at the pedagogical institute in Hradec Kralove. Teaching history was his second priority after goaltending.

As the bromide goes, "genius will out," and eventually Hasek accepted a Blackhawks contract and showed up at training camp in 1990. He may have been the best goalie in Europe, but he certainly was not the best in the Chicago livery. "He flopped around the ice like some fish," says Darryl Sutter who was a Blackhawks aide at the time.

Mike Keenan, head coach of the Hawks, hardly was enamored with Hasek either. And why should he have been? Chicago had a hot prospect in Jimmy Waite not to mention the redoubtable Ed Belfour as the workhorse starter. Hasek was demoted to Indianapolis of the International League and got his first taste of North American pro hockey.

Belfour was in his prime and that meant that Hasek had to bide his time in the minors. In many ways it was a bitter experience; so painful that Dominik actively considered returning to Europe and finishing his career on the other side of the Atlantic.

He finally got a break — of sorts — in the 1992 Blackhawks-Penguins playoffs when he was sent in to pinch-goal for Belfour against Mario Lemieux, Jaromir Jagr, and other members of the vaunted Stanley Cup champions. What at first appeared to be a case of a lamb being thrown to the wolves turned out to be an episode where the lamb intimidated the wolves. Nonplussed by the marquee opposition, Hasek repulsed some of the best shots Lemieux Ltd. had to offer.

It was the kind of performance that should have impressed the Blackhawks brass; and perhaps it did. But Chicago's number one goaltender still was Belfour, and in August 1992, GM Bob Pulford traded Hasek to the Buffalo Sabres — with Keenan's blessing — in an exchange that brought Sabres forward Christian Ruuttu to the Windy City.

The deal hardly raised eyebrows throughout the NHL. Hasek's playoff vignette was just a blip on the league's highlight video and Ruuttu was regarded as a prettyboy shooter who never would become a star. Hasek didn't help matters by tightening up as the 1992-93 campaign began.

By the time he found his groove, an injury sidelined him and by the time he returned to the ice, the Sabres had acquired future Hall of Famer Grant Fuhr. Dutifully, Hasek became the backup again and remained so through the start of the 1993-94 campaign when Fuhr went down with an injury that propelled Hasek to center stage once and for all.

This time he grabbed the golden ring. Armed with an indefinable puckstopping style, Hasek performed like a goaltender possessed. "I realized that my chances in the NHL were getting fewer and fewer," he says. "This was the time to do something."

What he did ranks with some of the more remarkable goaltending feats of any era. Never did he allow more than four goals in a game — he had four four-goal games — and Hasek completed the 1993-94 season with a 1.95 goals against average.

Perhaps the game that best defines Hasek's artistry occurred in the playoffs against the New Jersey Devils on April 27, 1994, at The Aud in Buffalo. Both Devils goalie Martin Brodeur and Hasek were invulnerable, and the score registered 0-0 after regulation time had expired.

As the Aud's clock ticked past the midnight mark, the teams were locked in combat. For a fleeting moment it appeared that Bobby Carpenter might have the winner on his stick, then Stephane Richer, but the Devils were foiled by Hasek.

By the time the fourth overtime period began, it was clear that the game would be decided when one of the goalie's lost concentration. Players from both sides were so exhausted they often appeared to be skating in mud, but on and on they went.

At last, a break occurred.

The Sabres moved the puck into the right corner of Devils' ice. A pass eluded Tommy Albelin stationed in front of Brodeur. The puck skimmed tantalizingly to Dave Hannan as Brodeur attempted to regain position. But he was too late. Hannan lifted the rubber over the Devils goaltender and Hasek was the winner at 65:43 of overtime.

"I remember him as three in the morning after that game," recalls Buffalo News columnist Jerry Sullivan. "It seemed that Dominik would rather have gone out and played some more than stand and talk about it."

By this time Hasek had commanded enough attention to inspire experts to closely X-ray his style. What they found was extremely confounding. At times he seemed like an Indian Rubber Man on skates, stretching in unorthodox ways but usually blocking the puck. Defining his game was difficult, even for Dominik.

"The game is so fast I don't think about style," says Hasek. "I have all my concentration on the puck, on the other guy's stick. I have always watched the other goalies and try the things they do. If I liked something they did, I would say, 'Oh, this is good.' Or, 'Oh, this is not for me.' I never had one goalie I copied, and I never had a goalie coach until I came to the NHL."

Hasek's moves are difficult to copy because they are so strange and often based on exercises that his mother supervised when he was a child. "He sits on the floor, spreads his legs, bends at the waist, and touches his stomach to the floor," says Buffalo center Michael Peca. "Dominik is like a contortionist."

"They say I am unorthodox, so maybe I am." Hasek explains. "I can't describe it. I do what is best for me."

Once Hasek had established himself as number one between the Sabres pipes, the club unloaded Fuhr and employed Andrei Trefilov and later Steve Shields as Dominik's little-used backups. Shields, a Michigan graduate, had less of a problem than Trefilov when it came to supporting Hasek.

"What amazed me — after I started watching Dominik — was how he would get into position," says Shields. "The crowd would roar when he would make a spectacular save, but I was most amazed at the ones that nobody else — but another goalie — would notice. The ones that seemed routine. I would be thinking to myself, 'How did Dom know to be *there*?'"

Although the Colorado Avalanche won the Stanley Cup in 1996 — and Patrick Roy was regarded at least in Denver as a saint among puckstoppers — Hasek continued to win more critical accolades as the NHL's best goaltender, although he remained a relatively quiet hero in his adopted city of Buffalo.

"Usually a team is built around stars," explains Hasek. "It's better built around forwards or defense because they are more in the game and on the bench. A goalie, by contrast, is a special person. I feel I'm an important part of the team, but the leader of the team should be a player not a goalie."

Nevertheless, almost by default, Hasek became the Sabres leader during the 1996-97 campaign. When the club's captain Pat LaFontaine suffered a career-threatening head injury early in the season, the Sabres appeared on the brink of collapse. A popgun offense produced precious few goals, yet Hasek constantly and tenaciously would preserve virtually any lead he had been given.

His most amazing save of the season was executed on January 29, 1997 against the

Pittsburgh Penguins in a game Buffalo won, 3-1. While he was lying on his side in the crease, Hasek reached up and made a glove save on a Mario Lemieux shot that was labelled "goal."

"Even in practice he couldn't stand to be beat," wrote Sullivan. "When a player flipped a puck casually at the net, he'd act as if the Stanley Cup depended on him stopping it."

Against enormous odds, Hasek helped orchestrate the Sabres Northeast Division championship symphony and won the Hart Trophy as the most valuable player in the regular season. It marked the first time the Hart had gone to a goalie since Montreal's Jacques Plante won it in 1962. Why did Hasek gain the honors? The reasons were many:

* He led the NHL in save percentage, stopping .930 of the shots hurled at him.

* Out of the Sabres' 40 wins, Hasek garnered 37, and in most games his club was significantly outshot.

* Although Buffalo did not have a scorer among the NHL's top 75, Hasek managed to keep his team in games with a 2.27 goals against average.

* He played 4,037 minutes, more than every goalie except Grant Fuhr of St. Louis (4,261).

"I like my numbers," said Hasek prior to the playoffs, "especially my save percentage. It's a great number. My goal at the start was to make the playoffs, and we did."

Buffalo's first-round opponent would be the Ottawa Senators, making their first appearance since the expansion franchise entered the league. On paper, at least, it appeared to be an easy assignment for Buffalo, considering Ottawa's lack of playoff experience.

"If I play well," Hasek said before the opener, "we can go a far way. There is much more pressure than during the regular season, but that pressure makes me focused for a game and really sharp. It's nothing that bothers me."

Whoa!

Those inside the Sabres dressing room had a different view.

They remembered an incident in Boston on April 9, 1997, when Hasek bolted from the ice and suffered a temper tantrum in the Fleet Center dressing room. They also were aware of tensions brewing between the goaltender and his fiery coach Ted Nolan.

Nevertheless, Hasek played competently in an opening game, a 3-1 win over Ottawa and was hardly to blame in the 3-1 second game loss. Rather, it was the following chain reaction of events that exploded across the Buffalo hockey scene.

For starters Hasek labored through a poor practice on the Sunday before Game Three and missed an optional game day skate, something he rarely would let happen. Insiders further reported that he skipped the team breakfast and ensuing meeting. "That was not optional," wrote Buffalo News hockey writer Jim Kelley, "and his absence worried a great many of his teammates. They were assured that Dom was just resting and that he would be ready at game time, but the fact was that nobody knew if that was true."

Hasek erupted with another tantrum in the pregame warmup at Corel Centre, smashing his stick against the goal post. Teammates attempted to calm their prize pal so that he could focus in time for the opening face-off.

"None of that seemed to matter once the game began," Kelley explained. "But the moment Ottawa put its first goal behind him, Hasek skated off the ice never to return. The amazing rubber man, Gumby in human form, fell backward, then forward. He kicked out

his left leg, then his right leg, twitched a bit sideways when the right leg popped out, then got up and left the game.

"He was untouched. He skated directly to the Sabres bench and walked off to the locker room. Steve Shields replaced him."

It later was disclosed that Hasek had mildly sprained the medial collateral ligament in his right knee. Some goalies might have been able to shake off the injury in the heat of playoff action and, perhaps, continue. Hasek's exit was determined and swift, with no hesitation whatsoever.

Hasek's departure left teammate Brad May "in shock." The goalie told May that he was hurt, yet he later returned to the bench in street clothes, smiled, and chatted with other Sabres. If he had suffered an injury it was not evident as he watched the game unfold. Nowhere could anyone detect crutches nor a cane. Were the wound to his knee, he normally would have nursed it with an icepack. He had none.

Thanks to Shields, Buffalo won the game, 3-2, and the Sabres public relations department called the goaltender's condition "day-to-day." Hasek was noticeably less optimistic. "My feeling is I won't be back until the end of the series," he proclaimed, and most of Buffalo went into mourning.

Meanwhile, the Sabres became more puzzled, especially when Hasek skipped the Sabres' hotel and motored to Ottawa defenseman Frank Musil's house. Although Hasek and Musil had been childhood friends, such fraternizing during the playoffs was taboo. Dominik's teammates not only were concerned, they were bewildered by his actions.

So was Kelley. In a detailed column which appeared the morning following Game Three, the columnist suggested that the pressure of carrying the Sabres had finally gotten to the goaltender. The Sabres' management, led by club president Larry Quinn, knew that Hasek depended on team support and hastily arranged a press conference in the club's locker room during which Hasek read a prepared statement while teammates stood behind him.

"It seemed too trite and cinematic to ring true," commented Sports Illustrated, while other media types mocked the staged event in other phrases and paragraphs. Significantly, Nolan apparently wasn't apprised of the event until the last minute.

The plot thickened the following Friday night in Buffalo where the teams returned for Game Five. Hasek, who obviously was incensed by Kelley's column claiming that he had sprinted from the arena the night of his injury met Kelly head-on in a corridor outside the Sabres dressing room after the game.

In front of several witnesses, Hasek taunted the journalist, alternately calling him a "liar" and "the worst person in the world." After Kelley suggested that the pair air their dispute in a calmer fashion, Hasek declined and eventually grabbed Kelley around the neck and tore his shirt before cooler heads intervened.

Hasek's assault was magnified by several factors, not the least of which was Kelley's role as president of the Professional Hockey Writers Association. Nolan deplored his goaltender's behavior and NHL commissioner Gary Bettman — following a hearing — imposed a three game suspension.

Meanwhile, Hasek-watchers debated precisely what event — or events — detonated his scatter-gun attacks. One friend pointed out that the goalie had suffered from sleep deprivation, a condition which became aggravated under playoff conditions. In an off-the-record conversation with a sympathetic reporter, Hasek pointed out that a goaltender cannot behave "like a stone" before 20,000 fans.

With Shields in goal, Buffalo lost Games Four and Five, returning to Ottawa behind in the series, 3-2. Considering all the turmoil surrounding the Sabres, most observers expected Ottawa to wrap up the first round tourney at home.

Instead, Hasek's stand-in blanked the Senators 3-0, enabling the Sabres to return home with a 3-3 tie. Dominik issued an apology to Kelley but was not in goal for the deciding game which Shields won in sudden-death overtime.

Dominik never returned to action. He served his 3-game suspension during the second-round series with Philadelphia and could have played in the fifth and final match. Instead, Nolan opted for Shields who lost as the Sabres departed on the short end of a 4-1 decision.

What wouldn't go away was the fallout over Hasek's curious deportment. "The behavior of Dominik Hasek added a bizarre twist to the playoffs," observed *Sports Illustrated*.

It also raised many question marks about his future in the NHL, especially with the Sabres. One of the goaltender's most ardent supporters, GM Muckler, was fired in May 1997 after a long power struggle with Nolan. Since the coach and his goalie had often been off the same wavelength, it was theorized that one or the other would be gone by the start of the 1997-98 season. Nolan left.

Bedevilled by the turmoil, Hasek told friends that he wished the fuss would go away. He said he was disturbed by the assertions that he had quit on his team.

"Maybe," he dolefully concluded, "it will take days, weeks, or months (before the trouble would go away). I don't know."

What is known is that the NHL's most valuable player entered a new season with a cloud over his career as big as Marine Midland Arena.

MIKE RICHTER

"I never had an ordinary growing up. I always had a series of tasks in front of me — to do well in this camp, or in that tournament. When one had been accomplished, there was always a second on the horizon."

Chico Resch considers Mike Richter the second-best goalie in the world.

Goalies' World magazine ranks Richter sixth overall and calls him a "steady man."

Yet when votes were counted for the 1997 Vezina Trophy for the "goalkeeper adjudged to be the best at his position," Richter was beaten by the winner, Dominik Hasek, 120 to 2.

Hasek received 22 first-place votes; Richter had none.

Runner-up Martin Brodeur had 18 second-place votes. Richter had none.

In third place Patrick Roy produced 11 third-place votes. Richter had but two.

It was hard to imagine that Richter lagged behind Guy Hebert in the Vezina balloting and was tied with Curtis Joseph.

This is the same Mike Richter who backstopped New York to its first Stanley Cup in 54 years and who out-goaled John Vanbiesbrouck and Martin Brodeur in the first and second 1997 playoff rounds, respectively.

If Richter was stung by any voting oversight, he certainly didn't betray any unhappiness. A philosopher and scholar as well as an athlete, Richter has the ability to see things clearly and see them whole. If the voters don't consider him one of the three best goalies, so be it.

"Getting individual honors certainly feels good," says Richter, who lives in an Upper West Side Manhattan apartment overlooking the Hudson River. "But if you were to ask me to trade something like an All-Star berth to a Stanley Cup Finals berth, I'd take the latter."

Part of Richter's problem when it comes to winning attention resides on the Rangers' roster. Ever since he became a regular on the Broadway Blueshirts, Mike has been overshadowed by the likes of Mark Messier, Wayne Gretzky, and Brian Leetch, all future Hall of Famers.

"That's not something that I don't like," says Richter. "I'm glad we have a very talented team. I'm surrounded by pretty good players. I understand the situation and that, for me, it's not a perfect situation."

Not that Mike is complaining. No sir. He is not the complaining type; never was, never will be. Richter is just happy to be between the pipes; tickled that any number of potential career road mines didn't blow up in his face and end his run on Broadway.

In 1995-96 he was shelved with a groin injury that, for a time, seemed deadly enough to force him into retirement. But the medics came through and Richter returned still able to perform the contortions that made him one of the most acrobatic goaltenders in the NHL and the goaltending star of the 1996 World Cup games.

When the underdog Americans defeated Canada in the final game, it was Richter who clearly made the difference and who once and for all established himself as a legitimate star without having Gretzky and Messier in front of him.

Mike Richter took aim at that great, glorious NHL over the horizon when he was growing up in an unlikely place called Flourtown, Pennsylvania, a suburb of Philadelphia. For some strange reason, Richter shied away from the traditional neighborhood sports such as baseball, basketball, and football. The Flyers were hot stuff at the time, and young Mike decided that he wanted to be like Philly's crack goalie Bernie Parent.

Goaltending, interestingly, best suited his personality.

"I was fairly shy," he reveals, "but goaltending gave me a lot to do. Having so much to do was a relief in some ways. Like I never went to a prom. I never had an ordinary growing up. I always had a series of tasks in front of me — to do well in this camp or in that tournament. When one had been accomplished, there was always a second on the horizon. One after another, they got me through my childhood."

He learned quickly and soon found himself on a team sponsored by an Atlantic City gambling casino. From there he moved to Lake Placid to play for the Northwood Academy, a prep school that had sent other players, such as Tony Granato and Chris Nilan, to the NHL.

When college beckoned, Richter could have gone to Harvard but chose the University of Wisconsin because he believed that he could better advance his hockey career there. It was a good choice. The Badger life fit Richter just fine and vice versa. In 1985 the Rangers liked what they saw so much that Richter was drafted 28th overall in the Entry Draft.

After two years, Richter moved to the U.S. National Team and then the U.S. Olympic Team. His partner was Providence College ace Chris Terreri. After a 2-2 Olympic mark, the Rangers shipped Mike to Colorado of the International League where he played so impressively that then GM Phil Esposito asked Richter to come east for a view of the Rangers-Penguins playoff series.

Mike hardly expected to face Mario Lemieux & Co., but when the Rangers appeared destined to lose their fourth straight game to the Pens — and this before disillusioned Madison Square Garden fans — Coach Michel Bergeron inserted Richter.

The smallish goalie looked particularly little as the Pens swarmed around him, and he did allow four goals to beat him. But he also displayed a certain poise and indomitability that captured the imagination of the local fans. Richter didn't know it at the time, but he was soon to be a Ranger to stay.

By 1990-91 Mike was sharing the New York goaltending with veteran John Vanbiesbrouck. The pair made NHL history by alternating for the first 76 starts of the season. Still, they were an odd couple and not altogether comfortable with one another.

Beezer felt he had earned the top spot and wasn't so crazy about the young intruder. Richter was feeling his oats but knew that as long as Vanbiesbrouck was around the Garden, he could never take over.

Mike didn't help his cause with a couple of classic non-saves that had some goalie savants wondering whether he could handle the more intense games. Richter's most egregious sin occurred in a 1992 playoff game against the Penguins.

With his club in command and steaming toward a series victory, Richter misplayed a 75-foot bouncing shot from the stick of Ron Francis. "That soft goal not only turned around the game," says Associated Press hockey writer Ken Rappoport, "but a series the Rangers thought they might have won."

The loss to Pittsburgh coupled with Richter's blunder on the Francis drifted raised an element of doubt about Mike's reliability. "He was unsure of his status," says teammate Brian Leetch. "If he gave up a bad goal, he would be out of the game."

During the 1992-93 season, Richter and Vanbiesbrouck were reaching a critical point in their careers. That year the Rangers missed the playoffs and, with expansion on the horizon, one would have to be sacrificed. New general manager Neil Smith put his faith in the kid and as did new coach Mike Keenan. Beezer was gone; Richter owned the net.

Not only did he put faith in Richter, but he played him over and over and over again. "Michael just had to have someone to believe in him," says Keenan.

He played in 68 games, won 42, lost 12 and tied six. His goals against average was 2.57, and he was named most valuable player in the All-Star Game which was played on his home New York ice. When the playoffs began, Richter was at the very top of his game and it showed. By the time the two-month tournament had concluded there was total bedlam in the Big Apple. Mike's Rangers had the Stanley Cup and Richter came away with a 2.07 goals against average.

"Keenan gave me a confidence boost," says Richter. "He was demanding, and he made it so there was a lot of peer pressure, but in a good way. I didn't want to let down my teammates. They were working hard for me and Mike let me know that."

No one has ever questioned Richter's work ethic; either on or off the ice. He has constantly schooled himself in the nuances of his trade and also has worked to complete his educational studies which were essentially abandoned after two years at Wisconsin.

"I felt bad about leaving the college part half-done," he admits. "I've always wanted a sense of completion, of finishing what I started when I was an undergrad. I didn't even pick a major. I was only there two years, then I went to the Olympic team."

Once established in New York, Richter resumed his studies at Columbia University which is located two miles north of his apartment. The long season allows him only enough time to enroll for summer courses.

"Taking one credit per summer is not an awful lot," he confesses, "but it does add up. It's interesting. It keeps you up on events and it certainly is a great way to get away from a season if I want to. It's almost a mental break and it convinced me that I haven't scratched the surface in terms of what I can do as a student."

When Vanbiesbrouck left the Rangers, he was replaced by Glenn Healy, an affable veteran who seemed secure in his position as number two. They failed to repeat as Stanley Cup champions in 1995 but Richter's game remained solid.

"Mike has attitude, skill, effort, and determination," says Calgary Flames defenseman James Patrick. "He's the quickest goalie I've ever seen. He's the hardest working player and he has a great attitude."

Richter's lateral movement is about as speedy as anyone who has put on a set of pads. His knack for doing a perfect split — planting one skate at one goal post and one at the other — is unsurpassed in the business.

His goals against average is another story. In 1996-97 it was 2.69 on a Ranger team whose graph dipped and rose like a roller coaster until the playoffs.

"We had nine guys out on the World Cup," Richter explains. "That's not an excuse because that just means that you have nine pretty good quality players. The problem was that we hadn't played together as a group. Especially with Wayne Gretzky coming in, a lot of our players were waiting and watching to see what he could do. We were just not on the same page and we lost a lot at the beginning. And lost our confidence.

"Then we started playing better hockey and began to deserve to win some games and began to develop more confidence. That allowed us to have even more success and we went on from there."

New York entered the playoffs in a curious position. The Rangers featured Gretzky, Messier, Leetch, Richter, and other high-priced talent, but they were not expected to last very long.

Richter changed all that. He out-goaled Vanbiesbrouck in the playoff between the Panthers and Rangers and then repeated the performance against the Devils. No doubt about it, Mike was in a goaltending zone that made him look like the best goalie in the league, Dominik Hasek included.

His luster was dulled somewhat when Philadelphia knocked the Rangers out of the Conference Finals in only five games. Nobody blamed Richter for the defeat.

As *Goalies' World* concludes, "Mike Richter gets a grade of A in almost every department!"

Everyone seems to know that except the voters for the Vezina Trophy.

MARTIN BRODEUR

*"I know exactly what I'm doing in a game.
Everything is instinct with me."*

Few goaltenders in National Hockey League annals can claim that their genes were directly responsible for their being in the majors but Martin Brodeur is a notable exception.

The son of Denis Brodeur — a goalie for the 1956 Canadian Olympic Team — Martin learned the netminding trade from his dad who was regarded as one of North America's finest blockers outside of the National Hockey League.

"Whenever I could," says Denis Brodeur, "I would bring Martin down to the Montreal Forum and have him watch the Canadiens on and off the ice."

This was easy for Denis Brodeur since he has been one of the finest hockey photographers in the business and for decades has taken pictures of Les Canadiens for both the Habs and Montreal newspapers.

Martin's first memory of a Forum trip dates back to his third year. The Habs staged a Christmas party for players and media. Denis placed Martin atop a net and took a picture of him. When Martin was old enough to hold a camera and a tripod, Denis taught his son how to photograph hockey action.

"I'd go to NHL games with my dad," says Martin, "and he'd get me a seat right next to the glass. I'd set up the camera and start clicking away. All I did was take pictures of the goalies."

His fascination with the padded skaters began after a short detour on the front lines. At age four, Martin began a tour of duty as forward on a neighborhood team. He liked scoring goals and probably would have been a sharpshooter forever had another team of older boys not asked him to sign up as a stand by goalie. Marty accepted the invitation without telling his mother.

When Mireille Brodeur learned about her son's decision to play goal for one team while still playing forward for another, she did the motherly thing and offered some good, maternal advice. *Don't be a goalie!*

"It was a Saturday," Martin remembers. "I came home and mentioned I was playing up front. My mom couldn't believe it. She said, 'What are you doing? Play forward, not goalie.'"

This was a tough decision that Martin solved by doing both; forward for one team, goal for the other. He did it for a year with absolutely no problems except for one thing. His goaltending had improved to a point where he had become a first-stringer and the coach wanted more of him in the nets than at center ice.

"One day," says Martin, "my coach said, 'You have to choose. What are you going to do, be a forward or a goalie?' Up until that point it was the biggest decision of my life. Finally, I said, 'Okay, I'll be a goalie.' I was a little kid making a big choice but it worked out."

Not without considerable time, patience, fortitude, and a smidgen of fatherly advice here and there. If anything, Denis Brodeur was an easy father. No pushing or yelling at his son that he should do this or that in goal — just play.

"I only went on the ice three or four times with him," Denis recalls. "When a kid does that well, you don't change his style, you just add to it. The only thing I ever helped him with was the wandering aspect of being a goalie — going behind the net and coming out to clear the puck."

"My father never got too involved and never forced me into anything." Martin observes. "He never forced me to go to hockey school. A lot of my friends couldn't play golf or baseball in the summer because they had to go to hockey school. The most he would do was after games. He would say little things like 'Try this,' or 'Try that.' But he was never like a coach. He wouldn't tell me to play the way he did because he was a little guy who was a lefty and I'm a big rightly."

Martin progressed up a familiar hockey ladder, from Montreal amateur leagues up to the Quebec Major Junior Hockey League where he starred for St.Hyacin the. "I kept telling people around The Forum that Martin was on his way to the NHL," says Denis. "I could see that as a Junior, he was doing things that the big-leaguers were doing. I knew the moves from my own experience and I could tell that Martin had NHL written all over him."

So did a fellow French Canadian named Patrick Roy, except that the latter was then a rookie with the Habs. It was 1985-86 and Les Canadiens were en route to a Stanley Cup, thanks to Roy's remarkable goaltending which garnered him the Conn Smythe Trophy. In a sense Roy became Brodeur's idol and role model.

"Watching Patrick, I kept saying to myself, 'Maybe, someday, I can do that,'" Brodeur remembers. "Patrick was a young guy from Montreal — like me. He showed he could do the job and made me see the possibilities of doing it myself."

There was one more obstacle to overcome; confidence.

At age 14, Martin was dropped from a Bantam league team. Stunned to the very core, he seriously considered quitting hockey. The NHL was further from his mind than Siberia and he made his feelings known to older brother Claude.

The brother was unimpressed. In fact, he was angry. He sat down with Martin and, eye-to-eye, laid it on the line. "You go back and play. You suck it up for a little bit. You never know what's going to happen."

To this day, Martin insists that he never would have returned to the ice had it not been for his session with Claude. Not that he zoomed to the top. Quite the contrary. He was totally bypassed in the 1989 draft and returned to Junior suitably discouraged but more determined than ever to work his way to the top.

He bypassed the possibilities of college scholarships because he was convinced he could get more ice time in Junior. At the 1990 Entry Draft the New Jersey Devils selected Brodeur 20th overall, and by the age of 19 he was making his first appearance for the Jerseyites, a 4-2 win over the Boston Bruins.

That wasn't enough to permanently secure a first-string job for Marty, but it was a start. He played four regular season games in that 1991-92 season, coming away with a 3.35 goals against average. He also appeared as a replacement for Chris Terreri in a playoff game against the Rangers that turned into a shootout. Brodeur gave up three goals in the Devils defeat.

His apprenticeship continued in 1992-93 with the Devils' American League farm team in Utica. It was impressive enough for GM Lou Lamoriello to promote Martin to the big club in 1993-94. Alternating with veteran Chris Terreri, Brodeur compiled an admirable 27-11-8 regular season mark and a 2.40 goals against average which included three shutouts.

By playoff time he had won the number one job from Terreri and appeared in 17 play-off games. "Everything happened so fast," Martin says. Unfortunately, the last playoff game was the most traumatic. This was Game Seven of the Conference Finals against the New York Rangers, a classic match which extended into double sudden-death overtime.

Brodeur had matched save after save against his New York counterpart, Mike Richter, until the Rangers' Stephane Matteau managed to come out from behind the net and find an opening on the unlikely wraparound.

With advice from Devils' goaltending coach Jacques Caron — himself a former NHL netminder — Brodeur honed his game to sharpness in the Lockout-shortened 1994-95 season. When the playoffs began, New Jersey opened as an underdog to the Bruins in Boston. Brodeur seemed more adjusted, more confident and more mature than before.

"He had the poise of a guy over 30," Caron recalls. "And it was so early in his career. Even then he was controlling the game more than anyone in the league."

In fact, New Jersey was the underdog in every one of its four series, culminating with the club's first Stanley Cup championship in June 1995. Martin played in 20 games, winning 16 and losing only four. Three shutouts and a 1.67 goals against average underlined Brodeur's dominance.

"When I go out there," Brodeur explains, "it's a different world. I don't feel you've got to be nervous to be able to perform. I try not to put extra pressure out there. Sometimes I'm nervous, but it probably doesn't show. I've got my mask on. I can do whatever I want.

"When I hear the music going and the fans going crazy, I say to myself, 'It doesn't get any better than that.' Nobody can buy that. If you're not a hockey player or a sport person, it's hard to live that experience."

For someone who is not yet 25, Brodeur has endured many dramatic experiences in goal. In 1994, he battled Dominik Hasek into a fourth sudden-death overtime during Game Six of the second playoff round. It wasn't until 65:43 of overtime that the Sabres' Dave Hannan lifted the puck over Brodeur's fallen body during a scramble in front of the New Jersey net.

This set the stage for the decisive Game Seven at The Meadowlands on April 29, 1994. Buffalo went ahead 1-0, but the Devils counterattacked for a pair against Hasek. Try as they might, the Sabres could not dent Brodeur again and his club took the game, 2-1, and captured the series.

"The secret of a goaltender is positioning," says Caron, "and Martin positions himself well. He doesn't run around; he places himself early. If you place yourself on a proper angle early, then the second angle is easier to get. He sets himself and just goes to what the play develops, and he's there again." As much as Brodeur has admired Patrick Roy, he also has had a soft spot in his heart for Ron Hextall, especially when the latter made waves as a young Philadelphia Flyer in the 1980s. Martin admired Ron's frequent use of the stick to trap the puck and transmit it to teammates. "When Hextall came in the league, it was such a big change from other goalies," says Brodeur, who was 15 when Hextall won the Conn Smythe Trophy. "He was so different. That's what I liked about him. He was so different."

Ironically, Brodeur faced Hextall in the 1995 playoffs and significantly out-goaled him in a six-game Conference Final series, leading up to a Brodeur-Mike Vernon match-up in the Red Wings-Devils Finals. Although Detroit was the heavy favorite, Brodeur's puck-stopping enabled New Jersey to string two victories together at Joe Louis Arena. From there, the Devils cruised to a four-straight sweep and New Jersey's first Stanley Cup.

The trek to the Cup was fascinating because it revealed the manner in which super-stition affected Marty's life. In this case, it was all about the movies.

"Before the first game in Boston I went to a movie — and we won the game." Brodeur admits. "So I go to the movies again — and guess what? We win again. So now we're 2-0, and the guys say to me, 'Hey, now we're back in New Jersey, let's go to a movie.' Wait a minute! "We didn't go to a movie before the third game — and we lost. We lost! So then we lost once and we all say, 'Hey, gotta go back to the movies.' We do — and we win all the games. Then we go to Pittsburgh, but it's a 35-minute drive to get there, so I tell the guys, no problem, we'll rent a movie. I make the hotel room as much like a movie theater as I can, popcorn and everything — but it doesn't work. We lose. So guess what happens next? In the end, everyone knew about it, even the coaches who came to us and said, 'Listen, go to a movie!' We saw so many movies we had to sit through *Casper* the night before we won the Cup."

Despite being pelted with octopi, which landed all around him at Joe Louis Arena, and assaulted with all manner of shots from the likes of Steve Yzerman, Sergei Fedorov, and Paul Coffey, Brodeur maintained a calm throughout the series while dazzling onlook-ers with amazing saves.

"Marty's confidence level goes up in the playoffs," says teammate John MacLean. "He rises to the challenge. He wants to be known as a bigtime goalie." He certainly could not become a big time photographer like his father, or his brother. No matter how hard he tried, Martin couldn't get the hang of the cameras. "I even switched to an automatic one and I still mess up," he laughs. "I would much rather be in goal than taking pictures of goalies.

"I love to be in goal — to be the last line of defense — to be all alone," he says. "But being all alone, talking to no one, so intense, you can drain your mental energy. So I try not to think too much, not to invent what will happen before it happens, not to get nervous by thinking, 'If they score now, it's tied, and then they'll score again and beat us.' So I just go with the game, take what it gives me and try to give it back."

Caron adds: "Martin tells me he plays his best when he feels like he's playing road hockey. He's the loosest guy I've ever seen play goal."

Not that Brodeur has enjoyed an unequivocally smooth career. The 1995-96 season loomed as a glorious year for defending the Stanley Cup. Instead, the Devils found them-selves in a life-and-death struggle to make the playoffs; one which lasted to the final game of the season in New Jersey. Pitted against the lowly Ottawa Senators, Brodeur played a mediocre game as his team not only lost the match but blew a playoff berth.

However, his resiliency was evident in 1996-97. He played so well that the Devils fin-ished first at the end of the 82-game schedule and Marty was prominently mentioned as a candidate for both the Hart Trophy as well as the Vezina. He wound up winning neither.

No season is picture perfect even if your father is a professional cameraman and 1996-97 had its glitches as well. One was the fact that Marty had to share the net with equally young prospect Mike Dunham, the understudy who had to play 25 games in order for the Devils to ensure that he would not become a free agent. From time to time, Brodeur was yanked from games so that Dunham could finish and add to his game total.

For the most part Marty took it well, although he was somewhat perturbed before a game at the Molson Centre in his native Montreal. In the expectation that he would play before family and friends, Brodeur had purchased a block of tickets. However, Coach Jacques Lemaire decided at the 11th hour that Dunham would play instead.

The decision stunned many in the Devils' camp, including Marty and Denis Brodeur. Dunham, however, played well in a tie and the incident was eventually forgotten. When the Devils returned to Montreal for a rematch, Marty was back in the crease — and the winner.

By the end of 1996-97 he had clearly established himself on a plane with such elite goaltenders as Dominik Hasek, Mike Richter, and Patrick Roy. His style lacked the ambiguity of Hasek and the elasticity of Richter, but it worked.

"There are goalies more spectacular than me," says Brodeur, "but I don't think I'd be better if I put mustard on my saves. I'm too big to sprawl around. And I have such good teammates. They take care of the passer and I take care of the shooter."

Brodeur's stickhandling capabilities put him in position to attempt the end-of-game shot into the opponent's empty net whenever the Devils lead a close game late in the third period. As a former forward, he yearned for the opportunity to put one in and, in fact, came close several times. But it wasn't until a playoff game against Montreal in the first round on April 17th, 1997, that he realized his ambition.

With the score 4-2, for New Jersey and the clock ticking down toward the end, Montreal coach Mario Tremblay pulled his goalie, Jocelyn Thibault, for an extra attacker. Brodeur was keenly aware of the open net when the Habs dumped the puck in from the neutral zone on Marty's right side.

He skated around his right post and behind the net to finally take control of the puck close to the left post. With one hand, he brought the puck back just as Mark Recchi swerved toward him. Brodeur released the shot and fired it up ice as 19,040 fans gasped in anticipation. The puck slid right into the opening as Marty lifted his goalie stick in his right hand and saluted defenseman Shawn Chambers with his left. As the crowd toasted him with deafening applause, Marty leaned forward on his stick, tilted his head to his right and laughed.

"I was freaking out. It was unbelievable," said Brodeur afterward. "When I shot it it went over everyone and I lost sight of it. Then the guys in front of me moved to the side and I saw it go in. I'll never forget that moment."

Marty remained a happy goalie as New Jersey eliminated Montreal in five games. The Devils then encountered New York in what had become a bitter grudge series. The Rangers had beaten the New Jersey in their 1992 playoff meeting and again in the seven-game 1994 classic. It was time for what Marty likes to call playoff goaltending.

"For a month and a half of playoffs, you need the goalie to give you a chance to win every game," he explains. "A quarterback in football has to win one game a week. Here, every two nights you have to do it. But I like the pressure. I like dealing with it, learning from it, succeeding with it."

In Game One of the New Jersey-New York series, Brodeur threw a 2-0 shutout at the Rangers. Actually, it was a 1-0 game down to the wire when the Devils added an open-netter courtesy of John MacLean.

Richter, his opposite, was beaten on only one shot — a strange shot by Scott Neidermayer from a severe right angle — that sneaked between the Ranger goalies' pads.

The feeling was that if the Devils could put just one goal on the board for Marty in Game Two, it would be sufficient. Certainly, in the first 15 minutes his teammates seemed to be thinking just that. They thoroughly overwhelmed the Rangers both territorial and numerically — with shots, that is — but the score remained 0-0 until New York obtained a power play.

As the Rangers mounted an attack, New Jersey's penalty-killer, John MacLean, was hauled down at the blue line. No call was made as the power play invaded Devils' territory. The pass went from Wayne Gretzky (behind the net) to Brian Leetch and before Brodeur could move, the puck was behind him.

Martin did his job but his mates could only score once on a play that was disallowed because of video replay. The game symbolized the rest of the series. Richter did what he had to do to thwart the Devils. Brodeur was splendid in goal — but not perfect.

With a 3-1 lead, the Rangers wrapped up the series in sudden-death overtime in Game Five. Ironically, it was a wrap-around shot by Adam Graves that, somehow, eluded Brodeur. The play had overtones of the 1994 Stephane Matteau score, a fact that was quite apparent to the victim.

"It was almost the same type of goal," explained Brodeur. "When I got scored on, that's what I thought. Then I thought 'Hey, they are going to ask me that question.'"

Where Brodeur goes from here is a moot point. His Stanley Cup ring and his goals against average suggest that the sky is the limit. "In my fifteen years of coaching," Caron concludes, "I have to say that Marty has the most talent of anyone I've seen."

How he employs that talent will go a long way toward determining when New Jersey celebrates its next championship.

JOHN VANBIESBROUCK

"I'm really drawn to the games we lost. I want to see how we reacted to those situations."

On the first day of training camp in the first season of the Florida Panthers in September 1993, John Vanbiesbrouck approached coach Doug MacLean with an interesting question.

"Who's got a really, really good shot at making the team?"

MacLean shot back, "Why do you want to know?"

"Because," smiled MacLean, "I want to take them out to dinner."

As it happened, the Panthers should have taken their goaltender to dinner — many times. No single player ever made a brand-new expansion team more respectable, more quickly than this Detroit native.

Originally drafted from the New York Rangers by the Vancouver Canucks, Beezer — as he is known throughout the National Hockey League — was promptly dropped by Vancouver and claimed by Florida general manager Bryan Murray in the Expansion Draft. To this day it remains the best thing that ever happened to hockey in Miami.

With Vanbiesbrouck guarding the crease, the Panthers emerged as a playoff threat in the first year of the franchise and, incredibly, marched all the way to the Stanley Cup Finals in June 1996 before bowing to the heavily favored Colorado Avalanche. Most of the credit belonged to Beezer who stands among the best half-dozen goalies in the league.

"Beezer," says longtime goaltending coach Francois Allaire, "is the best small goalie in the NHL since Rogie Vachon played for the Kings. He's always in good position and uses his body well to cover as much space as possible. John is always 'square' to the puck."

Those who have studied the evolution of Vanbiesbrouck from his teenaged hockey days hardly are surprised at his ability. The son of a Belgian immigrant, who worked as a bricklayer, and an Italian mother, John learned his hockey in the working-class East Side of Detroit along with his older brothers, Frank and Julian.

He says he played goal because it was the only position the older guys would let him play. Once between the pipes, he realized that he was a perfect fit for a goaltender. "I liked the idea that there was a lot of intuition and anticipation involved," Vanbiesbrouck remembers. "It was one thing to work on the mechanics of goaltending in practice but when I got out there for the real games, it was all natural.

"When all is said and done the real reason I wanted to play goal is because my oldest brother, Frank, was a goalie. He was my inspiration to play and to be like him, to try to be as good as him. I never thought of myself as being as good as he was at playing goal because he was, in my eyes, the best. I also played a lot of baseball in the summers and I had a lot of fun doing it. I enjoyed hockey and wanted to keep playing, but the next thing you know I am in high school, and people are actually cutting me from their teams."

Beezer likes to tell people that "timing is everything." The philosophy is rooted in his earliest days as a goalie when he was playing on the Midget level and had absolutely no visions of the NHL at the time. "I was 16 and we played in a tournament, 'we' being the Little Caesars hockey club, and my jersey either got forgotten or stolen. I had a good tournament, but every game I had to wear this guy Mike Affholter's jersey. We ended up going to the finals and we lost in the tournament, but I had a real good tournament and they had programs printed with my name in it, but I was wearing Affholter's jersey. There were scouts from the Junior leagues there and the Toronto Marlies from the Ontario Hockey League drafted this guy Mike Affholter in the fourth round. Sam McMaster, who became the general manager of Los Angeles, picked up on it. He was the general manager of the Sault Ste. Marie Greyhounds at the time, and he called and he spoke to my coach and spoke to my mother and asked if I wanted to go for a tryout. My eyes were set on going to college maybe at some time, but I still had one more year of high school to go. So I made a decision to go up and give it a try and I ended up beating out a bunch of goalies and making the team. It was a weird ride."

Still, Beezer had doubts about his professional potential. He was back in school sitting in a classroom while the Entry Draft was being held. A broadcast of the draft was hooked up to the school loudspeaker system. Suddenly, the announcer proclaimed, "Selected in the fourth round, John Vanbiesbrouck of the New York Rangers."

Beezer couldn't believe his ears. "I threw my papers up in the air, bolted out of the room and ran all the way home," he recalls. "Just as I got into the house, the phone rang and it was (Rangers general manager) Craig Patrick. It was one of the happiest moments of my life."

Since he was only 18 years old, Vanbiesbrouck was returned to Sault Ste. Marie. The big club promoted him once and he defeated the Colorado Rockies 2-1. Patrick was impressed enough to turn Beezer pro with the Tulsa Oilers of the Central League. It was the strangest experience of John's career.

For one thing the Oilers were on the brink of financial collapse and for another, when they did fold, the club had to play the last half of the season — and the playoffs — on the road. Conditions were primitive both before and after the folding but Beezer survived through the whole ugly mess.

"Our 'dressing room' was a joke," he chortles. "We had a hose for a shower — one hose for 20 guys — and no heat in the dressing room and no fans in the stands. When we practiced, the club had to take a bus to a mall some 120 miles away."

When the dust had cleared from that vagabond season, Vanbiesbrouck was voted co-most valuable player in the CHL (along with Bruce Affleck) and Minor League Player of the Year by *The Hockey News*. Finishing with a 2.50 goals against average, Beezer helped his vagabond Oilers to the playoff championship.

His move up to the bigs was inevitable. In 1984-85 Patrick promoted him to New York where he out-goaled his close friend and former teammate Ron Scott for the backup spot behind veteran Glen Hanlon. "John perseveres and has confidence," explained then Rangers assistant coach Wayne Thomas. "He can become one of the best goalies in the league."

History has demonstrated that Thomas was perceptive, to say the least, although the climb up the ladder was neither swift nor easy. He finished his rookie season at 12-24-3 and managed to dispel the "sophomore jinx" in the '85-86 season. A sense of controlled

arrogance, which would mark his play in later years, occasionally surfaced. Some Rangers fans claimed that he seemed more like a New Yorker than the natives of Manhattan.

"I took on the qualities of a New Yorker," he asserts. "I loved the energy of the people there. They don't back down from anybody. But they're like the Chihuahua — once you get past their bark, they are as warm as anybody in the world."

Vanbiesbrouck was warmly treated by the Big Apple fandom. He treated them to some golden moments including upset playoff series victories over Washington and Philadelphia and a Vezina Trophy as the NHL's best goalie in 1985-86. Despite the fact that he stood only five foot eight, Beezer constantly came up big; a factor he attributed in part to his anticipation.

"That (anticipation) is a goalie's greatest asset," he says. "You anticipate where the puck is going to go — low, high, or the top corners."

What John could not have anticipated since establishing himself as a premier goalie in 1984-85 was the front-office turmoil that would bedevil the Broadway Blueshirts. He was frustrated by two general manager changes — first Craig Patrick then Phil Esposito departed — and the fact that Esposito traded for Philadelphia Flyers goalie Bob Froese to be John's sidekick

Beezer, to put it mildly, was uhappy having Froese share the netminding with him. "We had a big rivalry with the Flyers at the time," he explains, "and that (having an ex-Flyer sharing his duties) didn't sit well with me."

Nor did it sit well when his next general manager, Neil Smith, imported young Mike Richter as the third Rangers goalie during the 1989-90 season. Froese eventually was unloaded leaving Beezer and Richter as the somewhat odd couple between the pipes. If John was uneasy at first, he appeared after a while to smooth his feathers and accommodate his rather pleasant sidekick.

"I began to see the benefit of having a fresh guy out there every night," he says. "Always having at least a few days between starts gives you a chance to refocus and build up some determination for your next game. By this time I had the experience to know that it was not bad to share the limelight."

To a point he was right, except that Richter's game improved to a point where he was virtually on a par, qualitatively, with Vanbiesbrouck. General Manager Smith was in a quandary: Should he trade one of his crack goalies for a stellar forward or defenseman?

"At first I was reluctant to let either of them go," Smith remembers, "because of my previous experience with goalies. When I was with the Red Wings, I drafted goalies for years (as Red Wings director of scouting) and came up with only one big-leaguer, Tim Cheveldae. Good goalies are too valuable to let go."

Vanbiesbrouck was frustrated on two counts. Richter was crowding him for games and the Rangers still had not won a Stanley Cup since 1940, the longest non-Cup drought in the league. After seven full big-league seasons, he had begun to wonder whether he ever would sip champagne from the silver mug. "Not a day went by that I didn't think about being on the Ranger team that finally ended that 1940 stuff," says Vanbiesbrouck.

But the days — and months and years — went by, and finally, Smith was forced into a decision; make either Beezer or Richter available in the Expansion Draft. One argument had it that Richter was too high-strung to handle the number one assignment alone; that only Vanbiesbrouck was capable of that. On the other hand, Richter was younger and, as such, boasted a longer shelf life as an NHL goaltender.

In the end Smith opted for the kid and Beezer was on his way south, which was not the worst destination in the world. Hockey interest in Miami and environs was a lot more intense than Vanbiesbrouck had imagined, and Murray drafted more character players than many established teams had on their rosters. Once he acclimatized himself to the continuous Florida warmth, Beezer found new happiness in the Southland.

"I'm having as much fun now as I've ever had," he insists. "And I feel I have a lot left in me. Since coming to Florida, I've learned a lot about myself and have improved my ability to focus. That's vital for someone who plays my position.

"In the past I may have been too pressure-packed on myself, a little too hard on myself and sometimes too easy on myself. Now I focus differently. Preparing for a game, I can still have expectations I place upon myself, but I can now focus on what I have to do. It is not wishful thinking, but rather 'doing' thinking."

In an era of "butterfly" goaltending, Vanbiesbrouck remains in the minority. Oh, yes, he will drop to the ice when necessary but his basic style is stand-up, playing "square" to the puck and as much from the "book" as possible while anticipation always is at the core of his best stops.

Extremely talkative off the ice, John is contemplative once he gets to the arena and, as *Sports Illustrated* once noted, "impassive in the net and during the 12 hours before each game." Sometimes his concentration reaches extreme limits as in the episode involving the man who pays his checks, Panthers owner Wayne Huizenga.

According to witnesses, the billionaire businessman affectionately patted the thoughtful Beezer on the shoulder before a game, whereupon the goaltender delivered an elbow to Huizenga. (Pressed later about the episode, Vanbiesbrouck pleaded temporary amnesia.) Too small to be so aggressive on the ice, Beezer nevertheless will attack the puck whenever possible, although he lacks the playmaking skills of a Martin Brodeur or Ron Hextall.

He suffers losses badly but not nearly as intensely as he did in younger years. Call it maturity or a new philosophy, but John handles the totality of hockey now better than he ever has, and it was reflected in the glorious 1995-96 season when the club made the playoffs for the first time in its existence.

"What made that season so special were my teammates," he says. "I really liked them. Hockey is a real tough game and when you throw a bunch of people together from different countries and backgrounds, you're not always going to end up with a perfect scenario.

"In that sense, the Panthers became as close to perfect as anyone could imagine. As far as teammates and the quality of people we had on this team, it was just a great place to go to the rink every day. It was a major factor in my developing the positive attitude I took to my game, and it helped me be better and my game be better."

Beezer's goaltending never was better than the period from mid-March 1996 through the Stanley Cup Finals. The Panthers had surprised their foes by maintaining a playoff berth through more than half the 1995-96 campaign. But when they began faltering a number of critics believed that the Panthers would drop right out of playoff contention.

"Actually," Vanbiesbrouck reflects, "that late-season slump was the best piece of

adversity we could have had. We overcame something that in years past would have sunk us, but we overcame it. That made our team very strong."

The decisive turnabout game occurred at Miami Arena on March 17, 1996, against the New Jersey Devils. The visitors had come to town on a hot streak, threatening to overtake and pass Florida. Beezer halted their surge with a 3-0 shutout that sent the Devils reeling out of the playoffs, while putting the Panthers in for the first time.

Boston was Florida's first round opponent. The Bruins had finished the homestretch with 13 wins out of 16 games and seemed to be a formidable foe, but Florida marched into Beantown and successively topped Boston, 6-3 and 6-2. The Panthers won the series in five games and qualified to meet Philadelphia, led by Eric Lindros, in the Eastern Conference Semifinal.

Beezer recorded the first shutout in franchise history, 2-0, to open the series, but the Flyers retaliated with the next two wins. Game Four was a classic in Panthers annals. A sudden-death goal by defenseman Ed Jovanovski gave Florida a 4-3 win. From there Florida reeled off two more wins and ousted Philadelphia in a major six-game upset.

"That series was special," says Vanbiesbrouck, "because the Flyers were the big favorites and we were able to come back from being down 2-1. Our character was never tested more than it was then."

After beating Lindros & Co., Beezer encountered the equally powerful Penguins led by Mario Lemieux and Jaromir Jagr. The Panthers were not flustered even after Pittsburgh went up 3-2 after five games. A pair of wins, 4-3 and 3-1, thrust the remarkable Floridians into the Stanley Cup Finals.

"What was so great about that one was that we best them in Game Seven in Pittsburgh."

Vanbiesbrouck stopped 39 shots to ensure the victory, which was Florida's last of the playoffs. The eventual Stanley Cup champion Colorado Avalanche simply had too much power for the Panthers, although Beezer's performance in Game Four ranks among his all-time best.

A scoreless tie lasted into the third overtime period before Colorado's Uwe Krupp beat Vanbiesbrouck on a shot from the blue line at 4:31 of the third overtime. John had made 55 saves until the game ended at 1:06 in the morning. "They won the game," concludes Beezer, "but we won a lot of pride."

That feeling of pride extended through the 1996-97 season, during which Vanbiesbrouck maintained his high quality level while his hockey club made the playoffs for the second consecutive season. This time, however, there was a playoff glitch, although it hardly was apparent in Game One of the first round against the Rangers fortified with the likes of Wayne Gretzky, Mark Messier, and Brian Leetch.

Beezer slapped them down 3-0, stopping 34 shots and beating his one time dressing roommate, Mike Richter. Meeting the press after the fray, John was pressed about the supposed joy in defeating the team that had unloaded him.

"It's not time to be sentimental." Vanbiesbrouck warned. "I'm out there focused. I'm out there playing a team, knowing they have superstars."

Those superstars stopped Beezer and the Panthers from having a super post season as they had a year earlier. New York rebounded for four straight wins over a Florida team that had been ravaged with injuries. Vanbiesbrouck betrayed signs of weariness as the

Panthers went out in the first round. Nevertheless, John Vanbiesbrouck was secure in the knowledge that he had securely planted ice hockey in an area where people doubted that it ever could survive.

"We played the best hockey we could," Beezer concludes, "and we made the play-offs two years running. We've created a good environment and the people are liking it."

How can one not like John Vanbiesbrouck?

CURTIS JOSEPH

"I want to perform well and have the guys know I'll be back there to make the big save so they can work just as hard at the other end of the rink."

Some goaltenders are practically born with pads on their legs and goalie paddles in their hands. Martin Brodeur is a case in point. Others come to the game later in their athletic life.

In the case of Toronto-born Curtis Joseph, it was almost too late.

While other netminders his age were making names for themselves as teenagers, Joseph was totally inconspicuous. Scouts ignored him during his highschool years and might have bypassed him completely had he not elected to take a precollege, postgraduate semester at a Saskatchewan boarding school.

While playing goal there, he attracted the attention of scouts from the University of Wisconsin. In 1988 he accepted a scholarship offer from the Badgers and suddenly emerged as a freshman sensation on the collegiate level, named to the Western Collegiate Hockey Association First All-Star team. Undrafted, he became an unrestricted free agent at a time when promising goaltenders were as coveted as fine grapes in a vineyard.

The Blues, who then had goalies Greg Millen and Vincent Riendeau as their one-two combination, signed Joseph to a four-year, $1.1 million contract.

Breaking into the bigs was another story. Millen was still hot and Riendeau displayed signs of being a very competent replacement. When Joseph did play — 15 games in 1989-90 with a 9-5-1 record — he was adequate at the very least but hardly coveted by the brass.

After two season the Blues tried to package him, along with forward Rod Brind'Amour, to the Devils who were owed compensation because the Blues had signed free-agent forward Brendan Shanahan. Instead, the arbitrator awarded All-Star defenseman Scott Stevens to New Jersey. "I realized it was a business decision," says Joseph. "I was very expendable."

Up to a point. St. Louis traded Millen to Quebec in 1990-91, and the next season Riendeau was sidelined with an injury. Joseph moved to the crease, played 60 games, and suddenly looked like a legitimate first-string netminder. So much so that the Blues had no compunctions about dealing Riendeau to Detroit in 1993.

By playoff time it appeared to be an excellent move. CuJo, as he became known to both teammates and fans alike, faced Chicago's vaunted Ed Belfour in the first playoff round; one which had the Blackhawks as heavy favorites to dispatch the Blues.

Joseph not only out-goaled Belfour, he came up with zeroes for eight straight periods as St. Louis swept the then Norris Division champions. "If Curtis Joseph continues to play like this," said Blackhawks coach Darryl Sutter after the series had concluded, "anything can happen. It just did."

Goalies' World wrote: "Joseph reached such a high level of play that all NHL goalies eventually got better. It was as if he was the first guy to run a sub-four minute mile."

The Blues didn't win a Stanley Cup that year but CuJo came out of the playoffs with seven wins against four losses and a 2.24 goals against average. "Goalies always get so much attention in the playoffs," says Joseph. "Maybe it's because there's such tight checking that your stars don't get to shine as much. Every time Brett Hull stepped out on the ice two guys were on him. The goalie can't be shadowed or checked more tightly. He has more of a chance to affect the outcome of the game."

Until Mike Keenan arrived in St. Louis during the summer of 1994, CuJo appeared to be a fixture with the Blues. Despite a goaltending style that can best be defined as styleless, Joseph won over his teammates with his ability to keep the rubber out of the net. *Goalies' World* magazine put it simply: "Joseph was perhaps the greatest goalie in the history of the St. Louis Blues."

Jeff Norton, who teamed with Joseph in both St. Louis and Edmonton, puts it another way. "CuJo has a charisma about him. He can carry a team. That's how good he is."

In 1994-95 the Blues were mediocre, to say the least, yet Joseph rang up 20 wins against 10 losses and one tie. Somehow, it failed to impress Keenan. Not only that, but Joseph found himself in the coach's doghouse. "There was no line of communication with Mike and me," says CuJo. "We never talked. I just played. `

"But after a while, I found I was just one guy out of favor. I quit trying to figure him out. With Mike there was always a lot of tension and that's not for everybody. Some guys need a push, some guys don't. Me? I don't think I need a push or the controversy. That's how I'd describe Mike best — controversial. I like to have fun and enjoy the games."

Who can blame him? Life has not always been fun for Joseph. Born Curtis Munro, he was raised by a nurse, Jeanne Joseph and her husband, Harold, after his 17-year-old mother, Wendy Munro, handed him to Jeanne five days after he was born. Although he used the name Joseph for the most part during his childhood and teen years, he didn't officially change it until 1989 when he signed with St. Louis.

"It was," he admits, "a big decision for me."

No less big was his decision that he could no longer play for Keenan. Although he had become one of the most popular hockey players in St. Louis, CuJo permanently fell into Keenan's disfavor when he struggled against Vancouver in the 1995 playoffs. He swore he never would play for Keenan again and went on an anti-Mike strike.

"I spent six years stopping pucks in the NHL," says Joseph, "then he (Keenan) comes in and tries to destroy my character." Keenan eventually dealt Joseph to Edmonton — along with forward Mike Grier — in exchange for draft picks. After a 15-game holdout stint in Las Vegas of the International League, Joseph became an Oiler to stay on January 12, 1996. Oilers general manager Glen Sather had to decide whether to sign just Joseph and trade Ranford or to trade Joseph.

He traded Ranford to Boston and then signed CuJo to a three-year contract. Joseph responded with a 5-4 overtime win over Buffalo, a 5-1 victory over St. Louis and a 4-3 win over Dallas. "He's had one of the top five save percentages in the league over four years," says Sather. "He had run into problems with Keenan but that was not unusual."

Playing in front of a young but rapidly developing Edmonton team, Joseph found new joy in goalkeeping again. His coach, Ron Low, knew that he had a gem in the crease and did precious little to disturb his main man. "I didn't worry about my goaltending," says

Low. "CuJo is the kind of goalie who can stop 17 in a row off his head. But if the puck goes into the net, he thinks it's his fault. He shoulders the blame. If he has a bad night, he's the first guy to tell you he had a bad night."

"I always feel that there is something I can do to prevent a goal." Joseph states. "I'm competitive. I don't like to get beat."

Nevertheless, Edmonton missed the playoffs in 1995-96. Of course, CuJo hardly could be blamed for that; nor could anyone for that matter. The rebuilding Oilers were not considered a playoff-caliber team at the time, but by the start of 1996-97 they were being viewed with more optimism.

For the first time CuJo would be actually starting the season for them and for another, they were showing signs of maturing from the defense up to the front lines. Still, it would be goalkeeping that would make or break their chances of reaching the postseason and a game against the eventual Stanley Cup champions helped set the tone for Joseph's team.

This was on the night of December 10, 1996. It was a 0-0 tie, the first such result in the history of the Edmonton franchise. "Joseph was heroic," wrote *Edmonton Sun* sports editor Scott Haskins. "He was larger than life in a five-foot-eight, 180-pound body, stopping 52 shots, many of them deadly blasts by people like Steve Yzerman, Brendan Shanahan, and Igor Larionov."

Sitting at his locker after the game, Larionov — once a teammate of Hall of Famer Vladislav Tretiak — told reporters that Joseph's performance was "the best goaltending I have ever seen."

Larionov made the observation based on the fact that CuJo began the game with a series of outstanding stops and kept getting better as the night evolved. It reminded some of his followers of a similar game against the then Stanley Cup champion Colorado Avalanche. In that game he allowed one goal.

"Sometimes the puck misses you," says Joseph. "Sometimes you lose your curve ball. When you go through bad times, you just sit there and wonder."

Bad times for CuJo were few and far between in 1996-97. His superior play in December 1996 catapulted the Oilers into serious playoff contention. He had become a fan favorite at Northlands Coliseum and reciprocated by purchasing a private skybox for underprivileged children and their families.

"I was amazed at how the fans took to him," recalls Kevin Lowe, the veteran Edmonton defenseman. "I never saw anything like it. His popularity was incredible."

Late in the 1996-97 season Joseph's play had reached such a high level he was being favorably compared with the best goalies ever to put on an Oilers jersey. Coach Low was a good judge, having played for the Oilers and having seen all the great players.

"Some nights," says Low, "it just seems like the puck is never going to go in the net. In the case of Grant Fuhr, Andy Moog, and Billy Ranford, they all had some great nights and won a lot of games, but there never were really nights like the ones in 1996-97."

Terry Jones, the hard-nosed *Edmonton Sun* columnist, virtually melted in his praise of CuJo. "The greatest of the greats have played here and were worshipped. But this is different. This isn't hero worship, it's more like love."

The love affair continued through the regular season as Joseph rubber-stopped Edmonton to a playoff berth and then — his finest hour — out-goaling of Andy Moog and the seven-game opening round victory over the heavily favored Dallas Stars. It was an arresting development in that CuJo had reached that ethereal level which athletes call "The Zone."

"It's a feeling that's hard to explain," says Joseph. "I don't know how I get into The Zone and I don't want to know how I get out of The Zone. It's just that I am seeing the puck and it looks awfully big. The puck always seems to just hit me."

Low explained: "To be in The Zone, you have to be a super-skilled goalie where suddenly it gets better than it usually is. The puck seems so big, you can always find it, even through a screen. At other times you couldn't find it with a spyglass."

During the Dallas-Edmonton series Joseph had a cavalcade of extraordinary saves but one in particular is recalled by goaltending students. It was an overtime stop on Stars' ace Joe Nieuwendyk after CuJo was seemingly at the mercy of his foe.

"The play started with a wraparound by Darryl Sydor," CuJo recalls. "I knew that he had a good step coming around the net, so it was going to be a good wraparound chance. I covered everything low. My stick went up in the air; it went over, and I could see Nieuwendyk falling, and he was going to get a good swipe at the puck. I tried to meet him over at the other side of the net, and I tried to get both hands across as fast as I could. Sure enough, it hit me and I was able to smother it just before it went in."

Joseph was unable to smother the defending champion Avalanche in the second play-off round but he played capably as usual and reiterated with his efforts that he ranks among the NHL's finest.

"I'm a better goaltender than I was four years ago," he concedes. "I'm a little wiser and a little stronger, mostly in the mental aspect. And I am 30 years old!"

GRANT FUHR

I've got an old body that needs to be twisted, bent and stretched.

Considering that he ranks among the best goaltenders since The Great Expansion of 1967 — and, perhaps, among the finest ever — Grant Fuhr has received less respect than he deserves.

There are many relevant reasons for this unfortunate state of affairs. In his prime as an Edmonton Oiler 1981-89, the man they call Cocoa simply was overshadowed by the likes of Wayne Gretzky, Mark Messier, and Paul Coffey.

The Oilers emphasis on offense was executed at the expense of defense and, of course, Fuhr. Yet through it all, he guarded the twines for four Stanley Cup championships in Edmonton before his hockey world began crumbling around him.

"When I played with him as a teammate, I found that Grant read the game as well as any goalie who ever played," says Oilers coach Ron Low who once was Fuhr's roommate. "In Edmonton we knew that his goal against average would never be the best and he'd give up the occasional soft goal.

"But in the big moment — for the big save — he was ninety-five percent unbeatable. Under pressure there was none finer. He was, at one time, the finest goaltender in the world."

His glove saves were without peer. His instincts were virtually flawless. From the mid to late 1980s he was said to have the fastest reflexes of any NHL goaltender. During that period he also was regarded as *the* man you would want between the pipes in a money game.

Different people have different views of Fuhr's source of greatness but those with the most insight are goaltenders themselves.

"When he came to Edmonton," Low recalls, "Grant was a natural, yet he had no style. Or rather his style was all styles. He would come out 15 feet to challenge the shot on one offensive rush. The next time he would be back in his crease. He could read the game so well but he was different from anyone I'd ever seen. From the first day of camp we knew he would be great."

Although Edmonton entered the 1980s with a competent goalie in Andy Moog, Fuhr would eventually displace him as number one. With Grant in goal, the Oilers won five Cups in 1984, 1985, 1987 and 1988. (Fuhr was also a member of the 1990 Cup winning Oilers, but didn't appear in the playoffs that spring.) He also starred in the 1987 Canada Cup in which Canada defeated the Soviets two games to one. Kelly Hrudey — then an Islander — and the Flyers Ron Hextall also were on Team Canada but their services were not needed. "Grant was utterly magnificent," Low remembers.

The glitter of Fuhr's magnificence became tarnished with time and a series of off-ice setbacks that included a 60-game suspension during the 1990-91 season for using an illegal drug. The Oilers decided they had had enough of him and dealt Grant to Toronto before the 1991-92 season. What appeared to be a promising situation crumbled under a knee injury and the emergence of Felix Potvin as a goaltending sensation.

Neither Fuhr's numbers nor his two seasons in Maple Leaf blue were particularly glowing. Meanwhile, Fuhr's former coach John Muckler had moved to Buffalo where he eyed Grant. After intense lobbying, Muckler persuaded his general manager, Gerry Meehan, to deal for Fuhr.

It was a major trade. Buffalo dispatched Dave Andreychuk, Daren Puppa, and the Sabres' first-round draft choice in the 1993 Entry Draft to Toronto for Fuhr. "The price was high," Muckler allows, "but we got what we needed: a goalie who knew how to steal a few big playoff games."

Buffalo took on Boston in the first playoff round in the spring of 1993 and Fuhr did precisely what was expected of him. He stopped the Bruins in the first two games at Boston Garden but saved his best performance for Game Three — won in overtime — when he thwarted crack shooter Cam Neely. To do so Fuhr dove to stop Neely's point-blank drive and then executed a backward somersault to get back on his skates.

Fuhr was knocked out of Game Four with a strained right knee — Dominik Hasek stepped in — as the Sabres completed the four-game sweep, giving Buffalo its first play-off series win in a decade. "If Fuhr wasn't standing on his ear," said Bruins coach Brian Sutter, "we'd have won it."

However, the Buffalo huzzahs were short-lived. He teamed with Hasek in 1993-94 to win the Jennings Trophy for the lowest goals against average but Fuhr's record was 13-12-3. Hasek made him expendable, and in 1994-95 he was dealt to Los Angeles where he recorded a dismal 1-7-3 mark and a 4.04 goals against mark.

Fuhr's career appeared to be over. The Kings wanted no part of him and the unrestricted free agent knew that other clubs took a dim view of his past and his medical records. They showed that he had a surgically repaired left knee and screws in both shoulders from an assortment of separations. Despite these debits, Mike Keenan figured that Fuhr was worth a contract and for that Grant is eternally grateful to his old pal, Gretzky.

Actually it was Gretzky's wife, Janet Jones, who did the urging. Mr. and Mrs. Gretzky had noticed Keenan dining at an outdoor Manhattan restaurant that summer of 1995. Over wine, Keenan asked whether they thought Fuhr had any good hockey left in him. "Of course he can still play," chirped Janet. "He just needs some confidence," added Wayne.

"That's good enough for me," concluded Keenan.

Mike signed Grant to a two-year $2 million deal after refusing to re-sign Curtis Joseph who had become a free agent. It was a noble gesture that blew up in Keenan's face. Despite the precarious nature of his career, Fuhr had egregiously neglected his diet to a point where he had become plain fat. Some say he galumphed into camp 30 pounds overweight although Grant insisted that it was no more than 15 pounds over his playing weight of 190. Whatever it was, Fuhr retained the services of conditioning consultant Bob Kersee and, as teammate Tony Twist discreetly noted, "got a spark under his ass."

Kersee crafted a new diet that banished fatty food and virtually eliminated between-meal snacks. Better still Grant stuck to the new regimen. His body fat content was reduced from 20 percent to 12.1 percent and he lost an estimated 20 pounds. He had his suspension lifted and then proceeded to play some of his best goal in years. He had to because

Keenan kept starting him — over and over and over again. "Almost every night," remembers then Blues assistant coach Bob Berry, "Grant was one of our top players." By the All-Star break he had more wins than he had accumulated over the previous two years.

"He's become the best goalie in the league again," said Keenan.

In a sense this was an imperative. The Blues' spare goalie at the time was Bruce Racine, a 29-year-old career minor-leaguer who never figured in Keenan's plans to start even a single game. Fuhr was resigned — if not enthused — to playing a full season without break. "I figured that if the old body would let me, then I'd play all of them," says Fuhr. "I hadn't been so light since my rookie year in Edmonton."

The coach underlined his point by giving his ace almost no respite. When the 1995-96 season had ended, Fuhr had established a league record for games played in one season by a goaltender (79), surpassing by three his own mark set in Edmonton. He also set a record for consecutive starts by a goaltender (76) and led all NHL goaltenders with shots faced (2,157). "The iron man was born to be a number one goalie," said *Goalies' World* magazine. "Fuhr is playing like the ace he once was."

When newsmen questioned him about the possibility of enervating himself before the playoffs, Fuhr responded that the more he plays in the regular season, the better he performs in the postseason. And it certainly seemed that way. Grant opened the playoffs against Toronto with a 3-1 win but suffered a devastating knee injury in the second match at Maple Leaf Gardens and was sidelined for the remainder of the playoffs.

Fuhr recovered sufficiently to play in 73 regular season games a year later and, despite a mediocre team, to record a 33-28-11 record along with a 2.72 goals against average. *Goalies' World* rated him the 10th best in the NHL right behind John Vanbiesbrouck.

"Grant saved Keenan's life for a year," says *Goalies' World* editor Gilles Moffet. "Then Fuhr came back with a very good 1996-97 even after Keenan left. The problem is that Grant is aging and there's no young star in the Blues' farm system. Which means that Fuhr's aging body must do it all."

In the 1997 playoffs Fuhr demonstrated that the fire still was in his belly and the talent in his pads. Facing the eventual Stanley Cup champion Red Wings, Grant gave his club a chance by blanking the Detroiters 2-0 in Game One and staying at the top of his performance chart throughout the series (eventually captured by Detroit in six games).

"Unless St.Louis gets a really hot goaltender out of the blue," says Moffet, "the Blues had better hope that Fuhr emulates other greats like Glenn Hall and Jacques Plante and plays until his 40s."

Knowing the way Grant loves stopping pucks, we can imagine him doing it into his 60s.

FELIX POTVIN

"Patrick Roy is a very good goalie and I'm really happy to be compared to him."

There have been occasions when goaltenders enjoyed too much success too soon.

Jim Carey is one example and Blaine Lacher another — not to mention Mike Moffet, Jack Gelineau, and other goalies who came and went faster than you can say Georges Vezina.

One might legitimately wonder whether Felix Potvin suffered from the too-much-too-soon affliction.

This much is certain: The French Canadian from Anjou, Quebec became an overnight sensation in Toronto; so good, in fact, that he displaced future Hall of Famer Grant Fuhr from the number one goaltending slot on the Maple Leafs.

An even more astonishing aspect of the Potvin saga was the rapidity of his rise. He was a second-round selection — 31st overall — in the 1990 Entry Draft after being virtually overlooked by most NHL clubs.

"I remember that none of the scouts in the NHL liked him at first," says Gilles Lupien, who has been Potvin's agent. "The first time he was eligible, no one even drafted him. Three rounds, not one team in the league took a chance. I remember thinking, 'Am I crazy or are they crazy? Don't they see what I see?'"

Many scouts had seen how Patrick Roy emerged as a Quebec-nurtured superstar in Montreal's net but Potvin was buried on the Chicoutimi Sagueneens of the Quebec Major Junior Hockey League and being bombed virtually every night. In an easy game, he would face 40 shots but on most nights it was up to 65 pieces of rubber flak.

Even after he had virtually single-handedly pushed the Sagueneens into the 1990 Memorial Cup playoffs, there was doubt about Potvin's true NHL potential. Those scouts with a knowledge of goaltending were critical of Potvin's style. One claimed that he bent over too much, another knocked him for improvising all the time, and a third criticized his use of the goalie stick.

"He plays short," one scout lamented. "He scrunches up too much and always is on his knees. He looks short."

His agent found that knock particularly amusing since Potvin stands 6'1" in bare feet. But Felix managed to grab more attention when he paced Chicoutimi to the Memorial Cup Finals and was named the Quebec League's best goaltender.

This was good enough for Maple Leafs scout Pierre Dorion who drafted the youngster and was prepared to give him about three years in the minors to develop. But Potvin wouldn't let that happen. His play was so remarkable with St. John's of the American League that Felix made his big-league debut in 1991-92.

Maple Leafs general manager Cliff Fletcher had paid dearly for Fuhr and fully expected the former Edmonton Oiler to remain the cornerstone of Toronto goalkeeping for several years. Fuhr's backup was another veteran, Rick Wamsley.

Incredibly, Wamsley was injured during training camp and Fuhr went down with injury early in the 1992-93 season. With no choice, Fletcher ordered Potvin to find an apartment in Toronto until the top bananas were ripe again. Felix started 10 consecutive games, winning six and losing only two while tying two. With a goals against average of 2.20, he immediately qualified for his bromidic nickname, Felix The Cat.

Fletcher's intention was to one-way Potvin back to St. John's at the earliest possible opportunity but the more the manager watched the prodigy, the more his intentions wavered. When Felix registered a 1.33 goals against average in the last six games of his 10 game stint, the boss was befuddled.

In time Potvin was moved back to the Maritimes, but before he had time to put new linen on his dining room table, Fuhr suffered another injury and Felix was back in Toronto.

"Originally," says Fletcher, "we wanted Potvin to remain in St. John's for another season. We wanted him to get about 3,000 minutes playing time with St. John's. We didn't want him on the bench in Toronto, we wanted him to play."

Uncertainty over Fuhr's future was just the lever Fletcher needed. That, plus Potvin's continued excellence. Starting three games in five days, the kid continued his superior stopping, allowing one goal in each of the first two games before tossing a 4-0 shutout at the Montreal Canadiens.

Potvin had made it impossible for Fletcher to send him east again. Instead, the manager made a startling move, trading Fuhr to Buffalo for Dave Andreychuk, Daren Puppa and the Sabres' number one choice in the 1993 draft. Fletcher explained that with expansion on the horizon, he was concerned about losing Potvin to a new team.

"What made us keep him," Fletcher remembers, "was his youth as well as his maturity. He's a very serious young man who works on a very even keel. He's the prototype of the modern goalie."

Until this point, playing Potvin was easier when Fuhr was off in the wings, available when the wounds healed. Now The Cat was on his own and liking it very much, thank you.

He demonstrated his independence with kick saves, glove saves, butterflies, and the brand of confidence that was transmitted throughout the lineup. In a powerful show of force, the Leafs defeated the Detroit Red Wings and St. Louis Blues to sweep the Conference playoffs.Then they extended the Wayne Gretzky-led Los Angeles Kings to seven-games before The Great One, himself, deposited the winner behind The Cat.

Wamsley describes Potvin's unique style: "Felix is unorthodox, stays back in the net, and puts the paddle [stick] on the ice a lot, but it's very effective. All the teachers, all the years, said you never lay the paddle on the ice, that it's too easy for someone to lift the puck and go to the top shelf against you. But Patrick Roy came into the league and did it, and Eddie Belfour does it, and Felix does it, and it works. It might not work so well in practice, when players have time to shoot, but in a game, when there's all that activity and someone's always tuggin' at a guy, hitting him, it's a lot tougher to put the puck in the top shelf."

Fletcher's confidence in Potvin was manifested in many ways and supported by two straight All-Star game invitations. By the end of the 1995-96 season The Cat was numbered among the NHL elite goaltenders virtually as secure as the Maple Leaf Gardens steelwork. More importantly, he seemed immune to pressure.

"There's always pressure when you play, and I've lived with that pressure since I was young," The Cat purrs. "I don't think what happened earlier in my career put any extra pressure on me. Both Grant Fuhr and Rick Wamsley helped me a lot with the shooters and in other ways."

By the start of the 1996-97 season Potvin had a lucrative new contract and 104 regular season wins, tied for fifth on the Leafs' all-time list. His 25 playoff victories put him third on the Toronto chart behind Turk Broda (58) and Johnny Bower (34). Individually, the stats looked good but in relation to a declining hockey club, they were less impressive.

The feeling was that the Leafs would go as far as Potvin would take them which, in the end, was not very far. He came away from the season with the most losses, 37, after a previous high of 26. He had never played in 74 games before nor was he ever backing such an inept NHL team. The Cat faced an NHL-leading 2,438 shots as well as a league-high 34.3 shots per game.

He also was the subject of innumerable trade rumors to such an extent that *Goalies' World* magazine editorialized that Toronto should not deal him. "Potvin is young, experienced and can play under pressure," says editor Gilles Moffet. "Keep him, Leafs!"

Moffet, who believes that Potvin is "taken for granted," rated The Cat the fifth-best goalie in the NHL at the conclusion of 1996-97.

"He was the busiest man in the NHL," Moffet asserts.

Perhaps, but The Cat entered the 1997-98 season with a new boss who just happens to be Ken Dryden, a Hall of Fame goaltender and president of Maple Leaf Gardens. Dryden's Argus eye for netminding will be focused on Potvin.

If Dryden disapproves, it could mean an exit from Toronto. But based on past performance, it appears that The Cat will have a home in Canada's world-class city for years to come.

NIKOLAI KHABIBULIN

"I play the puck more than I ever did in Russia. But I have to do that in the National Hockey League."

When Nikolai Khabibulin was growing up in Sverdlovsk, a city in the former Soviet Union, he received an interesting book at the age of 14. It was all about a goaltender named Vladislav Tretiak.

By the time young Nicky had finished the book, he knew that he wanted to be just like the Russian goaltending legend.

The rest — as the bromide goes — is history.

Tretiak never made it to the NHL. Khabibulin did.

He arrived in Winnipeg for the 1994-95 season, playing for a Jets team that was already earmarked for Phoenix. In due time Nikolai beat the Detroit Red Wings, 3-2, and stopped 39 shots. Then, he defeated the Ottawa Senators, 3-1, and neutralized 30 shots, followed by a 4-0 blanking of Edmonton. The Oilers threw 34 shots at him to no avail.

Experts ranked him the best goalie 22 years of age or younger in the NHL and in the 1995-96 season, Nicky was one of the few positive advertisements for Winnipeg hockey. He played 53 games for the Jets and finished with a solid won-lost mark of 26-20-3.

The Jets took on heavily favored Detroit in the opening playoff round. Many forecasters expected a four-game sweep but Khabibulin stunned the Red Wings so effectively that the series lasted six games before the Detroiters finally prevailed. Nicky was so good that some Detroit writers began calling him the "Bulin Wall."

Keith Tkachuk, who captained the Jets, summed up the series thusly: "If we didn't have Nik, that series doesn't go six games. He came up huge for us. The Red Wings were the better team but Nik helped us give it a run."

"After that," commented *Goalies' World*, "Khabibulin won't be overrated anymore."

Upon moving to Phoenix and becoming a Coyote, Habby — as he's known to his teammates — played well enough for *Goalies' World* to rate him seventh overall among the NHL's best netminders. He was right behind Mike Richter and ahead of Curtis Joseph. (Chico Resch had Habby in 10th place overall.)

The Coyotes thought enough of Khabibulin to offer up a handsome $3 million contract over three years. "The Coyotes were telling the hockey world they thought Khabibulin was the guy to lead them to the Stanley Cup," says Scott Bordow, sports columnist for the *Mesa (Arizona) Tribune*.

Whether it was the security of the big, fat contract or the fact that he faced increased scrutiny, Nicky did not start the season the way he had ended his career in Winnipeg. In plain English, he was struggling.

"Not to worry," insisted the Coyotes' general staff. "All will be well."

All wasn't well in too many critical games to suit too many critics. Some suggested that Nicky really wasn't all that good after all and, perhaps, Coyotes' executive vice-president Bobby Smith was both wasting his club's money and the fans' time.

Smith disagreed. "If he's as good as we think he'll be in the future," said Smith, "we don't have to get another goalie to win the Stanley Cup."

Khabibulin played 72 games for Phoenix in 1996-97, posting seven shutouts and a 2.83 goals against average. This with a team that was defensively weak; and that may be giving the Coyotes back line the better of it.

Khabibulin's challenge was maintaining a positive attitude through the whole ugly mess. It was not easy but he impressed not only his teammates but his boss in the front office.

"When you're a goaltender," says Smith, once a star NHL forward, "the whole building is looking at you whenever you make a mistake. I don't think you can be a top-notch goalie without being mentally strong."

The more they saw him, the more his foes agreed that Habby was both mentally and stylistically strong. Unlike most of his European-taught counterparts, Nicky comes out of his net to challenge shooters. Quick reflexes and a nimble glove hand are among his assets.

"The difference between the way I play here and the way I played in Russia is that I'm using my goalie stick more," says Khabibulin, "playing the puck more than I ever did in Russia, and maybe waiting on the puck a little longer. Otherwise, I haven't been trying to do anything different. What I have learned is that the best teams bring out the best in me. When I beat a good team I feel good about myself."

Chances are that he will continue to feel good about himself. He certainly will if he believes the ranking accorded him by *Goalies' World*. The magazine has tabbed him "the next superstar."

"The guy is for real," says editor Gilles Moffet.

Perhaps that explains why he is being paid a million dollars a year!

ED BELFOUR

"The eagle on my mask represents strength, excellent vision and strong leadership."

There was a time when the Chicago Blackhawks believed that their hopes for winning the franchise's first Stanley Cup since 1961 rested on the pads of goaltender Ed Belfour, alias Eddie The Eagle.

This was especially so during the Windy City reign of Coach Mike Keenan who so steadfastly believed in Belfour he played him in virtually every game.

The Eagle never complained. He likes work the way bears like honey. "I hate being pulled," Belfour allowed. "I figured that if I did my job for Mike I wouldn't be pulled. He made me bear down."

Keenan rejected two promising prospects, Dominik Hasek and Jimmy Waite, for Belfour, a decision that infused The Eagle with immense confidence. "Goalies draw energy from the confidence a coach shows in them," says Keenan. "For a guy like Eddie, goaltending wasn't work, it was fun."

To a point.

Keenan and teammates learned that Belfour took his goaltending more seriously than most. On game days he became a virtual recluse, tending to his equipment the way a concert violinist prepares his Stradivarius.

"I'm very picky," Belfour acknowledged, "especially when it comes to my professional life. Anything I care about is really precise and detailed. I want it to be perfect."

Belfour wasn't exactly perfect but he did play splendidly for Keenan and even reached the Stanley Cup Finals against the Pittsburgh Penguins in 1992. But he never won a Stanley Cup in the Windy City and after Keenan's departure, the fun wasn't the same. Nor was Belfour's relationship with his backup goalie Jeff Hackett.

Whereas Keenan had been unequivocal about Belfour's right to the goaltending throne, Craig Hartsburg was not. After moving behind the Chicago bench, Hartsburg perceived something worthwhile about Hackett and reduced The Eagle's ice time accordingly.

When it became apparent during the 1996-97 season that Hackett was a keeper, Belfour took a dim view of the situation and made his feelings known to management and Hackett. One report, which leaked to the media, had Belfour slurring Hackett as "nothing more than a backup."

By mid-January 1997, the dressing room friction had reached the point of no return. Blackhawks general manager Bob Pulford contacted his counterpart in San Jose, Dean Lombardi, and traded Belfour to the Sharks for Chris Terreri, Ulf Dahlen, and Michael Sykora on January 25th.

Much as he had been a favorite in Chicago, Belfour was pleased by the move. He instantly became numero uno again between the pipes and was warmed by Lombardi's support. "We realized that at some point if this franchise is going to get to the top level, we had to acquire a goaltender of Belfour's caliber," said Lombardi.

Ironically, The Eagle never intended to become a goalie when he was learning the ice game in Carmen, Manitoba (pop. 3,500). During his preteen years, Eddie skated at center while playing a rather boisterous, Marty McSorley-style that incurred penalties by the dozen.

By the time the kid reached age 12, the coach was fed up with his penalty minutes. "You're playing goal," Belfour was told, and therein was the start of a new career.

One could not say that Eddie took to puckstopping like an eagle to flying. He failed to make the varsity team in 11th grade at Carman High School, and even in his senior year was used sparingly. His transition was slow but young Belfour was committed and worked diligently at his new position. However hard he tried, he still was not able to capture the attention of Major Junior A scouts and wound up with a Tier II team, as obscure as one could be. "I don't think anyone knew who I was," Belfour recalled.

No matter. He applied himself, stayed in excellent shape by competing in triathlons, and eventually won a scholarship to the University of North Dakota.

The collegiate experience was precisely what Belfour required for his major leap toward the majors. As a freshman he lost only four games out of 33 — with no ties — and was a principal reason why the Fighting Sioux annexed the 1987 NCAA championship.

It was then that Belfour's meticulousness became evident. He began spending 15 to 20 minutes before each game simply sharpening his own skates. "I wanted to make sure that my edges were just right," he asserted, "and that there were no chips in the blade."

His performance did not go unnoticed by NHL clubs, especially the Blackhawks whose goaltending in 1987-88 was being handled — not very successfully — by Darren Pang and Bob Mason. Chicago signed The Eagle as a free agent since he had not been drafted and put him to work in the 1988-89 season.

With a 3.85 goals against average and a 4-12-3 won-lost-tie record, Belfour was not exactly a gang buster on West Madison Street. The Blackhawks thought nothing of allowing him to goal for the Canadian National Team in 1989-90 but welcomed him to Chicago Stadium for the 1990-91 season.

This time Belfour displayed the maturity that a year of facing European shooters imparted. He played in a career-high 74 games, trimmed his goals against average to 2.47, and finished at 43-19-7. Unfortunately, a 4.07 GAA in the playoffs removed a lot of the regular season luster as Chicago exited the first round in six games.

Nevertheless, Belfour had carved out a permanent position in the Blackhawks' goal and also established himself as one of the more accomplished butterfly-style netminders. In addition, scouts became more and more aware of his mental toughness not to mention The Eagle's willingness to scrap with enemies who crossed his crease.

"Ed has to win, even at home playing Scrabble," explained his wife, Rita.

With Belfour in goal, the Blackhawks reached the Stanley Cup Finals for the first time in 19 seasons when they went up against the defending champion Pittsburgh Penguins in 1992. Although Chicago was swept in four games, Belfour was hardly to blame.

"I have to realize I can't do it by myself," he said when the series ended at Chicago Stadium. "Sometimes that's part of my downfall — I put too much pressure on myself. I want to win and I overdo it sometimes."

Occasionally, Belfour would betray a hint of enmity toward more acclaimed contemporaries, particularly Patrick Roy. Once, The Eagle remarked, "If you win the Stanley Cup, people are going to love you. Patrick's won the Cup three times, and he deserves a lot of recognition. But he had a lot of help, too."

Some journalists, who would interview Belfour, learned that he had an edge in his attitude when he would discuss certain goalies; and an even sharper edge when he believed he was unfairly criticized. In 1993 when *The Hockey News* surveyed pro scouts for a ranking of every NHL player, it reported that Belfour didn't rank among the top ten goalies in the league.

"Eddie took it personally," said *Hockey News'* reporter Mike Brophy.

"*The Hockey News,*" Belfour stated, "has never been good to me. It's getting like *The National Enquirer.*"

Even while Belfour was leading the NHL in goals against average, save percentage, and shutouts, critics railed at his style, claiming that he spent too much time on the ice. His boosters retorted that he anticipated well, squared himself to the shooters with the best of them, and his quickness was second to none.

"Eddie got ticked off when other goalies were applauded simply because they played a textbook style," said Pang, who then did color commentary for the Hawks' games. "Nobody had seen the 'V' style of goaltending before Tony Esposito broke in.

"People said that style wouldn't cut it; he was too low to the ice, his legs were too far apart.

"Well, Esposito was successful and I'd say Eddie Belfour is the Tony O of the '90s."

"When people talk about Eddie," said San Jose Sharks general manager Dean Lombardi, "the first or second thing that comes out of their mouths is 'competitive.' If you want to get his goat, tell him, 'Dominik Hasek is better than you.' He'll hit the roof."

While The Eagle never sipped Stanley Cup champagne, he compiled a handsome 2.49 playoff goals against average with a save percentage of .912. Those who follow Belfour understand that The Eagle takes his business seriously and does not suffer fools — including some in the media — gladly. "I usually have two or three real good friends on the team that I like to hang out with," said Belfour.

Among his pals in Chicago were Greg Smyth and Darin Kimble, two of the tougher players on the Blackhawks. "I like their company," he explained. "You always know those guys are going to be behind you when you need their help." Belfour was a big help to the Blackhawks until Hackett arrived in the Windy City. At first, the newcomer was hardly considered a threat to The Eagle, but within a two-year period two things happened that changed the course of Chicago's goalkeeping history. First, Hackett began playing better than expected, and second, Belfour's winning trend began declining. His goals against average went up in 1995-96, the same year that Hackett began recording better numbers than The Eagle.

"That was real bothersome for me," Belfour admitted. "I don't like to take a backseat and not be involved game after game. That was hard for me to take."

By 1996-97 friction between Eddie and Jeff peaked. Belfour is said to have told Hackett that he didn't want to have anything to do with him. Some Blackhawks sided with Belfour; others didn't. Now it was a question for management to decide who would be top banana between the pipes. On a Friday evening late in January, following a 10 game winless streak, The Eagle had the answer. He was dealt to San Jose.

"I had spent my whole NHL career in Chicago and gave my heart and soul to the Blackhawks," he said. "I really wanted to win the Cup for those fans but it just seemed like Chicago was not making the commitment to win the Stanley Cup."

After dealing the two-time Vezina Trophy winner, Blackhawks general manager Bob Pulford described the trade as one of the most difficult he had ever made. Others argued that Pulford unloaded Belfour at precisely the right time. Many general managers considered Eddie a flawed goalie by this time and one who had benefited as a Blackhawk during the 1990s behind a tight Chicago defense. They considered him overpaid at $2.75 million per year and they eagerly awaited his challenge in California.

It was less than magnificent. Much less.

He was ripped, 5-2, in his debut against the Vancouver Canucks. "I was a little rusty," Belfour explained, "but it was good to get one under my belt. All of us had a bit of butterflies out there. When I'm on my game, I can come up with a few more saves than I did in that one."

Belfour's problem was more than one game as a Shark. He hardly comported himself like someone who was talking Patrick Roy numbers ($4.55 million), who soon would be injured, and who would do no better for the Sharks than second goalie, Kelly Hrudey, or Chris Terreri, who had been shipped to Chicago in the trade.

Nevertheless, his teammates supported him. Bernie Nicholls, who played alongside Belfour in both Chicago and San Jose and who is considered a mature evaluator of goaltending, endorsed the deal. "In the last two playoffs (1985 and 1986) I can honestly say I've never seen better goaltending — ever," Nicholls insisted. "Eddie is as competitive as any player I've ever met."

SEAN BURKE

"There is always the fear when you're not playing that they'll come to think they don't need you."

Before the Hartford Whalers dismantled their tent and moved to North Carolina, Sean Burke promised that helping keep the franchise in Connecticut would be his greatest "save."

It was a noble gesture on the goaltender's part but hardly within his hockey powers. What Burke does best is prevent vulcanized rubber from entering the twine-covered steel goal, not prevent National Hockey League teams from moving from North to South.

What Burke has done best ever since his rookie NHL season has been to bail out seemingly hopeless teams. In one magnificent campaign actually thrust the New Jersey Devils into the franchise's first playoff (1988).

Since then he has been a netminder underblessed when it comes to the performers in front of him; one who could have been treated for "rubberitis," the affliction that confronts goalies who face too many pucks in too short a time.

Superficially, at least, the Windsor, Ontario, native appears to be lacking when it comes to delivering playoff berths. After the 1988 push, Burke played only two more playoff games for New Jersey — both losses — in 1989-90. When he arrived in Hartford for the 1992-93 season the Whalers expected at least a couple of playoff berths for a franchise that desperately needed a boost of some kind.

Instead, for five consecutive seasons the Whalers got nowhere fast, missing the playoffs each season, although Burke hardly could be blamed for that sad state of affairs. His goaltending, if not his teams, have been of high quality from the get-go, starting with the Jersey experience.

"When I came to the Devils," says Burke, "they were struggling and hadn't ever made the playoffs in the history of the franchise. Right off the bat our coach, Jim Schoenfeld, let me play almost every night. And we just kept winning."

The Burke experience at The Meadowlands has become one of the richest aspects of Devils lore. Drafted by New Jersey in 1985, Burke had starred for the Canadian Olympic team and was regarded as one of the most promising young goalies on the continent. When he arrived at East Rutherford after the 1988 Olympics, the Devils were going nowhere fast and appeared destined to miss another playoff berth.

In his first start, Burke was less than impressive, yet he beat the Boston Bruins, 7-6, in overtime. Schoenfeld went with Burke the following day and he beat Philadelphia, 4-2. By late March it was apparent that the Devils had found a lucky charm in the big goalie. He beat Washington 4-2, for the team's first-ever victory at Capital Center and won enough games so that New Jersey still was a contender on the final night of the regular season, April 3, 1988.

A victory for New Jersey over the Blackhawks at Chicago Stadium would thrust them into the playoffs. Burke played well enough to keep the Devils in the hunt, and at 2:21 of sudden-death overtime, John MacLean beat Darren Pang to enable the Devils to beat out the Rangers for the final playoff slot.

En route to the playoffs, Burke had posted a 10-1-0 record and a 3.05 goals against average. His mental toughness was remarkable considering that he joined a club which literally could not afford to lose more than *one* game. He played his angles confidently and skated fluidly in the crease.

Burke's playoff performance would be another story. Was he just lucky in the stretch run or could he repeat his heroics in the playoffs?

The answer was supplied in the opening round against the heavily favored Islanders which the Devils won, 4-2. A strong Washington Capitals club was next on the agenda. This time the series went to a full seven games but Burke had been wobbly in Game Six, a 7-2 loss, and Schoenfeld was considering backup Bob Sauve for the decisive seventh game.

The coach's decision was done in a strange way. After the Friday day-of-game skate, Schoenfeld walked into the locker room and found Burke taking a shower. "Schony threw me the soap," Burke remembers, "and I dropped it. Then, he threw it at me again — and I dropped it. But I caught it on the third try, and he said I was playing."

Burke played a cool, calculating game and kept New Jersey tied at 2-2 into the third period. At 13:39 MacLean deflected a shot behind Capitals goalie Pete Peeters to give New Jersey the lead. Now it was Burke's game to preserve.

"I had something to prove to myself and to everybody that I could fight back from a game like Game Six and be a plus for my team," says Burke.

He blanked Washington the rest of the way and the game ended 3-2, for the Devils' second consecutive playoff upset. Sean Burke was fast becoming a new NHL hero. His next challenge would be the Boston Bruins and it was in Game Two of the series that he may well have established himself as a permanent number one goalie.

The score was 2-2 going into overtime but the Bruins were conspicuously stronger. In the first sudden-death period Burke robbed Cam Neely on a breakaway and also made outstanding saves against Rick Middleton, Craig Janney, and Randy Burridge. "Burke's goaltending was the difference," says Terry O'Reilly who was Bruins coach at the time.

The game finally was decided at 17:46 on a long Doug Brown shot. At this point in time Burke's record as a Devil was 17-6 in regular season and playoff games.

Sean's bubble eventually burst in the seventh game which the outmanned Devils lost 6-2, but he had become New Jersey's main man in goal. In 1988-89, his first full year in the NHL, he became the first NHL rookie and first Devil to start an NHL All-Star Game. Over two seasons Sean set a team record with 54 career victories.

Precisely what went wrong after that is a moot point. In the 1989-90 playoffs Burke played two games, lost them both, and came out of it with a 3.84 goals against average. Meanwhile, the Devils' second goalie, Chris Terreri, had shown enough improvement to earn more playing time — at the expense of Burke. After the 1990-91 season, Burke decided not to return to Jersey and signed on with the San Diego Gulls of the International League as well as the Canadian Olympic team.

Burke won a silver medal with the Olympians and eventually was traded by New Jersey to the Hartford Whalers for Bobby Holik and Jay Pandolfo, a second round 1993 draft choice.

"Coming to the Whalers was the best thing that could have happened," says Burke. "I liked being with an organization that was building and I liked being asked to take a leadership role."

The growth pains may have been more intense than he had imagined. For five straight years Hartford missed the playoffs, yet Burke remained the workhorse when not sidelined by injury. In 1995-96, for example, he played a career-high 66 games for a 3.11 goals against average. Despite a mediocre team in front of him, his won-loss record was a respectable 28-28-6.

"He is part of the underrated goaltenders club," says *Goalies' World* editor Gilles Moffet. "It has nothing to do with theme individual but everything to do with the team for which he plays. He's one of the top goalies in the league."

Others who were Burke's teammates in Hartford — specifically Brendan Shanahan and Paul Coffey — found the small-city, non-playoff environment bothersome, asked to be traded, and were granted their wish. Burke never leaned away from his position as a team leader and Hartford supporter.

"It can be dangerous playing on a team that doesn't have a lot of success when you have success as an individual," he explains. "You can get too comfortable with your situation and get lazy. In Hartford people appreciated that I was one of the top players. That was nice. But if the team didn't have success, what good was it?"

In the spring of 1997 owner Peter Karmanos moved Burke and the rest of the team out of Hartford to Carolina where the Whalers suddenly became the Hurricanes. The change of venue and change of name did not instantly make Burke an All-Star nor did it make the transformed club a playoff contender. But Sean's focus remained unchanged and his philosophy as solid as ever.

"I've taken my situation as a personal challenge. When you come to a team that was struggling, as I did, and you are a good player, you have a responsibility to help turn that team around.

"I've learned how to self-motivate myself when performing under less than great conditions. Sure, it's great for a goalie when he doesn't have to play the best game of his life to win. It's great knowing that with good goaltending, you're on a team good enough to beat any team in the league."

For five years that luxury has eluded Burke. Whether he finds such happiness as a Hurricane — or on any other NHL team — remains to be seen.

What is known, however, is that Sean Burke on an underdog or on a winner, will deliver every bit of goaltending he has to offer. Quite simply, it's part of his make-up.

ANDY MOOG

"It's going to not be fun at some point. But now it's still easy to do because it's still so much fun to come to the rink and play."

If you ask Andy Moog he won't hesitate to tell you he's something special.

"I might be the first guy in a new breed of goaltenders. I'm talking about people who have come through the 1980s and have had longevity. It was myself, Grant Fuhr, Mike Vernon, Patrick Roy, and Eddie Belfour; the new breed that came through. I was one of the first guys in that group that ushered in a new era in goaltending."

That he did.

It was an era in which goaltending standards were lifted to all-time highs and one in which Moog demonstrated a longevity that has made him the envy of his peers. Conceivably, the man whose name carried across Canada and the United States in the spring of 1981 could play 20 years of big-league hockey.

"Andy's style gets simpler as the years go by," says Anaheim Mighty Ducks goalie coach Francois Allaire. "He has eliminated a lot of unnecessary moves from his game. His biggest asset is that he knows his limits and he plays accordingly."

Goalies' World magazine was less generous in its appraisal at the conclusion of the 1996-97 season, although Moog had a handsome 2.15 goals against average. It placed Moog in 16th position overall, behind Rick Tabaracci and in front of Chris Osgood.

"He may have the best goals against average," says *Goalies' World*, "but he is also well-protected."

Moog also is well-endowed with goaltending lore, being the son of a professional goaltender who had the courage to play professionally before the era of the mask.

"My father taught me when I was 13 and 14 years old and he emphasized that I should never get rattled," Andy remembers. "He taught me not to give the other team an advantage by reacting in any way to what happens on the ice. Those pointers have helped me to this very day."

Battered Don Moog was not a pleasant sight for his son to see. "His nose was a big piece of jelly," says Andy. "It was all over his face. His teeth — they were false." Eventually, Don Moog concluded his hockey career and became a Greyhound bus driver. The old pads were placed in the basement of the family home in Penticton, British Columbia, and remained there with the gloves and other equipment.

By the time Andy was 10, he was invited to play hockey with his neighborhood chums. Where would he play? No question.

"I already had the equipment," he laughs, "so I became the goaltender."

The path toward professional goaltending went from Penticton to Billings, Montana, where Moog played for the Billings (Junior) Bighorns. He was named to the Second All-Star team in 1979-80. That induced the Edmonton Oilers to select him 132d overall in the 1980 Entry Draft on their sixth pick.

He was sent to Wichita of the Central Hockey League a year later to ripen for the big time. All signs suggested that he was at least two or three years away from "The Show." But strange things were happening in Edmonton where the goaltending was in a state of turmoil prior to the opening playoff round against the Montreal Canadiens.

Oilers coach Glen (Slats) Sather had two veterans, Eddie Mio and Ron Low, but neither was healthy so he went with untried Moog.

Teammate Kevin Lowe, who later authored a book about his Oiler experience, put it this way about Moog:

"Andy came in and stood on his head. While he was doing that, he got a little help from his friends. He needed it. In our earlier two games at Montreal we scored a grand total of one goal. No way Moog would win for us if we didn't score for him but our new kids obliged in a hurry. Glenn Anderson and Jarri Kurri beat Richard Sevigny in the first while Slats encouraged us to keep taking the play to them. He figured that the Habs could be had by throwing them on the defense. Glenn figured that if we jumped into the lead and held it for a bit, the rabid Montreal crowd would turn on the Canadiens and screw them up even more.

"He couldn't have been more right. We beat them 6-3, and Moog kept making saves. The more saves he made, the more reassured we felt in front of him. We relaxed, realizing we didn't have to play defensive all the time and as we opened up, the Canadiens backed off. It was hard to believe that this wonderful Andy Moog had a 14-13 record with Wichita in the Central League and a 3.33 goals against average. Overnight, he had become a Canadian national hero — except, of course, in Montreal.

"But could Andy Who do it again? The test came in Game Two and Moog passed it with as much ease as he had in the opener. Staked to a 2-1 lead after two periods (Coffey and Siltanen had scored for us, which shows you we had offense on the defense!), Moog shut the door on the Habs in the third. Kurri put the game away, thanks to Wayne's pass late in the third, and we walked out of The Forum with an incredible two games to none lead.

"And to top it all, Montreal's goaltending was mediocre compared with the magnificent Moog. We dominated them in Game Three and Moog continued to play like Georges Vezina. 'Maybe I was in a daze,' said Andy, 'but who cares, it was working.'

"Lafleur was invisible and Gretz was all over the place. Wayne scored a hat trick and we just cruised at the end, holding a 6-2 lead. At the end the fans began a countdown and went out of their minds. Actually, I couldn't help but feel sorry for the Canadiens. Guys like Lafleur, Larry Robinson, Rejean Houle, Savard and Lapointe were names I revered growing up in Lachute — and they had just gone under.

"It was, as the *Edmonton Sun* proclaimed the next day, INCREDIBLE!"

Moog became as much a fixture in Edmonton as Northlands Coliseum. In 1982-83 he played in 50 regular season games and 16 playoff matches as the Oilers went to the Stanley Cup Finals, where they were beaten in four by the New York Islanders.

On another team Andy would have been *the* goalie but the Oilers also felt comfortable with a youngster named Grant Fuhr. In 1983-84 the battle for top spot was neck and neck until the final playoff round when Fuhr took the lead as well as a Stanley Cup ring.

That did it. Fuhr had become the go-to guy while Moog was, for all intents and purposes, the back up. This was an intolerable situation for a professional who believed he was equally competent. After playing on Stanley Cup champs in 1984, 1985, and 1987, Andy asked to be traded.

Sather refused, and Moog left Edmonton to play for the Canadian National team and the 1988 Canadian Olympic team. "I felt that I was not being challenged," Andy explains. "I was not developing as a player. It was time to move on."

The Oilers cooperated by trading Moog's rights to the Boston Bruins. In Beantown he became a hero of sorts over five full seasons. In 1990, 1991 and 1992, he played 20, 19 and 15 playoff games, respectively. He was deified in the manner of past Bruins goalie heroes such as Frankie Brimsek but there was one essential difference: When Brimsek played there was no NHL Players' Association. Now there was and Moog stood front and center as its vice-president. He was outspoken on labor issues to the point of angering his Bruins bosses. Still, it was difficult for general manager Harry Sinden to dump Andy. His record was too good.

In 1992-93 he finished with a career high 37 wins and went 17-1 in his last 18 games with a 1.88 goals against average. He was, as Dallas Stars GM Bob Gainey says, "able to carry his team."

Carry them, that is, up until the playoffs.

Perhaps it was an overload of work; perhaps it was just bad breaks. Whatever it was, Moog played uncharacteristically poor in the 1993 playoffs but there were good reasons. Don Moog had been stricken with lung cancer and his life was ebbing. Andy, who previously had missed three regular season games, returned to be at his father's side. "It was a very difficult time," Andy recalls. It was equally difficult for the Bruins. Andy was not in top form and Boston quickly lost the first round playoff to Buffalo in four consecutive games. Moog started three games and lost them all. His average climbed to an unsightly 5.22.

That was just the lever Sinden required. He sent Moog packing to Dallas in June 1993 for Jon Casey. "Hockey is a humbling game," says Moog. "You have to earn respect for yourself every time out. Every night."

Respect was restored in Texas. He became one of the top stars on the Stars and one of the NHL's workhorses. By 1996-97 he had chalked up 16 big-league years and 35,077 minutes played. That was the equivalent of over 580 hours or close to 24 consecutive days. If the end was in sight, Andy was seeing it.

"I figure it's going to not be fun at some point," he says. "But it's easy to come to the rink, go through some of the grueling practices and the travel and all the lows that come along with a hockey season. It's easy to do because it's still so much fun to come to the rink and play."

Under Coach Ken Hitchcock in 1996-97 he played in 48 games, winning 28, losing 12 and tying five. The Stars enjoyed a very appetizing regular season run, ranking among the NHL's best.

Hitchcock states: "Andy adds an understanding of what it takes to win. The team rallied around him because they have confidence in his ability. If players feel confident around a goalie, the club stands a good chance of being successful. He's still very focused and very competitive and wants to play in the big games. The only thing is that he won't be able to play in as many games as he did when he was younger."

But there is the matter of Moog's more recent playoff records. With Andy in goal the Stars missed the playoffs once and have never escaped from the first round on three other occasions.

During the 1997 Stanley Cup opening round, Dallas was heavily favored to oust Edmonton, but Curtis Joseph, plain and simple, played extraordinary in goal while Moog did not. The Stars were over and out in seven games.

Which is not to suggest that Andy Moog is an antique. Quite the contrary. With prudent use, he can still be a significant asset and with his motivation, he should be a solid goalie for a few more years.

Andy Moog retire? No way.

"I've never dreamed of doing anything else but play goal," he says.

Case closed.

JIM CAREY

"I had an obsession with winning. I couldn't handle losing. I'd get so upset, I'd bite myself."

At this point in time it's almost impossible to believe that Jim Carey won the Calder Trophy in 1995 and the Vezina Trophy a year later.

This is the same Carey who, in the last six weeks of the 1995-96 season, not only was the National Hockey League's best goaltender but also maintained an astonishing 96 percent save percentage while recording no less than five shutouts for the Washington Capitals.

Carey's unexpected tailspin from Caps hero to unsteady Boston Bruins blocker ranks among the most abrupt turnabouts in modern goaltending memory.

Which is the real Carey?

Supporters of the Dorchester, Massachusets, native note that he starred at Boston's Catholic Memorial High School, the University of Wisconsin and Portland of the American Hockey League.

"When I had him, he was very consistent, very levelheaded in the net," says Wisconsin's coach Jeff Sauer. "It almost got to the point where some of our guys would get mad because they didn't see any emotion from him."

With Carey in goal the Badgers reached the Final Four in 1993-94 after which he signed with the Capitals who had selected him 32nd overall in the 1992 Entry Draft.

The Caps had hoped to season him in Portland for the 1994-95 season but after he recorded a 30-14-11 mark in Maine, he was called to Washington and merely startled the civilized hockey world with save after save. In no time at all his big-league stats were 13-3-2 accompanied, by a 1.89 goals against average and a .923 save percentage.

Jim was voted NHL player of the month, the first rookie ever to be solo winner of the prize. Then Washington coach Jim Schoenfeld had opted for Carey after his three other choices — Byron Dafoe, Olaf Kolzig, and Rick Tabaracci — had failed in one way or another.

"At the time we called up Jim we had the lowest shooting percentage in the league and the lowest save percentage," Schoenfeld recalls. "A team can't have both and be successful."

Carey's success story was originally authored at Nassau Coliseum where he topped the Islanders on March 2, 1995. It didn't seem like much at the time although teammate Jason Allison perceived some good ahead. When he noticed Carey shaving in the dressing room after the win, he suggested that Jim retain the beard for good luck purposes.

"I'm thinking, 'Yeah, right, one in a row, ha-ha-ha,'" says Carey. "But Jason was serious."

So was Jim. He totaled 28 regular season games for Washington (18-6-3) while opposition scouts puzzled over what got him to the top so fast.

"I worked hard on what I had." Carey notes. "I was not extremely quick. My whole life I worked on positioning and rebounds. Check out how many goals are rebounds. If you can eliminate that, you've done a lot as a goalie. If I can force a guy to shoot wide, that's one for me as far as I'm concerned."

David Poile, the Capitals' general manager who had originally drafted Carey, believed that he had finally found the stopper that had eluded Washington for so long.

"During my tenure," says Poile, "goaltending had been our Achilles' heel in Washington. "When it came to crunch time, the playoffs, it wasn't there. You could say the Capitals lost, or the Capitals choked. But nine times out of 10, it was the other team's goalie outshining our goalie. It was always the other goalie who would steal a win. We were hoping that Jim could do that for us."

But the Capitals collided with Pittsburgh in the opening playoff round and after amassing a three-games-to-one lead, lost the next three straight and the series. Carey's playoff save percentage slipped to a pathetic .834 compared to .913 over the regular campaign but his coach at the time, Jim Schoenfeld, absolved the rookie of any blame.

"We lost the last game of the Pittsburgh series, 3-0," says Schoenfeld. "The guys who were the scorers should have had the sleepless nights that summer, not Carey."

If the traumatic playoff had any long-lasting effects on Carey, it wasn't apparent in 1995-96. He ousted all competition and played 71 regular season games. Among them were nine shutouts and a 2.26 goals against average. Still, there were critics. One knock was that he dropped to his knees a little too early and a little too often.

"His assets were his demeanor, his attitude, and his composure," says Dave Poulin, coach of Notre Dame who had been a teammate of Carey's in Washington. "He was controlled in the way that he played."

Part of his success was rooted in his family. His father, Paul, was a high school all-American football player. Jim's brother, Paul Jr., was a first baseman in the Baltimore Orioles' system. His mother, Beverly, stoked her son's competitive fires with an assortment of games as pedestrian as coin-flips.

"If we flip a coin," says Beverly Carey, "I'll beat Jim five times out of six. I don't even consider him a lucky goalie."

Whatever the cause, Jim's luck ran out in the 1996 playoffs. Entering the opening round against Pittsburgh for the second straight spring, Carey appeared to be in excellent shape. He was a top Vezina Trophy candidate and the hottest goaltender in the homestretch.

Something went wrong in the playoffs. Very wrong. In Game One, Carey relinquished four goals by 11:09 of the second period after making but a dozen saves. Coach Schoenfeld gave him the hook, inserting Olaf Kolzig between the pipes. Washington rallied and won the game 6-4.

Kolzig also captured Game Two and seemed set in the net. Why would a coach upset a winning combination? Yet, before Game Three had begun Schoenfeld went back to Carey.

In the first period Carey gave up two goals on three shots in the first period. He settled down as the game unfolded but the damage had been done. Pittsburgh came out of it with a 4-1 victory, although the Capitals had outshot the Penguins 39-19.

Schoenfeld went back to Kolzig in Game Four, and Ollie The Goalie played one of the games of his life. The score was tied, 2-2, after regulation time and then extended through four overtime periods before Kolzig was beaten on a screened shot. In Game Five Schoenfeld stayed with Ollie but this time his luck was bad and he lost 4-1.

Now down 3-2, Schoenfeld switched again to Carey. Under the circumstances it was a difficult move, especially for the young goalie. "Carey had to be thinking about his last two games and the last thing you want in a big game is a thinking goaltender," says *Goalies' World* editor Gilles Moffet. "Everything has to be instinct. Kolzig had played three great games in his last four and was the man who could save the Capitals."

Carey started, gave up two goals, and was yanked in favor of Kolzig. But it was too late. Pittsburgh went on to win, and Carey finished the season a confused goaltender. "That series will have a lasting effect on Carey," says Moffet. "He will have flashbacks of his nightmarish 1996 playoffs and of his two hooks. He will have to be very, very strong mentally. The wounds of the 1996 playoffs will be very tough to heal. In fact they may last for a long time and maybe for his entire career. You even have to wonder if Carey will ever be the same. Goaltending is a matter of confidence."

The only confidence booster for Carey arrived in June 1996 when he won the Vezina Trophy as the best goaltender during the regular season. Jim was the first goalie to be nominated in both of his first two seasons. In 1996 his competition came from Detroit's Chris Osgood and Daren Puppa of Tampa Bay. Osgood finished second, six behind Carey.

But the award merely cloaked the playoff debacle. Against the Penguins he had a 6.19 goals against average and a .744 save percentage in parts of three games. He returned to Washington at the start of 1996-97 but hardly played like a Vezina Trophy winner. Whether it was Carey's fault or the injury-riddled Caps fault is debatable, but late in the season GM David Poile included Carey — along with Jason Allison and Anson Carter — in a blockbuster deal with Boston. In return Washington received goalie Bill Ranford as well as forwards Rick Tocchet and Adam Oates.

"For me Boston was a whole different ball game," says Carey. "Washington was not a sports town and Boston is. I know that, having grown up there. In Boston the fans live and die with their teams. In Washington there's politics and a million and one other things you can do.

"In Boston, I walk down the street and people recognize me. There's no hockey tradition in Washington. The Bruins certainly have one and the players in Boston feel it. You can see it in the crowds. Late in the season we were essentially out of the playoffs, yet we beat Florida and the place went crazy. That's a hockey town. In Washington if they were out of the playoffs at that time, they would have drawn 9,000 people."

Carey's play as a Bruin was mediocre, to say the least. "He looked awful," says Moffet. "He looked like a goalie who needs help."

Nobody had to tell Jim how his game had suffered. It was there for all to see. "All I wanted to do was start over at the beginning of the season (1997-98) and start winning," he says. "I want the Bruins to be a solid contender and see what it's like playing in Boston then."

Can Carey recover his lost Vezina form?

Goalies' World rated him "The Most Disappointing Goalie of 1996-97." Editor Moffet concludes: "Carey is still one of the most talented young goalies in the game but if the Bruins do not take good care of him quickly, his career will be short-lived. Carey needs a solid veteran backup and a full-time goalie coach!"

GUY HEBERT

'I feel like every shot that comes my way I have an opportunity to stop."

The venerable city of Troy, New York — just up the Hudson River from New York's state capital, Albany — never has been known as a goaltending production center.

The one exception is Guy Hebert who, since 1994, has been the difference between the Mighty Ducks of Anaheim keeping their heads above water in the National Hockey League or sinking to the very depths.

It was not easy.

It's never easy when you are the last line of defense on an NHL expansion team.

The first player chosen by Anaheim (second overall) in the 1993 Expansion Draft from St. Louis, Hebert came to the Mighty Ducks after only 38 total NHL games spread across a mere two seasons.

Moreover, nothing that he had done for the Blues was particularly noteworthy beyond one shutout and two consecutive .500 records with a rather uninspired hockey club.

"Any goalie will tell you that regardless of how the shots come on you, you always feel responsible for them," says Hebert. "A save here and there can always turn a tie into a win."

Usually, Hebert required more than a save or two. Because of Anaheim's ineptitude over its first three seasons, Guy usually was more overwhelmed by shots than under-whelmed. Even in 1996-97, the Mighty Ducks first playoff year, Hebert looked at more rubber than his counterpart at the other end.

A game against St. Louis in January 1997 comes to mind.

On a night when freezing rain, sleet, and snow engulfed the city, the Blues incessantly bombarded the Anaheim goal. A grand total of 39 shots were fired at Hebert but only one eluded him.

"We had them where we wanted them all night," chuckles former coach Ron Wilson in retrospect, "hemmed in our end. When that happens my hope is that goaltending is up to the task and on that night it was."

It was precisely that brand of goaltending which would allow Anaheim to reach the playoffs for the first time in April 1997 although his play had been superlative long before that while the Mighty Ducks were missing the playoffs.

"Hebert was the most underrated goaltender in the NHL while Anaheim was a non-playoff team," says Gilles Moffet of *Goalies' World* magazine. "In 1995-96, for example, the Ducks had enough points (78) but Winnipeg, with an extra win, got the last playoff spot.

"Guy had been fantastic in February and March with seven straight wins, allowing only seven goals on 236 shots in the last six wins. Hebert is good under pressure and was dying to show it in the playoffs."

He didn't have to wait that long. The months of February, March and half of April

1997 were just like the playoffs. Virtually every game played by the Mighty Ducks had the veneer of postseason about it. Despite the pressure-cooker atmosphere, Hebert kept his cool and revealed a mental equilibrium that impressed friend and foe alike.

"I always try to keep a happy medium," Hebert insists. "Sometimes it's difficult. In 1995-96 we had too much of a roller coaster ride and it made for a really difficult time. One day you start to feel good and the next day you're down in the dumps. I got caught doing that a little bit and after that happened, I refused to do it again."

Earlier in his career Hebert had been ridiculed in *The Hockey News* for being one of the most overpaid goaltenders in the NHL. By 1996-97 he had learned to handle his critics as well as the odd bad game.

"I'm upset when I don't play well and don't win," Hebert admits. "But I try to keep things in perspective. I'm confident in my ability and I know that I have Mikhail Shtalenkov so if I can't play or am not playing well, and Mike's playing well, then he plays. We look at it as 'What can I do for the team?' That was an important lesson I learned."

Essentially, Hebert learned how to be a winner as did his teammates. The Mighty Ducks had never made the playoffs before 1996-97, a fact that made their accomplishment that much more enriching when it finally happened. Especially for Guy.

"I wanted the playoffs very badly," he says. "Getting there had been my only goal for the (1996-97) year. Naturally, I wanted a lot of wins and good personal stats but I was willing right from the start to trade all that in just to make sure we made it into the playoffs."

How well Hebert comported himself was evident by the Mighty Ducks' resounding finish. "The Ducks owed that finish to the scoring of Paul Kariya and Teemu Selanne," wrote Elliott Teaford of the *Los Angeles Times*, "but they also couldn't have done it without Hebert."

Brian Bellows, who had seen considerable goaltending over a long NHL career, rates Hebert among the top 10 goalies in the league. "He's certainly one of the most unsung goalies in the league," says Bellows.

Perhaps, but if one sings about someone long enough, he no longer is unsung and that is precisely the case with Guy Hebert.

BILL RANFORD

"My first year in Boston was a blur. I was playing on Cloud Nine; happy to be there and excited every time I was on the ice."

The excitement has changed for Bill Ranford but the IQ — as in Intensity Quotient — remains the same.

More than a decade after he broke into the big time as a Boston Bruins rookie, Ranford still produces the kinds of "Ooohs" and "Ahhhs" from fans that only a very special athlete can induce.

Now, however, they come from Washington and not Boston nor Edmonton where he previously established his high-quality goaltending credentials.

From the very start, he has been very special. Independent, he calls it. "I always have been," he says. "You can't be a follower all your life."

Ranford's first decision not to follow occurred when he was a 16-year-old goalie in Red Deer, Alberta. Opportunity had knocked. He had gone to his first training camp for the Junior A team in New Westminster, British Columbia.

He didn't figure to make the big club. In fact, he was all set to return to Red Deer when he was told to stay in New Westminster and join the Junior A team and not play Tier II hockey anymore.

"I chickened out," Ranford remembers. "My father was with me and told me I could go home to Red Deer with him if that's what I wanted. It was a situation where I didn't feel I was ready to leave home."

He returned to Red Deer in time for supper the next night. The following morning found Bill on a plane for the 1,000-mile trip back to British Columbia. "It was a 30-second decision for me," he chuckles. "When I got back to Red Deer, I realized I wanted something better than Tier II hockey and that better brand was in New Westminister."

On the surface the Ranford expedition to New Westminster was hardly an artistic success. In 1985-86 he registered a 4.84 goals against average and a hardly encouraging 17-29-1 won-loss record.

Then, a strange thing happened. Despite his inexperience and modest credentials, Ranford was summoned to the Boston Bruins. It was the final week of the regular season with the Bruins perched precariously in third place and in danger of missing the playoffs for the first time in two decades.

General Manager Harry Sinden and Coach Butch Goring believed they needed a fresh ingredient in the mix, so they designated Ranford as goaltender for a crucial game against Buffalo at Boston Garden on March 29, 1986.

Just about everyone but the general staff thought the Bruins high command had gone nuts.

"It sure as hell was a crapshoot," acknowledges Sinden. "But when Butch and I talked, we said, 'If this could help the team, we'd be wrong not to take a shot.' It was a calculated chance. Billy had had a great camp. He'd faced a ton of shots in Juniors and sometimes that's better for a developing goalie.

"He played with courage. There always was the chance that it wouldn't help the team and that Sinden and Goring would be exposed as foolish. But was that any reason not to make a move?"

During his brief run that spring, Ranford galvanized the Bruins. He beat Buffalo, 2-1, in his debut and followed that with a 5-3 victory in Buffalo. Pat Riggin, the regular Boston goalie, suddenly found himself warming the bench.

When the dust had cleared, the Bruins were in the playoffs again and Ranford was credited as the catalyst. However, the playoffs were less conducive to success. Bill lost both starts and finished with a 3.50 goals against average. "After that season had ended it finally came into reality that I had gotten a chance and I made the best of it," Ranford recalls.

Boston couldn't wait for his return and when training camp opened, the *Boston Globe* ran a five-column headline, CAN RANFORD, THE BRUINS WUNDERKIND LAST SEASON, PICK UP WHERE HE LEFT OFF?

To a certain extent he did. After 41 games he established himself as NHL-worthy, if not among the best in the bigs. What was evident to one and all was his intensity both on and off the ice.

"I'm a bad loser," he admits. "It's just the way I am. I'm not a sore loser, but I'm not a good loser. Before I came up to the Bruins, I had gone through a lot in New Westminster. I learned that even if you're down 10 or 11 goals, you've still got to try."

Nobody could question his effort but there were doubts about his ability. The 3.33 goals against average in 1986-87 after 41 games as a Bruin was not stunning enough for Ranford to win a starting assignment in the fall of 1987.

He was relegated to Maine of the American Hockey League and remained a Mariner for most of the season before *the* trade. On March 8, 1988, Ranford was dealt to the Edmonton Oilers with Geoff Courtnall and a 1988 second round draft pick for Andy Moog.

The move to Edmonton merely confirmed what Ranford followers had suspected all along: Give Bill a solid team in front of him and he'll respond with blazing trumpets.

He finished his last six games in Edmonton undefeated and kept getting better by the year. In 1989-90 Ranford recorded his first 20-plus win season and tied for fourth in the NHL with 24. He also stopped two penalty shots (Claude Loiselle and Tom Kurvers) before taking the Oilers on a 22-game odyssey to the Stanley Cup.

On the way to Lord Stanley's mug, Ranford tied the NHL record for playoff wins with 16 and won the Conn Smythe Trophy as the playoffs' most valuable player as the Mark Messier-captained team went the route. In time Ranford would become the only NHL goalie who could tell his grandchildren that he played for winners of the Stanley Cup, Canada Cup, and World Championship — and had a Smythe Trophy thrown in for good measure.

One can only guess as to the heights Ranford might have reached in Edmonton had the club's financially strapped owner, Peter Pocklington, not stripped the Oilers of their stars, Messier included. By 1994-95 Ranford was fronting a ramshackle club that had virtually the same trappings as the New Westminster sextet, only on a different level.

In 1993-94 the Oilers had missed the playoffs and were under .500 for the second

straight year. Ranford had lost a dozen more games than he had won and his goals against average had climbed to 3.48.

"In spite of the numbers, that season was one of my most consistent. The wins and losses may not have been there, but the consistency was. Even though we weren't winning, I was enjoying the game."

He also enjoyed the World Championships, posting a 6-0 record and backstopping a shootout win over Finland for the title. "My game matured," Ranford explains. "In other years I would be trying to break up plays when I shouldn't, trying to do too much. I was doing things that weren't part of my game and I had to go back to the way I play.

"I had settled down. I wasn't strictly a reflex goalie anymore. When I was playing my best in the mid-1990s, I was on my feet and challenging the shooters."

In 1994-95 he finished the season with a 3.62 goals against average and still managed to earn raves. "Ranford," says goalie consultant and author Ian Young, "is the best example in the world why you can't judge a goalie by his goals against average.

"In terms of his style, he reminds me of an old-fashioned stand-up goalie. He has that massive desire to be the best in every one of his movements."

One of the other movements was rather traumatic. On January 11, 1996 he was moved back to Boston for Mariusz Czerkawski, Sean Brown, and 1996 first round draft pick Matthieu Descoteaux. At the time of the deal the Bruins appeared incapable of reaching the playoffs. With Ranford between the pipes, they delivered a homestretch rush for their 30th consecutive postseason competition.

"Ranford didn't have his best season by any means," commented *Goalies' World* magazine, "but he reached within his immense potential to accomplish a mission thought impossible by many die-hard Boston fans. Ranford saved their honor."

At the time *Goalies' World* rated Ranford the 15th best netminder in the league, one behind John Vanbiesbrouck and one ahead of Tom Barrasso. "Away from the inexperienced Oilers, Ranford could be back among the top ten goalies in the league in 1996-97."

This was not to be; not even close. *Goalies' World* dropped Ranford to 26th position with the comment that he was "way below his standards."

Whether that was a bum rap or not is debatable. He played 37 games for a rather inept Bruins team and came away with a 12-16-8 mark and a 3.49 goals against mark. By the beginning of March it had become apparent that the Bruins were going nowhere fast and would likely miss the playoffs for the first time in three decades.

On March 1, 1997 Harry Sinden responded to the near calamity by dispatching Ranford, along with forwards Rich Tocchet and Adam Oates, to Washington in exchange for goalie Jim Carey and forwards Anson Carter and Jason Allison.

"Ranford is a battler," said then Capitals coach Jim Schoenfeld at the time of the deal. "He battles for every save. He makes teams beat him; he doesn't beat himself. He's definitely the guy we're counting on down the stretch."

The trade was hailed as a playoff-maker in Washington. The Capitals were playing on the bubble and required a boost to get themselves on track for the homestretch. Virtually every critic lauded the move by then general manager David Poile.

That is, virtually every critic but New Jersey Devils coach Jacques Lemaire. It was Lemaire's opinion that Ranford would have little impact on the Capitals' playoff run.

"He's a guy who went to a few teams," Lemaire explains. "When you're going to three, four teams, you can't be steady. You can be very good, but maybe not steady at the same time. Otherwise teams would keep him. Who wants to get rid of a valuable player?"

Lemaire's was the minority view but nonetheless was eminently prophetic. Ranford did little to impress and even less to nudge Washington into the playoffs. He played 18 games as a Capital and came away with a respectable 2.74 goals against average. But that was on a team that scored precious few goals. As a result the won-loss numbers were not impressive at all (8-7-2) and, lo and behold, Washington — like Boston — missed the playoffs.

Unquestionable, the dismal finish has cast a pall over Ranford's future. It also coast both Schoenfeld and Poile their jobs. Under new GM George McPhee and Coach Ron Wilson, Ranford will have an opportunity to bring his image back to its Conn Smythe Trophy-winning status.

Those who know Bill as the fighter that he is are convinced another career turnaround is not only possible but likely.

MIKE VERNON

"Most coaches are two-faced. They almost have to be. When things are going well, you're their guy. But when you're losing, well, they get paid to win. They'll turn on you on a dime."

If the National Hockey League had in its infinite wisdom produced a trophy for "Most Underappreciated Goaltender of All-Time," the hands-down winner would be Mike Vernon.

Respect has not come easily to the witty and wise veteran. Not even after goaltending his way to Stanley Cup championships in 1989 with Calgary and 1997 with Detroit. Occasionally, Mike betrays annoyance over this unpleasant state of affairs.

"I have my moods," said Vernon. "I can be a bear with a sore ass."

On the eve of the 1997 playoffs, Vernon was so lightly regarded by experts that *Goalies' World* magazine listed him in 38th place among big-league puckstoppers. Thirty-eighth! Mike was hidden behind Glenn Healy and ahead of Chris Terreri.

"NOT VERY IMPRESSIVE" was the *Goalies' World* terse observation of Vernon before he embarked on a playoff journey that would earn him the Conn Smythe Trophy as the most valuable player in the 1997 Stanley Cup run.

How, then, could Vernon be so egregiously undervalued?

It is a good question. After spending eleven mostly unheralded seasons in Calgary, Vernon was traded to the Detroit Red Wings in June 1994 for defenseman Steve Chaisson. Scott Bowman, who now was coaching the Motor City six, wanted Mike although he knew he was obtaining a short goalie who showed shooters a lot of net.

Bowman also knew that Vernon compensated for his dwarfish look with exquisite attention to his angles, exceptional speed for his age and general all-around smarts. He also gambled that Mike would be an improvement on the two previous Red Wing goalies, Bob Essensa and Chris Osgood.

In March 1994, then General Manager Bryan Murray guessed wrong and traded for Essensa, who had been with the Winnipeg Jets. Essensa was far from the goalie Detroit had expected and when he gave up two terrible goals in Game One of the playoffs against San Jose, he was pulled by Bowman who opted for young Osgood. It was youthful Osgood who blew the final game to San Jose but who survived the axe.

Bowman liked Osgood long-term but figured that Vernon would be the ideal veteran to ease the kid toward NHL stardom. Mike had been through the goaltending mill, starting at home in Southwest Calgary where he learned the business of puckstopping.

"As soon as I took him to the rink," Mike's father, Martin, once recalled, "he was about two or three years old at the time, he always stayed beside the goaltender."

Mike's mother, Lorraine Vernon, added, "In the dressing room, he'd try on the goalie's equipment and he'd drag it around with him. Even today he says he doesn't play hockey — he's a goalie. He always played goal. I don't remember him wanting to do anything else but play goal."

Martin Vernon adds: "Mike was always a good skater and he still is. If he took his goalie equipment off, he'd skate as well as half the guys."

Vernon played well enough as a youngster in Calgary to attract scouts by the time he had become a teenager. When he was 15 he was invited to the Billings Bighorns camp but he returned home and eventually starred for the Calgary (Junior) Wranglers. He was their starter from day one and twice was named the Western Canada Junior League's most valuable player.

Lorraine Vernon remembers: "He'd bring home those trophies and awards and he'd just put them in a corner and forget them. He was looking to the future, starting to really think he could get to the NHL."

The Flames selected Mike in the third round of the 1981 Entry Draft. He honed his game to sharpness in Denver, Moncton, Salt Lake City and Moncton again. He was summoned to Calgary for two memorable games: one an exhibition victory over a touring Soviet squad and the other a win which ended an 11-game Flames losing streak.

But it was the 1985-86 season which was the real grabber. Mike played in the American League for Moncton and the International League for Salt Lake City, and then he found himself writing a Hollywood style story for the Flames as they zoomed straight to the Stanley Cup Finals.

"When I was sent down to the "I" at the beginning of the season, people thought my chances of getting back to the NHL were slim and none," said Vernon. "After I came back up to Calgary, I proved I could stop the puck with the big boys."

Vernon played in 22 playoff games (won 12 and lost nine) as the Flames eventually were ousted in the Finals by Montreal. His Stanley Cup goals against average was 2.93 and he was being hailed as the Flames goalie for the next decade. But Mike had been burned enough and he had seen how other Cup phenoms such as Steve Penney of Les Canadiens had quickly disappeared.

"Goaltenders," said Vernon, "are usually the guys who come up and make it in the playoffs, but that doesn't mean they are set for life. Look at Penney. He was a playoff hero one year and then he wasn't even playing. This is a tough position. That's why people say it takes longer for a goalie to mature. Look at how many goalkeepers have long careers. Tony Esposito, for example. He learned to cope with the ups and downs of the position. But it takes time; it's a tough task."

There were charges early on that Vernon had an attitude problem, that he was too easy going, that he was this and that and the other thing. What he was, however, was a first-rate goaltender. He followed his sensational playoff with a starting position and 54 games in his first full year as a Flame. His record was 30-21-1, secure enough to be *the* goalie in Calgary.

"It was a helluva story," said Vernon. "From the press box to the power play. From the crap apple to the Apple. I began to have fun."

What he didn't have was a championship. That would come in the 1988-89 season. By that time Vernon had won at least 30 games for the past three seasons; a feat that no other NHL goaltender had accomplished.

In the 1989 Finals the Flames faced Montreal — Mike Vernon vs. Patrick Roy.

The Habs led the series 2 games to 1 and might have had a 3-1 lead were it not for an

extraordinary Vernon save on Mats Naslund. Flames coach Terry Crisp called it "the turning point of the series" and he was right.

Calgary went on to win its first Stanley Cup. Curiously, Vernon received less attention than his supporters, such as then general manager Cliff Fletcher, believed he deserved.

"The only difference between Mike Vernon and other top goalies is color," Fletcher explained. "Ron Hextall has notoriety for his stick work and Patrick Roy has notoriety for his twitching head. Others have colorful masks. Mike just has a plain mask. He doesn't have that notoriety. He just stops pucks."

Vernon stopped pucks well enough to last in one city for eight full NHL seasons. Not many goaltenders can make that statement. His move to Detroit was pockmarked with problems at first, including a 1995 Stanley Cup Final in which the New Jersey Devils defeated the Red Wings in four consecutive games.

Mike did not play badly for Detroit but he certainly wasn't on par with his opposite, Martin Brodeur, who ranked among the stars of the Stanley Cup champions.

Vernon finished the 1995 playoff year with 18 postseason wins and 12 losses. He had one shutout and a 2.31 goals against average, yet Scott Bowman decided that it was time for Chris Osgood to take over.

No problem. When Mike was needed, he delivered. Bowman used him in 32 regular season games and was rewarded with a 21-7-2 mark; not bad for a so-called second-stringer. The 2.26 goals against average, however, was not as good as Osgood's 2.17.

At playoff time, Osgood was used in 15 games and Vernon in only four. All signs indicated that Bowman wanted Osgood as his goalie for the present and future. Events during the 1996-97 season underlined Bowman's point. Vernon played 33 games while Osgood's number was 47. Vernon's goals against average was 2.43 as opposed to his younger partner's 2.30.

Throughout the campaign Vernon waited for the other skate to drop. Convinced that he was history in Detroit, he made all necessary plans for a trade. "I figured they had no reason to keep me if I wasn't playing so I'd be traded somewhere else," said Vernon. "We had four people interested in buying our house in Detroit and I told my wife, 'Maybe we had better call them.' This is how you think when you're not playing. Brace for the worst. I was trying to hold out my wife in the event we had to move."

One of the reasons why a move was a possibility were the numbers. Mike's won-lost mark (13-12-8) was not nearly as impressive as Chris' 23-13-9.

"Mike was abused by the fans many of whom considered Chris Osgood the man Scotty Bowman should have used," said Tony Gallagher of the *Vancouver Province*. "It looked for most of the year that Vernon would be moved at the trading deadline." Yet when the 1997 playoffs began, it was Vernon and not Osgood who was asked to backstop Detroit to its first Stanley Cup since 1954.

"I have no idea why Scotty started me in the playoffs," said Vernon. "I never asked him."

The reason was quite obvious. Bowman's instincts told him that Vernon still had enough experience, enough cool, and enough mental toughness to beat any opponent in the way, including the defending champion Colorado Avalanche. Bowman remembered how, in a late-season bloodbath, Vernon not only beat the champs but also beat up his opposite, Patrick Roy, in a bizarre bout at center ice.

It was Vernon's gumption that impressed Bowman and 20,000 Detroit fans. Goalies are not expected to fight, but Mike displayed a camaraderie and zeal that couldn't fail to rub off on his mates.

"It's good to be mean on the ice," said Vernon. "I always tell them, 'If you want to be a nice guy, get an office job. You can be a nice guy there.'" Mike had been exposed to enough coaching shenanigans not to be surprised when he was given the 1997 playoff goaltending assignment. Yet this time he was really taken aback and made no bones about it.

"When Scotty said I was starting the playoffs, I was as shocked as anyone. But some coaches prefer a guy with experience. It's not a deep, dark tunnel to me. I've been through it.

"Then again — and this may sound bad — but most coaches are two-faced. They almost have to be. When things are going well, you're their guy. But when you're losing, well, they get paid to win. They'll turn on you on a dime."

But Vernon would not turn on his buddy, Osgood. He understood precisely how deeply hurt the young goalie felt when he was bypassed for the 1997 assignment. "I knew what was happening to him wasn't fair," Mike allowed. "Not playing in those playoffs was probably the lowest point in his career. It's a slap. But it will make him a better goaltender. It will make him hungrier. And it will make life easier when he's my age and still going through this stuff."

Vernon would not allow Osgood to play; Mike was simply too good. He beat St. Louis in the first round and Anaheim in the second. But Colorado in the Conference Finals was another story. Before the series had begun Avalanche coach Marc Crawford had divined a method for beating Vernon; create gridlock in front of his crease so that he can't see the puck.

Mike was unimpressed. "That's the case with any goaltender," he replied. "If there's traffic in front of them, most goaltenders will have problems. It's no different how big or small you are. It's how good a goalie you are and if you're on your game or not. I've seen some great short goaltenders and some great tall goaltenders. It just doesn't matter."

It hardly surprised Vernon that his critics were eagerly awaiting some sign of collapse they could seize upon to put down his workmanship. After Detroit had taken a 3 games to 1 lead against Colorado the Avalanche blasted four pucks past Vernon in Game Five. That was enough for Bowman who yanked Mike and inserted Osgood who gave up two more in a 6-0 rout.

Vernon-watchers recalled that in 1994 the favored Flames jumped ahead of Vancouver 3 games to 1 in the opening round. Mike had been exceptional in the first four games but then his game regressed and the Canucks eliminated Calgary. Vernon, in a nutshell, had been out-goaled by Kirk McLean.

After the 6-0 debacle, Mike handled the newsmen with the testiness one expects from an embarrassed goalie.

"I've been pulled before in playoff games," he related. "It was just one game. We were all at fault. You can't pinpoint one individual as the culprit. This is a team game and the media has to realize that. If we're going to win, we're going to win as a team. If we're going to lose, we're going to lose as a team. As for starting again, I want to play and that's the only thing I can do. I'm looking to the next one."

And well he did.

Vernon and the Red Wings eliminated Colorado in one of the most excruciatingly tense playoff games of the 1990s. The victory dispatched Detroit to the Finals for the second time in three years. Nobody had to remind Vernon that he had been swept in four contests by New Jersey in 1995.

"Mike has never been fully appreciated," said Detroit columnist Terry Foster. "He was unfairly blamed for the 1995 Stanley Cup Finals loss to New Jersey, even though the Red Wings combined for a total team no effort. Vernon gets little respect."

That, however, was to change during the Detroit-Philadelphia Finals. With each match, Vernon out-goaled whomever was his opposite in the Flyers' net, be it Garth Snow or Ron Hextall. "We had it in the back of our minds how devastating it was to lose to Jersey," said Vernon.

The 1997 Stanley Cup final round ended almost as fast as it had begun — four in a row — and never did Vernon play anything but a competent championship game.

He finished with a 1.76 goals against average, the lowest ever recorded by a goalie in the playoffs. On top of that he lifted his playoff game number to 123, tying him for fourth place with Andy Moog behind Patrick Roy, Billy Smith, and Grant Fuhr.

Vernon was toasted as never before. At game's end NHL commissioner Gary Bettman presented Mike with the Conn Smythe Trophy as the Stanley Cup's most valuable player. Grabbing a long cigar someone had handed him, Vernon raised his arm to the Joe Louis Arena crowd and then joined his teammates for the traditional sitting-on-the-ice group photo.

To Mike's fans, the Smythe Trophy symbolized the recognition that had so long eluded him. To Vernon it was — just as it had been when he was a youth in Calgary — just another piece of silver.

"I really wasn't too concerned with the Smythe," he said. "I just wanted to win the Stanley Cup. That was the bottom line.

"We were all consummate winners in my mind and the team in front of me played a great round of hockey. Winning the Smythe never entered my mind. Just winning was the most important thing."

There were, however, some very tangible benefits beyond the Smythe. Vernon was in the final year of his contract and would have become an unrestricted free agent except for one clause. It stipulated that if Mike had won three games in the Stanley Cup Final, his contract would be renewed for one more year at $2.3 million.

Considering that he finished the playoffs with a 16-4 record, even Vernon's most venomous critics would admit that he deserved the bonus.

Near the end of Game Four someone close to the glass at Joe Louis Arena raised a sign in the direction of the Detroit goal: VERNON, I APOLOGIZE.

Mike saw the message and when the dust had cleared at the Joe, he concluded, "I don't know who the guy was, but I accept the apology."

Perhaps now Mike Vernon can be accepted for what he is — a splendid little goaltender.

RON HEXTALL

"Once you establish your ground as a goaltender, if they hit you, it's interference. Period."

Along with Hall of Famer Jacques Plante, Ron Hextall has done more to revolutionize the manner in which hockey is played — not to mention the position of goalkeeper — than any puckstopper in history.

It was Plante who introduced the behind-the-net maneuver and later refined it to include passes to teammates, but it was Hextall — by sheer force of personality and physique — who advanced the technique of goalie-as- defenseman.

Hextall turned passive puckstopping into aggressive puck moving. He not only fielded the rubber and turned it over to teammates but began using his big goalie stick to dispatch passes to center ice and even ice the puck.

"Ron was the first goalie to put his team on the attack," says John Vanbiesbrouck of the Florida Panthers, "especially when the Flyers were killing penalties." Not surprisingly, Hextall became the first National Hockey League goalie to actually lift the puck out of his zone and into the enemy's empty net. And this, no less, in a playoff game.

He is a Vezina Trophy winner, a First Team NHL All-Star and the recipient of numerous awards. Yet with all these kudos, Hextall, now in the twilight of his playing life, comes across as a tragic figure. The reason for that is simple; he has had two playing lives. In Part I he was a veritable superstar. In Part II — the one in which he is currently suffering — he has failed to live up to the image created in Part I.

A career-threatening injury in 1989-90 was the line of demarcation between the outstanding Hextall and the average-to-mediocre one who followed in Part II. Hextall played only eight games that season amid reports that, because of physical constraints, he never again would be able to play a full season of NHL goal.

If nothing else, Hextall is a battler. He fought back against steep odds and returned to the Flyers goal, although he hardly was the Hextall of yesteryear — and, unfortunately, never would be.

The early Hextall was one of a kind. That is precisely why — as a rookie — he was able to fight his temper as well as the enemy and take Philadelphia to the seventh game of the Stanley Cup Finals before losing to the Wayne Gretzky-led Edmonton Oilers.

"Ronnie was the real thing right from the start," says Chico Resch who was Hextall's partner in 1986-87. "At the time there were young goalies in the league like Patrick Roy, Tom Barrasso, and Grant Fuhr whose skills were not that developed but were compensating with enthusiasm and adrenaline. Ronnie wasn't making those mistakes. He wasn't playing on his knees or using tricks. At the time he had the best feet and hands and lateral movement of any big goalie I had ever seen. I figured then that he had a chance to be one of the all-time greats."

One season does not a career make, but Hextall had become so proficient, so fast,

there was every reason to expect that his upward curve could reach the goaltending stratosphere. Even his coach, Mike Keenan, always spare with a compliment, likened Hextall to Hall of Famer Ken Dryden.

Like Dryden, Hextall was a long shot who made good. Ron came to the Flyers' training camp in September 1986 expecting to be farmed back to the American League, but he turned so many heads in exhibition games he was given the opening night starting assignment against Edmonton.

Hextall allowed the first shot by Jari Kurri to beat him and then foiled the Oilers the rest of the way for a 2-1 win. It was the start of something big. Ron won the regular starting assignment away from ex-number one Bob Froese and soon earned a second, less-adoring, reputation as a woodchopping goalie.

In fact Hextall turned truculence into a goaltending asset as he did battle with any foe who intruded in his crease (or its environs). During a game at Maple Leaf Gardens, he took exception to Toronto's Brad Smith and chopped him down with a two-hander. On the next night at The Spectrum, Hextall swatted Troy Murray of the Blackhawks.

No less impressive, but in a more positive way, was Hextall's stickhandling. "When I was coaching the Maple Leafs then, I was so impressed with the way he handled the puck I figured he could play the point on the power play," says John Brophy. "Every time a team would dump the puck into the corner, Hexy would dump it out. It got pretty frustrating for our forwards."

Up until then no NHL goaltender had actually — physically — scored a goal by firing the puck into the opponent's net. In 1979 Bill Smith of the Islanders was *credited* with a goal against the Colorado Rockies. He received the honor only because he was the last Islander to touch the puck before it made its way — accidentally — into the Rockies' goal while Colorado had possession.

Hextall was keenly aware of Smith's record and vowed that he would go one better and actually pump one about 180 feet down the ice into the yawning net. In the meantime his NHL experience made him a better goalie each year. During his sophomore season he played 62 games and finished with a 3.51 goals against average. A year later it was 64 games and 3.23 mark.

He was being hailed not only for his own play but also for continuing a tradition. His grandfather, Bryan Sr., had starred for the 1940 Rangers Stanley Cup championship team and his father, Bryan Jr., had played for several NHL clubs including the Rangers, also as a forward.

The difference between the goal-scoring Hextalls and the goal-stopping Hextall was temper. Both Bryans were able to contain their emotions while Ron was explosive as a minor and major-leaguer. Eventually his histrionics thrust him into the NHL's hot water tank.

During the 1987 Stanley Cup Finals he chopped Edmonton's Kent Nilsson so hard that the league sent Hextall down for eight games at the start of the following season.

Did Hexy learn his lesson?

Hardly.

During the 1988 playoffs he charged 40 feet from his net to clobber Canadiens defenseman Chris Chelios with his blocker glove. Hextall was seeking revenge for a

Chelios elbow on teammate Brian Propp earlier in the series. This time Hextall was hit with a dozen-game suspension.

"There's a limitation to what a guy could do," Vanbiesbrouck recalls. "I couldn't figure out then why he wanted to take it upon himself to do everything. I wondered why he wanted to be portrayed as such a bad guy."

It was not that Hextall wanted to be painted the scrooge, it simply was his competitive nature compelling him to keep his crease as enemy-free as possible. Away from the ice, he was more like Mister Clean, a devoted family man married to the former Diane Ogibowski, a one time top senior figure skater in Canada. Those who were acquainted with the laconic off-ice Hextall found it difficult to meld the two personalities as one.

"I'm not a good loser," Hextall admits. "After the two suspensions, I knew that I had to cut out that stuff."

Flyers longtime scout Jerry Melnyk remembers an even wilder Hextall as a 17-year-old playing Junior hockey in Brandon, Manitoba. "There were teams who thought he was loony," says Melnyk.

All of the so-called craziness went out the window when his career appeared in danger during 1989-90. Even the goal he actually scored — a full-length ice shot into the empty net — on April 11, 1989, against Washington in the playoffs paled to insignificance as Hextall worried about his future.

His concerns were resolved when he returned for 1990-91 and played 36 games and compiled a decent 3.13 goals against average for a nonplayoff team. The Flyers were enduring difficult times and would continue to do so while Hextall struggled to find the form that had won him accolades during the preinjury years.

But on June 20, 1992, Hextall got the shock of his career. Along with Peter Forsberg, Steve Duchesne, Kerry Huffman, Mike Ricci, Chris Simon, et. al., Ron was dealt to the Quebec Nordiques.

It was a shocking switch for Hextall who had become as identified with Philadelphia as historic William Penn. To his credit, the goalie adapted to his new environs, playing a solid 54 games for Les Nordiques (29-16-5) — good enough to produce a playoff berth.

When Hextall won the first two opening round playoff games it appeared that Quebec would wipe the hated Montreal Canadiens out in a sweep. It was then that Hextall betrayed the flaws that would haunt him not only then but in playoffs ahead, both with the New York Islanders and, later, the Flyers once more.

Montreal reeled off consecutive wins — 2-1, 3-2, 5-4, and 6-2 — and eliminated Quebec. The Nordiques were not only disappointed but anxious to unload Hextall. They found a buyer in Islanders general manager Don Maloney. The Isles, who had failed to re-sign popular goalie Glenn Healy, dealt Mark Fitzpatrick, also a very promising young goaltender, and their first round draft pick, Adam Deadmarsh, to Quebec for Hextall and Todd Bertuzzi.

As an Islander, Hextall was as unsettling as the weather along the Suffolk County beaches. On some nights his play was as beautiful as a shorefront moonlight and on others, it was as disastrous as a hurricane.

In the final weeks of the season it appeared as if the Isles would be knocked out of a playoff berth by the expansion Florida Panthers. The homestretch race crystalized during

the final week. Florida lost to Quebec at Miami. On the next night the Islanders were at Tampa Bay. If New York could win that game, the Isles would clinch a playoff berth.

Hextall was never better. Although the team around him seemed gripped with tension, Ron stopped wave after wave of Lightning attackers. In time teammate Steve Thomas produced a pair of goals and Hexy delivered a 2-0 shutout and the coveted playoff berth.

Ron seemed not only as sharp as ever but good enough to even produce a first-round upset against the powerful New York Rangers. But once the playoffs began it appeared that Hextall had regressed to a level not seen in his big-league career. Clumsy at times, stiff at others, he was beaten often and easily as the Islanders exited, humiliated, in four games. Hextall was so weak that he was twice replaced by young Jamie McLennan.

When the Flyers offered Tommy Soderstrom for Hextall on September 22, 1994 Maloney couldn't accept the deal soon enough. Why the Flyers wanted Ron in the first place was another question. The Islanders experience suggested that he was too far over the hill to help Philadelphia but General Manager Bob Clarke — long a Hextall supporter — believed otherwise. In the end, after a strong regular season and a playoff run that took Philly to the Finals against Detroit, the team's goaltending proved to be their weak link. A series of soft goals in the first three games of the series — two of which were played by Hextall — dispirited the Flyers. They lost the series in four games, leaving many to question the future of Hextall with the team.

KIRK McLEAN

"As soon as you stop having fun, it's time to get out."

When Kirk McLean spearheaded a Vancouver march to the Stanley Cup Finals in 1994, the Canucks goaltender seemed poised to reach the Vezina Trophy level. The evidence was compelling on McLean's side.

Since arriving in British Columbia — he was dealt by the New Jersey Devils — in 1987, McLean carved a handsome niche in the Vancouver hockey foundation.

During the early 1990s he became a workhorse goaltender and in 1991-92 he played in 65 games, winning 38, losing only 17, and tying nine. His goals against average was a nifty 2.74 and a portent of good things to come.

Over the feverish spring 1944 playoff run, McLean played in 24 Stanley Cup games and finished with a 15-9 record including four shutouts and a 2.29 goals against mark.

He was never better. What's more there were hints that the Willowdale, Ontario, native could still improve on his game. A year later he lowered his regular season goals against average, suggesting that the healthy trend would continue.

Unfortunately, it never happened.

The quality of McLean's game plummeted — along with the Canucks — in 1995-96, and not so coincidentally, his goals against average soared. At the start of the 1996-97 season *Goalies' World* magazine had dropped McLean to a dismal 37th place, behind Tommy Soderstrom and ahead of Mikhail Shtalenkov.

"McLean is at the crossroads," said *Goalies' World*. "Either he comes out very big and shows without a doubt that he is the best goalie in Vancouver or he slowly molds himself into a backup man while his younger partner Corey Hirsch gets the number one job."

McLean played 44 games for Vancouver in 1996-97 and recovered slightly. He was over .500 (21-18-3) on an underachieving team and was moved up five notches by *Goalies' World* while his partner Hirsch was listed in 34th position. Nevertheless, the magazine's critic, Gilles Moffet, concluded, "McLean is playing way below his capabilities."

Nobody is quite sure why, especially when one considers Kirk's consistency in the past. When McLean was on his game he was the equal of Ed Belfour, John Vanbiesbrouck, and Patrick Roy. Canucks sports psychologist Wayne Halliwell once summed up McLean's success formula quite simply: "He has very good mental skills."

They originally were developed in Oshawa, Ontario, where he played Junior hockey for the legendary Generals. Kirk was drafted by the New Jersey Devils and played 10 NHL games for them before being traded to Vancouver, along with Greg Adams, for Patrik Sundstrom and a draft pick.

McLean claims that his turning point as a pro came when he realized the virtues of a stern work ethic. "I had a tendency to maybe slack a bit when I was younger," he says, "but I really worked on that and it's done nothing but improve my game."

Mental toughness — a bromide to some but a key to others — also became his hall-mark. When a shot eluded him, Kirk didn't treat the goal scored as if the world had collapsed on his shoulders.

"The way I see it," he goes on, "if the puck goes in, it's no big deal. Boom! Come back with a big save and, hopefully, the team will come back with a big goal.

"If I lose a game, I figure that I have more wins ahead of me. It's a long season and I know I'm not going to win every game. Naturally I'd like to, but I'm realistic. There's no sense getting uptight. I'm tense, but I'm also calm. It's important for me to keep an even, level head. I know I'm going to have my highs and lows so it makes no sense for me to get so uptight my game gets wrecked."

Halliwell agrees: "If you watch him during the national anthem, you'll see how calm he is. He doesn't even move while others are going through their moves. He's a very calm individual and that enables him to maintain his composure."

That composure never was more evident than on the night of January 30, 1997, when the Canucks hosted the New York Islanders at GM Place. It was a game in which the visitors were on top of the puck all night and did manage one goal out of 35 mostly difficult shots.

Midway through the second period crafty Islanders ace Zigmund Palffy broke free on a short-handed foray and had plenty of time to put the fake on McLean. But before Palffy could complete his move, McLean thrust his stick like a bayonet, hoping to disrupt the assault before it ever reached fruition. "I didn't know if I had the book on Palffy," McLean recalls, "but he has a great touch and he's very creative. As it turned out, that was the first time I've ever pokechecked on a breakaway. That's a 50-50 chance. It's high risk and as it happened, it didn't work. Palffy made a quick move and I got my arm on it."

It frustrated the Islanders almost as much as McLean's work during the overtime when he shut down the opposition long enough to enable his defense partner Jyrki Lumme to score the sudden-death goal.

"If it hadn't been for Kirk," says Lumme, "I never would have had the opportunity to score. He made some unbelievable saves. When he plays like that, it gives the team a lot of confidence."

Of course if McLean wanted to make excuses for any of his down periods, he could mention the fact that he had undergone two arthroscopic knee operations within a year. After missing two months following the surgery, he started a dozen of Vancouver's next 14 games and in that period the club registered a 7-4-1 mark.

"He kept us in games and gave us a chance to win," says Martin Gelinas. "If we hadn't had him in goal it would have been a different story."

McLean's performance dislodged Hirsch who had been number one while Kirk recovered. Even the competition couldn't help but admire the master. "I had seen Kirk play good games over the years," says Hirsch, "but never with so much consistency as he did in January 1997. He was great night after night."

McLean, who numbers Jaromir Jagr and Theo Fleury among his prime nemeses, still is young enough to maintain that form and once again become the goalie who went to the seventh game of the Stanley Cup Finals.

"I still think about that series," he says.

And some people still believe that Kirk McLean can become the goalie he once was when he came within a game of winning the Stanley Cup.

DAREN PUPPA

"I probably could have gone somewhere else, but I like the team, the players and the Tampa Bay area."

The Tampa Bay area happens to like Daren Puppa.

Fans at the Ice Palace would like him even more if he played once in a while; or at least more than he did during the 1996-97 season.

The oversized — sometimes awkward — hulk of a puckstopper was available for a grand total of six games.

A year earlier he performed nobly in 57 contests and proved to be the prime reason why the Lightning gained a playoff berth for the first time in the franchise's history.

This was a team that had been consigned to the National Hockey League depths by the preseason polls. That is, until Puppa stepped forward and posted a remarkable 29-16-9 record and a 2.46 goals against average. The arithmetic made him a Vezina Trophy finalist.

During that run, the Kirkland Lake, Ontario native began suffering back spasms and by playoff time, he seemed like a different goalie, as his 4.86 average suggests.

All seemed right with Puppa's world — not to mention the Lightning's — in October 1996: Tampa Bay produced a thrilling, come-from-behind win over the Penguins at Pittsburgh, Puppa was undefeated, and his club was in first place.

At precisely that point the walls caved in on just about everyone from the goalie to Coach Terry Crisp. Puppa's troublesome back capitulated to the constant strain produced by the continuous games. He finally had to step aside and begin an endless series of medical procedures that would last almost the entire season.

In November he underwent surgery to repair a herniated disk and that was followed by a painfully long recuperation. Too long in the minds of some Puppa-watchers.

"Each day," says *St. Petersburg Times* hockey writer Tom Jones, "the burning question was not, 'Whom do we play next?' but, 'When is Puppa coming back?' Days turned to weeks, weeks turned to months, first place turned to last. And Puppa couldn't even stand, let alone play savior."

Coach Terry Crisp estimated that the Lightning lost as many as 14 points because of inefficient goaltending after Puppa was sidelined. "The difference," says Crisp, "was our not having Daren. I can go around and around on the reasons for our downfall that year but when I lose my number one, I have a big hole to fill."

First he tried Corey Schwab and then Rick Tabaracci. Both played well in spots but neither was up to Puppa's standard. "Daren is our star," says General Manager Phil Esposito, "our best player. I don't care what team you have, if you lose your best player, how can you compete for the playoffs?"

Somehow, the Lightning managed to hang in there, staying close enough to the pack to make an earnest run for it in the homestretch. Sure enough, Puppa did return at the end of March, and when Tampa Bay played the Florida Panthers on the night of March 29,

1997, the Lightning general staff believed that a win would be just the tonic for the march to Playoffville.

For 58 minutes and 35 seconds, Puppa did everything imaginable to produce that victory at Miami Arena. Teammate Rob Zamuner had staked the Lightning to a 1-0 lead in the first period on a short-handed goal. "From then on," recalls Zamuner, "Poops stood on his head."

He did until there was a minute and 25 seconds remaining in the third period. That's when Florida's Tom Fitzgerald redirected Terry Carkner's floating wrist shot from the left point behind Puppa.

When the 1-1 tie had concluded an exasperated Crisp simply said, "Daren Puppa is not a messiah, but we sure hope he can give us a burst for the stretch run."

Esposito must have believed that Puppa was at least close to being a messiah. Shortly after the game with Florida, the GM picked up his cellular phone and called the goalie's agent. A few days later Daren owned a brand new three-year $6.9 million contract.

"He's been loyal to us and we wanted to show some loyalty toward him," said Esposito. "That game against Florida was all I had to see. We're just a different team with Daren."

No question.

Over two seasons the Lightning's record was 28-16-10 with Puppa guarding the twine. Those numbers make them a realistic playoff contender. But then again that's assuming that Daren is healthy and one never can be certain of that.

Until that uncertainty is finally lifted, Puppa will remain a potential Vezina Trophy winner or one of the endlessly walking wounded.

"When he's right," says defenseman Bill Houlder, "he makes the rest of the team look awfully good. That's what star players do."

They do it, as long as they are healthy.

KEN WREGGET

"I came to a point and said to myself, 'If this is what they want me to do (be a back-up goalie), I'm not gonna bang my head against the wall. I have to accept it and work as hard as I can.'"

No goalie in the long chronicles of the National Hockey League ever made a save quite like it.

In the 1996 playoff between the Pittsburgh Penguins and New York Rangers, the Pens were hanging on to a lead by a gossamer string as the Broadway Blueshirts stormed Ken Wregget's net.

The Penguins goaltender was down on the ice while legs churned all about him. Suddenly, he saw the puck sitting directly, tantalizingly on the goal line. A Ranger stick was about to swat it home for what could have been the turnaround score.

Courageously — some might even say stupidly — Wregget pushed his mask into the puck and shoved the rubber, face-first, out of imminent danger until the whistle blew a halt to the action.

Onlookers agreed that it was the most amazing face mask save anyone could have imagined in a Stanley Cup crisis situation. *Sports Illustrated* amusedly referred to it as "a heads-down play." More to the point, Wregget's clever move — using his head, one might say — enabled Pittsburgh to not only win the playoff game but also oust the Rangers from contention.

And through it all, Wregget is considered a "backup goalie." Or, as Rangers coach Colin Campbell puts it, "a flopper."

Never has that label been more unfairly affixed than it is when Wregget's name is involved. Over a National Hockey League career that dates back to 1983, Wregget has earned more than backup acknowledgment but he never will attain more because he always has been paired with another headline-grabber.

Although Tom Barrasso was the Penguins designated number one stopper in 1995-96, Wregget played in nine of the team's 18 games and produced a 2.30 goals against average.

"At playoff time," says *Goalies' World* magazine, "Wregget was fabulous. Once again he bailed out the Penguins in a critical situation."

Nevertheless, *Goalies' World* ranks Wregget 21st best, two behind Patrick Lalime who became an overnight sensation in Pittsburgh during the 1996-97 season when both Wregget and Barrasso were injured.

"Wregget," adds *Goalies' World,* "is a true reliever."

Oh, well. If you're pigeonholed, you're pigeonholed, and nobody knows that better than Wregget himself. He has accepted being typecast even though some goaltending experts long ago concluded that he would do very well, thank you, were he given a full-time role virtually anywhere.

Ken actually had it for a time in Toronto, although he had to grow into the role. His first full season wearing the royal blue and white was 1984-85, when he shared the goal-

tending with Allan Bester. By 1986-87 Wregget had won the job and remained at it until the Flyers gave up two number one draft choices for him — so that he could be back-up to Ron Hextall.

"I never actually lost a number one job," Wregget insists.

"On a lot of clubs Wregget would be the number one goalie," says his former coach Eddie Johnston who himself played goal in the NHL.

Wregget has been bailing out the number ones ever since he was backup to Hextall when the two were late-year teammates on the Philadelphia Flyers during the 1988-89 season.

The Penguins-Flyers playoff had been extraordinarily exciting that spring, winding down to a Game Seven that would be for all the marbles. Hextall was supposed to be the Flyers starter but had to be sidelined with a wounded knee.

Wregget, who had just shaken a bout of mononucleosis, had only played three games for Philadelphia and appeared so rusty that Flyers were were just about ready to concede the series before the puck was dropped in Game Seven. Even worse, several Philly stars — Rick Tocchet, Tim Kerr, and Derrick Smith, to name a few — also had been scratched because of injury.

The Penguins barrage began in the first minute and continued throughout the night. Wregget was absolutely nonplussed by the overwhelming odds against him. All he did was stop pucks.

"We threw 40-something shots at Wreggy," recalls former Pittsburgh goalie Wendel Young who was there that night. "He only let one go by, and they got four on us. Four-one for Kenny. What a performance."

That sent Philadelphia up against Montreal in the Wales Conference Finals. Wregget started the opener — and won. By then, Hextall had recovered and was back in the nets for Game Two. Wregget didn't return and the Flyers lost.

"It wasn't a case where I stepped into it and lost the starting job," says Wregget. "It was a case where I stepped into a role. And it all started there in Philadelphia."

Wregget has succeeded because of mental toughness and a technical game that ranks with the best. He has been around long enough to know the angles and the enemy shooters. But he also betrays debits. His stickhandling is nothing to write home about and his glove hand is carried a bit too low for the experts. Others criticize him for locking his right knee behind him when he slides across the crease to his left. Supposedly that makes it tougher for Ken to get back in time for a rebound.

"His attitude is his best asset," says Johnston. "He doesn't get upset, and that's a key. He can come off the bench and do the job for you and he doesn't complain. That's important for the team. We didn't want a guy bitching, 'Ah, I should be playing.'"

He finally reached number one in 1996-97; at least early in the season. Barrasso still was around but his game had turned rusty. WREGGET REAL NO. 1 PENGUINS GOALIE, BUT BARRASSO HAS THE JOB. That was the headline over Bob Smizik's column in the *Pittsburgh Post-Gazette* on November 7, 1996.

"Wregget has been significantly superior to Barrasso," reasoned Smizik.

The delightful run ended on December 26, 1996, when Ken pulled a hamstring in a game against Les Canadiens. It was a debilitating injury that idled Wregget for almost two months and, at first, sent the Penguins high command into panic mode.

Barrasso also had been hurt which meant that the club had to import untried Patrick Lalime. To the civilized world's amazement, Lalime posted a league-record 16, game unbeaten streak to start his career.

By the time Wregget was ready to return, Lalime had become the toast of the league while Ken, literally, was forgotten. After a 4-2 win over Florida on February 18, 1997, Panthers coach Doug MacLean couldn't even remember Wregget's name when questioned about Pittsburgh's goaltending after the game.

First he called him Tom Barrasso and when apprised of his error, referred to Wregget as "whatever-his-name-is."

That is not the problem in Pittsburgh. Members of the media who have covered the Penguins have grown to appreciate Wregget because he always has been available and affable, descriptions that did not exactly fit Barrasso during the mid-1990s.

"Maybe I'm just a regular guy who thinks people are people and people are good," reasons Wregget.

Which is not to suggest that Ken is without emotion or anger. The frustration of being labeled number two — while fervently believing you are number one — can take a psychological toll on an athlete.

It was particularly so in Wregget's case after Barrasso missed all but two games with a wrist injury during the Lockout-shortened 1994-95 season. Ken amiably stepped in and proceeded to lead the NHL with 25 wins. This, in his mind, should have been the ticket for more number one work the following season.

What's more, he let management know his feelings — in spades. General Manager Craig Patrick and Coach Eddie Johnston listened carefully and pleaded patience. Good man that he is, Wregget obliged. For the rest of the season it was the status quo for Ken who kept hoping that his day would come. It did.

Actually, it was night and day. On the evening of April 24, 1996 the Penguins and Washington Capitals faced off for the fourth game of their playoff. Washington led the series 2-1 and seemed poised to take a virtually uncatchable 3-1 lead. Barrasso, who had not been particularly strong in three games, had started for Pittsburgh but suffered back spasms at the start of the second period. The starter pulled himself out and was replaced by Mister Backup.

The next 345 minutes were Wregget's finest. Not only did he repel every form of shot by the Capitals in regulation time, but he repeated the feat in what was to become the third-longest game in NHL history. In the second sudden-death overtime period Washington's crafty Joe Juneau was awarded a penalty shot. Wregget stopped him cold.

Whether it was tension or simply overwork, by the time the third overtime had arrived, Wregget had been clenching his stick so hard that when a break in the action arrived he had to, as *Sports Illustrated* noted, "take the blocker off his right hand — his stick hand — and literally pry open his middle finger which was locked around the stick." The procedure had to be repeated in the fourth overtime.

Meanwhile, Wregget and his opponent, Olie Kolzig, were locked in one of the most delectable goaltending confrontations in Stanley Cup annals. The staggering Penguins understood that if Wregget faltered they were toast. It was now morning and still no score. Finally, Petr Nedved scored for the Penguins and Ken was numero uno again.

He started Game Five and held Washington scoreless into the second period. His total shutout streak — including Game Four — was 146 minutes and 30 seconds. And this for someone who had never had consecutive shutouts in his 13-year NHL career.

Wregget had not only stopped 73 straight shots but went on to pace Pittsburgh to a 4-1 win in a series they ultimately captured in six games. "His style may be awkward," says former NHL goalie Gilles Meloche, who was the Penguins goalie coach, "but he'll come far out of the crease and let the puck hit him. He's got a great head on his shoulders."

Perhaps if his coaches did as well, Ken Wregget wouldn't be, as the *Pittsburgh Post-Gazette* labels him, A BACKUP WITHOUT LETUP.

JEFF HACKETT

"No matter how hard you practice — or work — it's not the same as playing games."

Jeff Hackett simply was not National Hockey League caliber.

No way.

Not in a million years.

That, at least, was the brutally frank evaluation of many who watched the London, Ontario, native attempt to break in with the New York Islanders almost a decade ago.

Hackett twice attempted to make the grade in Nassau — once in 1988-89 and again in 1990-91 — and in neither case did he make even the slightest impression. A 4-7-0 record was followed by a 5-18-1 mark. The only positive to come out of it was that Hackett impressed everyone with his affability.

"We kept saying what a nice guy he was but that it was too bad he couldn't cut it as a big-league goalie," one of the Long Island hockey writers remembers. "Who could figure this turnabout?"

The turnabout was startling, to say the least, and a lesson to anyone willing to generate considerable energy to overcome stiff odds. The Islanders gave up on him in 1991, allowing the oft-smiling goalie to be made available in the Expansion Draft. San Jose, which had just been awarded a franchise, plucked him from the scrapheap and gave Hackett another chance.

Precisely what attracted the Sharks general staff to Hackett is a moot question, but it is quite likely that some remembered what he had accomplished in the minors during the 1989-90 campaign. Tending goal for the Islanders' American League farm team in Springfield, Hackett was voted the Jack Butterfield Trophy as the playoffs most valuable player as Springfield won the Calder Cup. Hackett sported a 10-5 won-loss record with a 3.85 goals against mark over 17 games.

"I knew San Jose would have a difficult time because the Sharks were an expansion team," he says, "but I also knew that I'd get a chance to play. The first year in San Jose was a positive experience. We were all thrown together and everybody was in the same situation. We were pioneers in a sense. There were no big stars, but we played hard and we were in every game."

He played 42 games for the Sharks in their maiden season, winning but 11 games, losing 27, and tying one. His average was a less-than-airtight 3.84 on a team that didn't come remotely close to making the playoffs.

Was Hackett downhearted? Hardly.

"I sure didn't enjoy losing," he admits, "but I did enjoy playing. I also understood what a lucky guy I was being in the NHL. Coming to the rink anytime is a lot easier than doing a lot of other things in this life. From time to time I would look back at friends I knew from back home in Ontario and realize that some of them didn't even have jobs.

When I look at life that way, I know that I'm a lucky guy."

Slowly, inexorably, Hackett gained experience and bettered his game. More than that, he was finally being recognized in a positive way. The Bay Area media selected him as the Sharks' most valuable player, and over a period of 10 games, his goals against average dropped to 1.90.

He played another season in San Jose under equally difficult circumstances. "Management took away the character players and replaced them with younger guys who weren't proven in the league and it became a bad situation. The franchise took a big step backward."

During a game against Los Angeles on December 26, 1993, he faced 59 shots and allowed only two goals for a 7-2 victory. Unfortunately, the lows outnumbered the highs, and on July 13, 1993, the Sharks traded Jeff along with Neil Wilkinson to the Chicago Blackhawks for Jimmy Waite and a 1994 draft choice.

"I was very excited coming to a team with the history and tradition that the Blackhawks have," says Jeff. "As a kid, I always dreamed of playing on an Original Six team. All I wanted to do was find out if I could play a bigger role in this league. I didn't want to look back and have any regrets."

In some ways this should not have been a good move for Hackett. As the backup for iron man Ed Belfour, Jeff figured to appear only in a limited number of games. As it happened during his first two seasons in the Windy City, he was called on to play only 29 times, starting just 18 of those games.

"I was rusty and my confidence wasn't as high as I would have liked it to be because I hadn't played — for the most part — for about three weeks," says Hackett. "I was like a fourth-line forward. It was hard for me to contribute."

That then coach Darryl Sutter lacked confidence in Hackett didn't help either. The combination of Belfour and Sutter virtually locked Jeff to the bench until Sutter was replaced by Craig Hartsburg for the 1995-96 campaign.

It was in that season that the real Hackett emerged; much to the detriment of the main man, Belfour. In fact, Hackett tied a club record with his eighth straight victory, yet he refused to personally challenge Belfour for the number one spot. "I always said that Eddie was the number one guy," says Hackett. "He was an All-Star, a legend. He had done it for years in the league."

But the advent of Hartsburg marked a major distinction in the manner in which goaltenders were handled by the man calling the shots. Sutter had been a Belfour supporter. Hartsburg wanted to wait and see.

"If I played a great game when Darryl was coach — or won a game or played well — I usually didn't get back in the net for two or three weeks," Hackett laments. "With Craig it was different in a lot of ways. He talks to his goalies and lets them know what he expects. He also lets us know at least a day before when we're going to play. It turned great for me."

So good, in fact, that he played 35 games for Chicago in 1995-96. His record was 18-11-4 with a 2.40 goals against average. Belfour's totals were 17-10-3 and a 2.74 goals against mark. What the numbers eloquently said was that Hackett was ready for prime time goaltending.

"Eddie was getting a little bit older," says Hackett, "and there was a new coach with different thoughts about handling things. For me it was a breath of fresh air."

But not for Belfour.

As the 1996-97 season approached, Belfour was making $2.75 million but believed that he deserved more like Patrick Roy's $4.55 million. When Blackhawks general manager Bob Pulford rejected the bidding of Belfour's agent, Ron Salcer, it marked the beginning of the end of The Belfour Era in Chicago and the beginning of the Hackett Era.

It also detonated one of the most explosive dressingroom dissension scenes in Blackhawks annals.

"Belfour was sulking from Day One as practice began for the upcoming campaign," says Chicago hockey reporter Rick Sorci. "He threatened a walkout at the conclusion of the season when he would become an unrestricted free agent. And as the year began, the contract situation festered leading to bitterness that spilled into the locker room.

"Perhaps if the team was having a good year the situation would have worked its way to a happy ending. This, however, was not the case."

By Christmas 1996 the coach had concluded that Hackett was every bit as good as Belfour; if not better.

Sorci explains: "The worse things went for Eddie, the better they went for Jeff. When Hartsburg began using Hackett more and more Belfour's ego got the better of him. One day at practice he confronted Hackett and told him point-blank, 'You're nothing more than a backup.' Stunned, Hackett walked away and refused to take the bait. It was obvious that something had to give. It was a bad team with a bad goalie and bad vibes."

Hackett remained remarkably cool about the insult. "There are arguments and confrontations in sports locker rooms all the time," says Jeff. "Unfortunately, this one leaked out and it really got blown out of proportion. It had nothing to do with the relationship between Eddie and me. It had everything to do with Belfour's contract offer. That's sports in the 90s. It's big business. It's tough and I still consider him a friend." Pulford called Belfour's diatribe with Hackett "unfortunate." The manager also knew that he had to make a goaltending decision — either Hackett or Belfour. He opted for Hackett and dealt Belfour to San Jose.

Hackett was the winner. He was given a new three-year contract for $900,000 a season and a new partner, veteran Chris Terreri, who was not about to complain about playing time.

Meanwhile, Hackett continued to improve. His save percentage climbed to .929, best in the league, although he refused to take credit for his performance. "Goalies are getting better in general," he says. "There are more teaching techniques, so much more available to the goalies to get better. Practices are more oriented so a goalie like myself can work on specific things.

"Plus, there's not as much offensive talent out there that there was ten years ago. There are still a lot of good offensive players in the league, but because of expansion the talent is more spread out."

Just how Hackett would respond to his new responsibility as number one was a concern to management but Pulford and Hartsburg were willing to wait; not that they had much choice.

"It wasn't as if I could just throw a switch," Hackett recalls. "It was something that I had to grow into, both in terms of confidence and the consistency of my game. People have to understand that this is the first time there's been a good team playing in front of me since I've been in the minors."

One of the best things to happen to Hackett was the opportunity to study under Vladislav Tretiak, the Hall of Famer and all-time best Russian goaltender who had become Chicago's advisor to puckstoppers.

"Working with Tretiak had a tremendous influence on my career," says Hackett.

So was the support supplied by Hartsburg and Pulford. Despite all the early season distractions, the Blackhawks gained a playoff berth while Hackett's play emphasized that Belfour's departure wasn't the calamity that some believed would be the case.

"Management has given me the opportunity to take my game to a higher level," Hackett concludes. "They think I'm capable of doing that and that gives me a lot of confidence. I'm going to work hard to take my game to the next level, but it's not going to be easy every night and it's not going to happen overnight."

But it *is* happening and those who remember Jeff as an awkward, floundering member of the Islanders still can't believe it.

TREVOR KIDD

"Everywhere I went in the regular season people were patting me on the back and telling me to keep it up. I didn't have   as many well-wishers after the playoffs."

When Trevor Kidd was drafted by the Calgary Flames in 1990 there was considerable debate as to who the best young netminders were that season.

Kidd, who had played three years of Junior hockey with Brandon and another season in Spokane, was regarded as a prize pick, a sure big-leaguer. With the eleventh pick overall, the Flames wasted no time nabbing Kidd. Whether they erred or not is a question still debated at The Saddledome.

In that same draft the New Jersey Devils selected Martin Brodeur. According to the 1997 *Goalies' World* magazine netminding rankings, Brodeur was listed second — behind Dominik Hasek — while Kidd was buried in 20th position. "He's not a top-notch number one yet," *Goalies' World* editor Gilles Moffet observed.

The Flames thought he was during the 1994-95 season, his second full year in the bigs. Mike Vernon had been numero uno in 1993-94, leaving 31 games for the aspiring Kidd. But the veteran was traded to Detroit in the summer of 1994 signaling faith in Trevor as top banana.

Kidd's response was admirable. He started Calgary's first 22 games and finished as the National Hockey League's busiest goalie with a league-leading 43 appearances and 2,463 minutes between the pipes.

What's more, his 22 wins tied for second best in the league with Ed Belfour of the Chicago Blackhawks and Ken Wregget of the Pittsburgh Penguins who had 25.

"Most people would say we took a big gamble trading Mike and going with Trevor," said Flames executive vice-president Al Coates at the time. "We don't feel that way. We had to go with our young goalies or we wouldn't be able to keep them. Besides, Trevor played in enough big games the year before that we had full confidence he could do the job."

Kidd's form contrasted markedly with Vernon's. The youngster used the butterfly compared with the angle style employed by Vernon. "Kidd had a flair for the dramatic," says *Hockey News* reporter Mike Brophy. "He made saves look harder than they actually were. But so did Belfour and he had won two Vezina Trophies."

Kidd was so good that he wound up in a neck-and-neck duel with Flames' ace Theoren Fleury for the unofficial title of Calgary's most valuable player. Kidd was the team's Molson Cup winner, for the most Three-Star selections after being named the game's first star eight times, second star six and third star seven.

That, however, was during the regular season. Heavy favorites in the opening playoff round against the San Jose Sharks, the Flames discovered that their goaltending wasn't as solid as Kidd had led them to believe.

"We didn't give Kidd the opportunity to play just an average game in the playoffs,"

says former Flames general manager Doug Risebrough. "We exposed him to more difficult shots than any goalie should have to face."

The expansion Sharks took two big bites out of Kidd & Co. in the first two games at The Saddledome, winning both games 5-4. In Game One, Rick Tabaracci was called in from the bullpen to relieve Kidd.

In San Jose the Flames rallied for two wins behind Kidd and then Trevor threw down a 5-0 shutout to put Calgary ahead 3 games to 2. But the Sharks rebounded, 5-3, at home, setting the stage for the decisive seventh match at The Saddledome.

"In Game Six," adds Risebrough, "three of our defensemen were beaten on one-on-one situations. Even if Trevor had been on his game for the entire series he would have had trouble the way the team played in front of him."

The 6-2, 190, pound Kidd would have an opportunity to correct all flaws by producing a victory in the rubber match which turned into a heartthrobber. A 4-4 tie extended into double overtime. And then it happened. Ray Whitney, an afterthought in the San Jose line-up, beat Kidd, abruptly ending the Flames playoff season almost before it got off the ice.

"Kidd did not play well," recalls Brophy, "and making things worse was the fact he was outplayed by Sharks goalie Wade Flaherty, a career minor leaguer who had stepped in to save the day when Arturs Irbe floundered."

While some questioned Kidd's potential, Risebrough remained confident that his draft pick would deliver. So did Trevor. "I proved that I could be a number one goalie. Now I have to prove I can do it in a long season." Not to mention the playoffs.

He followed the San Jose debacle with a 1995-96 campaign that best can be characterized as disappointing, although he finished with a 2.78 goals against average. His win-loss numbers were 15-21-8, and he had three shutouts, same as the previous season.

But the opening playoff round test against the Blackhawks was nothing short of a disaster for both Kidd and the Flames. They lost in four straight and by Game Four it was Tabaracci in goal not Kidd.

"He has not won the big games," says *Calgary Sun* columnist Mark Miller.

When the 1996-97 season began the Flames had three goalies from whom to chose — Kidd, Tabaracci, and Dwayne Roloson. The battle for top slot was between Kidd and Tabaracci, a situation that induced uneasy moments in their relationship for the first five weeks of the season.

When it became apparent that the three-goalie system was unwieldy, Flames general manager Al Coates dealt Tabaracci to the Tampa Bay Lightning where he played some of the best hockey of his life. (He was rated 15th overall by *Goalies' World,* five ahead of Kidd.) Kidd's play occasionally provoked oohs and ahs and led Flames followers to believe a playoff berth was possible.

In mid-season some members of the media placed the team's playoff future directly on Kidd's shoulders. "If the Flames are going to advance to the mid-April playoff party," wrote George Johnson in *The Sun*, "Trevor Kidd has to be Calgary's best player — not best goaltender, best player — from here on in."

He wasn't. And the Flames didn't make it.

In the end Trevor played 55 games and finished 21-23-6. Calgary missed the playoffs and the questions about Kidd are as perplexing as ever.

Mark Miller aptly summed it up: "Three years into a career built on much expectation, Kidd is still looking to achieve the big-pressure success that is the trademark of the game's great goalies."

Only time will tell whether he will change that appraisal.

JOCELYN THIBAULT

"My proudest accomplishment is making it to the National Hockey League at 18 after barely two years in Junior hockey."

The young man's "proudest accomplishment" may also prove to be his downfall as a major-league goaltender.

Only time will tell.

Too much, too soon is the story of Jocelyn Thibault's life as a professional hockey player. That and a series of poor decisions by the men in command of the Montreal Canadiens during the 1996-97 season.

Not that the Montreal native is a bad goaltender; far from it. But his style, psyche and future may have been so severely impaired by events out of the young man's control that it will take a monumental amount of work to re-shape him as a winner.

When Canadiens general manager Rejean Houle acquired Thibault from the Colorado Avalanche on the fateful night of December 6, 1995, he described Jocelyn as "one of the most brilliant young goaltenders in the NHL."

His pedigree was impressive. He had been Canada's best Junior goaltender in 1992-93 and was the eighth highest draft pick for a goalie in NHL history. Only 18 when he made his debut with the Quebec Nordiques, Thibault thus became the second youngest goalie in NHL history.

Houle no doubt felt obliged to eulogize his acquisition in excess because the Habs had transferred Patrick Roy and Mike Keane to Denver while also obtaining Andrei Kovalenko and Martin Rucinsky. Roy, until a personality clash with then coach Mario Tremblay, had been the darling of Montreal Forum fans.

"At first Thibault filled in admirably," noted *Goalies' World* magazine. "Jocelyn should be extremely confident going into his first full season with Montreal (1996-97). He should be one of the top 10 goalies in our ranking."

When he was on his game, Thibault offered a variety of assets. He was cerebral, had exceptional reflexes, and had good concentration. After suffering a weak game, he was able to rebound and come up with a solid effort. His style was simplicity itself; use the butterfly technique whenever possible. To some observers, he seemed to be a pint-sized version of Patrick Roy.

When he arrived on Ste. Catherines Street West, Thibault knew that he could rely on veteran backup Pat Jablonski for advice. An easy going, helpful type, Jablonski was an excellent instructor for Jocelyn as well as a sounding board in times of stress.

"Pat and I hit it off the moment we met," Thibault recalls. "I was really lucky to have a great guy like him to play alongside."

The numbers indicate that they were performing as well as could be expected, considering that the Canadiens had a modest lineup in front of them. But the Habs are under constant pressure to win big, and they weren't doing so.

The Thibault-Jablonski axis was permanently severed during the 1996-97 season following an episode which would have wide reverberations for the Habs. It began when Montreal's highly competitive newspapers carried stories that certain unnamed members of the team complained that goaltending was at the root of the club's problems.

Overreacting to the critique, Houle replaced Jablonski with young, inexperienced Jose Theodore in a move that raised eyebrows across the province of Quebec and in NHL board rooms across the continent.

"Houle and Tremblay poorly handled the goaltending situation," says *Goalies' World* editor Gilles Moffet. "Their ignorance of goaltending not only endangers Thibault's career but also that of Theodore, two very talented goaltenders who stepped on to very thin ice."

Despite the difficulties, Thibault's performances during the regular season were better on the whole than more seasoned goalies such as Bill Ranford, Ed Belfour, and Kirk McLean. What Jocelyn needed most of all was patience and a confidence boost.

Thibault carried a heavy load for the Habs in 1996-97, playing 61 games in front of one of the NHL's most unreliable defense corps as well as a team that was badly decimated by injury. Nevertheless, he finished with a 22-24-11 won-loss mark and a 2.93 goals against average.

Goalies' World rated him the twelfth-best netminder in the league, behind Jeff Hackett and ahead of Sean Burke. "Thibault has a great future," was the comment.

More importantly, Jocelyn pushed the Canadiens into a playoff berth! That seemed to have been overshadowed by the embarrassment caused by Patrick Roy's return to Montreal for the first time since his trade to Colorado. The date was March 5, 1997, and, in retrospect, it might have been the most important — in a negative sense — of Thibault's career.

Roy's return hogged the headlines and made it even more important for Thibault to look good or, at the very worst, not look too bad. The result couldn't have been worse for the kid or Coach Tremblay for that matter.

Colorado — and Roy — won the game 7-3 while Thibault relinquished six goals on only 20 shots. But taken overall, the regular season was a commendable one for Thibault, if not outstanding. It is noteworthy that among the goaltenders who played more than 40 games and were confronted with an average of over 32 shots per game only three played better than Thibault — Dominik Hasek, Guy Hebert, and Mike Richter, all mature veterans.

Thibault's downfall occurred during the 1997 playoffs. Facing a strong New Jersey Devils team, Jocelyn seemed neither sharp nor sure. After the Habs lost three straight games, Thibault was given the hook and replaced by Jose Theodore. The player who once was the best Junior goalie in Canada seemed stunned by his demotion. What's more Theodore played exceptionally well to beat New Jersey in a marathon overtime Game Four before losing in Game Five.

Shortly after the playoffs, Thibault's coach, Mario Tremblay, resigned and was replaced by Alain Vigneault. Whether or not the new Canadiens leader will be able to restore Thibault's confidence is a moot question.

Well under age 25, Jocelyn still has the potential to be a major goaltending force but it will only happen if he can overcome the many problems that arose when he followed in Patrick Roy's footsteps.

STEPHANE FISET

"It was frustrating when Colorado got Patrick Roy but I made my mind up to keep quiet, do whatever they asked me to do and hope we won the Stanley Cup. After that I asked them to trade me."

One can only imagine how high Stephane Fiset's star might have climbed had the Colorado Avalanche not obtained Patrick Roy from the Montreal Canadiens during the 1995-96 National Hockey League season.

"Colorado players told me that they would have won the Cup with Stephane because he was great when he played for them," says Los Angeles Kings defenseman Rob Blake.

That may very well be but this much is certain: The Avalanche — otherwise known as the former Quebec Nordiques — had just been transplanted from Quebec City. With Stephane guarding the crease for them, the Denver club had become the NHL terrors and Fiset ranked among the Avalanche's premier players. He had won a club-record nine consecutive games and over a period of 35 games he totalled an impressive 22 wins, with only six ties.

Any goaltender in the league would have loved to own such an impressive won-loss ratio. Nor was anyone terribly surprised by the Montreal native's ascent to the top. Since he had become a full-timer with Quebec in 1992-93 Stephane ranked among the finest products to emerge from the goalie factory that the Quebec Junior Hockey League had become.

Along with Felix Potvin, Martin Brodeur and, of course, Roy, Fiset articulated on ice everything that the Quebec goaltending gurus — Francois Allaire in particular — had preached. But Fiset quickly discovered that there's considerable difference goaltending for a team like the Stanley Cup champions and a rebuilding club like Los Angeles.

"I was excited coming to the Kings," Fiset says. "The club had good, young players, and when the team took me to be the number one goalie, it definitely showed that they had a lot of confidence in me. I hope to stay in L.A. for the rest of my career.

"The thing is, when you are an NHL goalie, you always have to prove yourself no matter who you are. I'll be proving myself for the rest of my career."

Rebuilding as the Kings were under Coach Larry Robinson, they were overcome with problems. Wayne Gretzky had left the club, injuries sidelined key players, and, at times, Fiset was so bombarded with rubber the Society For The Protection Of Cruelty To Goaltenders should have been notified.

Over his first dozen starts of the 1996-97 season Fiset was confronted with an average of 34 shots, compared to the league average of 30 per game. "He'll be our number one goalie for years to come," jokes Robinson, "if we don't wear him out first, forcing him to face 40-50 shots a night."

Not that Stephane was complaining. Throughout his goaltending career — it started in Juniors with Victoriaville — he has been a gamer. And he showed that spirit with a miserable Nordiques sextet in 1989-90. Even after his first six games left him with no wins, five losses and a tie, Fiset kept his chin up and his goalie stick on the ice.

The Nordiques wanted to determine how Fiset measured up against the likes of Ron Tugnutt, Jacques Cloutier, and John Tanner. After Stephane collected his first NHL victory on October 29, 1991, he proceeded to lead Les Nordiques in wins and save percentage.

"After I got that first win," he recalls, "the others seemed to follow."

When Ron Hextall moved to Quebec as part of the Eric Lindros deal, Fiset not only had an older goalie on which to rely but also someone who could tutor him on the fine points of puckhandling.

"Ron was the one who shouldered the pressure," says Fiset, "and that helped me a lot. I was ready to be the number one goalie, but I learned a lot from him — especially how to handle the puck.

"Hextall wasn't the type of guy who said, 'Do this' or 'Do that.' I just watched him work and learned from it. We had a good relationship."

Fiset benefited immeasurably as his 18-9-4 record indicates. "We weren't afraid to play any team in the league," he remembers.

By the time Les Nordiques became Les Avalanche, Fiset's club had grown even stronger. Peter Forsberg had come over from Sweden, aligning himself with the likes of Mike Ricci, Claude Lemieux, and others who would power Colorado to the championship.

"My name is on the Stanley Cup," Fiset enthuses, "and I can say that I touched it after we won the prize. I can say that I would rather have been a backup and experienced the moment of winning a Stanley Cup than have been traded to the Canadiens.

"Winning the Stanley Cup was the greatest experience of my hockey life. There's nothing like it in pro sports. It's what you live for and what you play for and being in Denver with Patrick Roy, I learned a lot. He taught me about game preparation, handling pressure, and the media."

But he had had enough of playing in Roy's shadow. Once Colorado had won the title, Fiset marched into General Manager Pierre Lacroix's office and asked to be traded.

Fiset remembers: "Pierre Lacroix was great to me, trading me to Los Angeles and not demanding too much in return. If he had asked too much, I would probably still be in Colorado, playing behind Patrick."

Then Kings general manager Sam McMaster knew all about Fiset's record in Junior hockey and that Stephane had been named Major Junior Goalie of the Year in 1989, two years before Felix Potvin. "When we got Stephane," says McMaster, "we were getting an established number one goalie who can play among the best in the NHL. He had a tremendous record with Colorado and Quebec and played a big part in their rise."

Whether it was the ineptitude of his teammates or simply an overwhelming number of shots to stop, Fiset did not enjoy a glorious 1996-97, his first full year in Tinseltown. Byron Dafoe, who played 39 games compared with Fiset's 44, came away with a better goals against average (3.12 to 3.18), won as many games (13) as Stephane, and had a significantly better won-lost percentage.

Nevertheless, Robinson ranked Fiset among "the top five goalies in the league," although *Goalies' World* magazine had Stephane in 18th position — Dafoe was 24th — at the conclusion of the 1996-97 campaign. "Hot and cold" is how Goalies' World editor Gilles Moffet reviewed Fiset.

"The thing everybody sees is him stopping the puck," Robinson concludes. "But it's

the little things Fiset does — like the positive attitude he brings to the dressing room — that makes him an outstanding goalie."

He did play on a Stanley Cup winner and he did perform splendidly with a solid team fronting him. Should the Kings eventually build to the level of that Avalanche outfit of 1996, Fiset could be kissing Lord Stanley's mug once more.

"Years from now people won't remember how many minutes you played," says Fiset. "What matters is that your name is on the Stanley Cup. I worked hard to help the team and was always positive. I felt like I was a big part of winning the Cup, just like anyone else on that team.

"My dream was always to win the Cup. It was a great experience in Denver but now I want to win it with me in goal!"

RON TUGNUTT

"All my career, I've gone to teams in decline. I went to Quebec when they were losing the Stastny brothers and Michel Goulet. I went to Edmonton after they'd lost Gretzky and Messier. I went to Anaheim when it was an expansion team. I came to Montreal after they'd won the Cup and were headed down. I was beginning to think it was me."

One evening, while tending goal for an inept Nordiques squad, the little man who wears spectacles when he's not standing in front of the goal, stopped 70 shots fired by the Boston Bruins.

The game concluded in a 3-3 tie and Ron Tugnutt was proclaimed a hero throughout the National Hockey League. The performance was so heroic that even the opposition — led by captain Raymond Bourque — skated one by one to Tugnutt and tapped their sticks on his pads to acknowledge the uncanny performance. Bourque, himself, had taken 19 shots at Tugnutt and, like so many other people, was moved to do a double take when he saw Ron in civvies later in the night.

"You just don't picture him as a goalkeeper," says Chico Resch. "He looks more like a college professor. A little one who's not very athletic."

But Ron Tugnutt is very much a netminder and a high-class one at that; although his arithmetic may not support that claim.

"When I'm wearing glasses and people come up to me, they're not really sure I'm the Ron Tugnutt they see on the ice," says the diminutive goalie. "I tell them, 'Yes, this is really me,' but they still don't believe me."

Disbelief in Tugnutt has followed Ron throughout his major league career which began in Quebec City (1987) and reach an apex a decade later when his work late in the 1996-97 season led Ottawa to the first playoff berth in the Senators' history as an expansion franchise.

In between, Tugnutt was an itinerant goalie whose most emphatic stint in the bigs was 1990-91 when he played 56 games for Les Nordiques. By 1995-96 he was completely out of the NHL and obscurely performing in Portland, Maine, with virtually no future as a major-leaguer.

However, late that season the Senators underwent a front office metamorphosis with Jacques Martin stepping in as head coach. The erudite Martin knew Tugnutt well and kept him in mind in the summer of 1996.

During the off-season Ron had been property of the Washington Capitals. He saw no future with them and had decided that he would spend the 1996-97 season playing goal in Sweden.

Four days before leaving with his wife, Lisa, and sons, Jake and Matt, the phone rang. It was Senators general manager Pierre Gauthier.

They weren't exactly close friends but Gauthier remembered scouting Tugnutt for the Nordiques and liked him as a netminder. The GM swung a deal with Washington enabling Tugnutt to become the Senators backup goalie to Damian Rhodes.

This was nothing knew to Ron. His backup credentials were lengthy. He was stand-in for Bill Ranford in Edmonton; ditto for Guy Hebert in Anaheim; and likewise for Patrick Roy in Montreal. That Gauthier was designating him number two in Ottawa hardly was insulting to the little man.

"All my career," says Tugnutt, "I've been looking for someone to believe in me. Maybe my name should be Ron Toughluck!"

But in October 1996 Ron hardly believed that Martin's belief in him would be as intense as it became in the spring of 1997. When the 1996-97 season started Rhodes was considered far and away *the* man between the pipes for Ottawa. He had finished the previous season in good form and was reaching the top of his game.

Rhodes played capably enough for a good part of the campaign but then suffered a mysterious calf injury that sidelined him for three weeks. The homestretch drive had arrived, and lo and behold, the Senators were still in the race. Even more surprisingly, Tugnutt was keeping them alive with some exceptional work.

"Jacques is going to go with the guy who is winning games," Rhodes admitted at the time, "and Ron is the guy who is winning games."

Tugnutt claims that when Martin stuck him into the major homestretch games he found himself in what goaltenders like to call "The Zone." He had become as hot as a goaltender could possibly want to be and he was loving every game of it.

"I'm sure it's the same kind of feeling batters feel in baseball," says Tugnutt. "A fellow like Wade Boggs, for example, says he can see the spin on the ball.

"People say the puck looks like a beachball but, really, what you see is that the puck is moving slower. When things are going that good, the puck can be picked up a lot easier. That includes deflections. You can see if a guy is going to pass or shoot. The pucks are hitting you and you know where they are going. You're seeing them well."

Those who remember Tugnutt the teenager were not wholly surprised by his superior play. Ottawa fans recall Ron as stopper for the Junior Peterborough Petes, beating the Ottawa 67s in significant playoff games. Others can still see him in his impressive early years with Quebec. But Ron will be the first to admit that his timing was not exactly exquisite in terms of his NHL development.

"All my career I've gone to teams in decline. I went to Quebec when they were losing the Stastny brothers, Peter and Anton, and Michel Goulet. I went to Edmonton after they'd lost Gretzky and Messier. I went to Anaheim when it was an expansion team. I came to Montreal after they'd won the Cup and were headed down. I was beginning to think it was me."

Obviously, it wasn't.

Rhodes, who was being paid $1 million to be the number one goaltender, had become an afterthought. He sat and watched as Tugnutt brought the Senators closer and closer to playoff respectability. On March 25, 1997, Rhodes had allowed four goals on 13 shots. He had to be replaced by Tugnutt early in the second period.

That game almost marked the "finis" for Rhodes' major work on Ottawa's get-into-the-playoffs project. Coach Martin had planned on starting him against Philadelphia on April 6 in a game that also would be playoff-decisive but, according to reports, Rhodes begged off, claiming that his injury had not completely healed.

Tugnutt admits: "I told my wife Lisa that if Rhodes doesn't come back for the long term, then it could make or break my career, if I don't go out and get the job done. I knew if I was able to do it that I might be around for a few more years."

Martin knew then and there that the 29-year-old Tugnutt was his man, and Ron knew that the brass ring was his to grab and hold. So did the Senators who steadfastly refused to fade in the final weeks of the season.

"This run had become both a great opportunity for me as well as the other players on the team," Tugnutt remembers. "Nobody really thought that we would hang in there as long as we did and when the pressure was on we came up with some of our best performances."

One of Ron's best was against the Florida Panthers. As so often happens, the game was virtually decided by big saves. Early in the first period the enemy had a pair of short-handed two-on-one breaks. Tugnutt blunted both of them and went on to a 3-2 triumph.

That victory seemed to be the catalyst for the final run to the finish line, during which Tugnutt was named both NHL Player of the Week and NHL Player of the Month. In the critical games between April 7-13, 1997, Ron posted a 3-0-0 record, including a shutout, a 2.00 goals against average, and a .915 save percentage for the week. His stats for the homestretch month included a record of 5-2-0 with three shutouts, a 1.86 goals against average, and a sparkling .920 save percentage.

The unique playoff run culminated with a 1-0 whitewashing of the Buffalo Sabres at Ottawa's Corel Centre. It was the last of three consecutive wins to conclude the season and vaulted the club to the seventh seed in the Eastern Conference.

"Tugnutt became the most unlikely hero on the most unlikely playoff team," noted Chris Stevenson of the *Ottawa Sun.*

In the euphoria of the winners' dressing room Tugnutt was asked about his late father, John Tugnutt, who had been a prime influence on Ron's pro career. John had driven a sanitation truck and snowplows when he wasn't in the stands watching his kid play goal during Ron's formative years as a goalie.

"I know he was watching this game," Tugnutt told the surrounding reporters. "I'm sure he enjoyed it. He stayed close to me for the last two years. Whenever I had to look for something more, look deeper, he was always the one I could look to. He was here today."

Those who watched Tugnutt up close and personal in the dressing room noticed that his voice was choking. He had to pause to get himself together; he seemed to some to be embarrassed by the situation.

"I'm not usually at a loss for words," he went on, "but I am today. To finally relieve all this stress is unbelievable. I guess I can get a little emotional. To come back and get an NHL job is one thing; not only to get a job but to contribute, that's a great feeling."

The feeling continued into the playoffs as the underdogs from Ottawa extended the favored Sabres to seven games — and sudden-death overtime — before being eliminated.

"This has been the highlight of my career," Tugnutt reflects. "The guys walked out after that final game with their heads held high."

No one's head was held higher than that of little Ron Tugnutt, the goalie who looks more like an academician.

TOMMY SALO

"The two times I played with the Islanders in my first time around the NHL it was terrible. I was so mad. I didn't have any confidence. I cannot explain it."

If ever there was proof positive that there's no correlation with Olympic heroics and its National Hockey League counterpart, Tommy Salo is Exhibit A.

The blond, Swedish goaltender paced his country to its first ever gold medal in the 1994 Winter Olympics at Lillehammar. To say that Salo was sensational would be the understatement of the half-century; especially his shootout stop on Paul Kariya.

Not only did he foil Kariya but Canada's Dwayne Norris, Greg Parks, Greg Johnson and Petr Nedved as well. Salo indubitably had established himself not only as Sweden's premier puckstopper but as an international hero as well.

"You have no idea what a big thing the win was for my country," says Salo. "But it also was the key for me coming over here and playing in the NHL. I was happy for Sweden that we won and happy for me that I got this chance."

What Tommy soon would learn is that there's no correlation between what a goalie does in Europe and what he does in the North American professional ranks or, to be more specific, the NHL.

Once the New York Islanders imported Salo to Nassau Coliseum, hopes were instantly raised among the Isles faithful that Tommy would step into the NHL with no trouble at all and continue the brand of netminding he displayed in Norway.

Alas, it was not to be.

Salo put on an Islanders uniform and proceeded to become the most ordinary goaltender one could ever imagine. Perhaps worse. But let us start with Tommy's North American debut with the Islanders' farm team at the time in Denver.

Introduced during the pregame festivities, Salo zipped on to the McNichols Arena ice with a flourish that befitted a Jay Leno, and then — with exquisite comedic timing — Tommy proceeded to lose his footing and fall on his face.

With a huge grin adorning his red face, Salo picked himself up, dusted himself off, and skated to the crease. From there he merely played a solid game and directed the Denver Grizzlies to a victory.

The International Hockey League did not see any better goaltending than the brand Tommy Salo offered in that 1994-95 season in the IHL. He played in 65 games, won 45, lost only 14 and tied four. His 2.60 goals against average coupled with his IHL rookie-of-the-year and goaltender-of-the-year *and* player-of-the-year awards were mighty powerful credentials.

But they made no impression on NHL observers because what the big-league folks had seen hardly was impressive.

He played six games as an Islander that same season and was singularly ordinary in losing five and winning only one. "It was tough believing in Salo," says Islanders publishing director Chris Botta, "because he didn't always seem to believe in himself."

Goals that he would have stopped while wearing a blindfold in the "I" suddenly became indistinguishable lasers in the NHL. Long-range, unscreened slap shots flew past him; pucks that sat comfortably behind his net were handled like land mines, and, as Botta recalls, "Tommy did not look like a National Hockey League goaltender."

This was particularly unfortunate for both Salo and the Isles because Tommy was enjoying the chance of a lifetime. At the time, New York owned two major-league caliber stoppers, Tommy Soderstrom and Eric Fichaud. The former was not favored by coach Mike Milbury and the latter was too inexperienced to handle a regular job.

There was a job for the grabbing but Salo simply wasn't ready. The way Tommy sees it, the first year doesn't count. In his mind 1994-95 was to be a learning experience and the learning had to be done in the high minors. Period.

"I played well in The I that first year because I knew I was going to basically stay in Denver for the whole season," Salo remembers. "I really didn't think about the NHL at all."

Tommy enjoyed a successful enough training camp in September 1995 to be given an opportunity to share the Islanders starting assignment with Soderstrom, his idol from Sweden. "Disaster" would be a fair appraisal of the 10 games (1-7-1) and 4.02 goals against average.

Some Islanders insiders believe that it was a mistake having two Swedish goaltenders as the one-two combination. The theory was that since Salo idolized Soderstrom, it was difficult for the youngster to relax with his mentor, so to speak, looking over his shoulder.

While the Nassau faithful kept hoping that Salo would find himself, he instead, would give up goals at inopportune times, fail to make big saves, and look merely ordinary on his best nights.

By the second week of November 1995, Milbury had seen enough and dismissed Salo to the Isles' farm team in Salt Lake City. With Soderstrom still in partial disfavor, Milbury wanted Tommy to find himself and finally recalled Salo during a four-game road trip to Western Canada.

No dice.

"The two times I played with the Islanders that year were terrible," Salo remembers. "I was so made. I did not have any confidence. I cannot explain it. It wasn't the shooters being better in the NHL.

"What it came down to was that I simply was not ready. I gave up the easy goals that I had never given up before in my whole life."

Dismayed and disillusioned, Milbury had no choice but return Salo to the Grizzlies with the usual "Thanks but no thanks" while wondering if he ever would see the Scandinavian lad in Islanders livery again.

Certainly, Salo fully believed that he had had it with Milbury & Co. When he returned to Salt Lake City, Tommy bluntly told a reporter, "I don't think I'll play for the Islanders anymore. I don't think they have a future for me."

Grizzlies coach Butch Goring had other ideas. He worked on Salo's head, on his style, and on his rebounds.

Goring states: "Tommy had a lot of growing up to do in professional hockey. The Islanders in no way, shape, or form had changed their minds about him."

Salo continued to try the Islanders' patience. Milbury sent a pair of scouts to Las

Vegas to eye Tommy against the Thunder in a two-game series. In the opener, Salo was awful, but after the game he went over to the bird dogs and declared unequivocally, "I know I'm going to be all right tomorrow."

The next night he pitched a 2-0 shutout against Las Vegas. It reminded Salo-watchers of the prodigy he had been in his hometown of Surahammar, Sweden when he was a teenager. At the time Tommy idolized Pelle Lindbergh who had become the first Swedish goalie to carve a niche in the NHL. Lindbergh was the toast of Philadelphia and one of the Broad Street gang's best-ever stoppers.

"I watched Pelle play against those great Edmonton teams in the 1980s and the Islanders and Canadiens," says Salo, "and I wanted to be like him."

It wasn't until 1996-97 that Tommy found the form that had made him so appealing in Scandinavia. Salo was impressive enough in training camp to win yet another opportunity. Soderstrom was given his walking papers and the new duet was going to be Salo-Fichaud.

Few would argue that this would be Salo's last true chance to make a positive imprint. He needed a few big games and he got them. On November 27, 1996, he recorded a 5-1 win over the Flyers. That was followed by his first big-league shutout, 2-0, over the Washington Capitals.

Teammate Niklas Andersson — a roommate of Salo when they were 15-year-olds on the Swedish National Junior team — was not surprised at his pal's progress. "If you could see him through the years the way I have," says Andersson, "you would know it was just a matter of time. It's not easy coming to the United States when you're 22 years old and you know very little about the language, the culture. Coming here forces you to grow up. Tommy has grown up a lot over the past few years. Here's an example: In 1995 he came over to my apartment on Long Island to do some laundry. You may not believe this, but Tommy told me it was the first time he had ever done his own laundry in his entire life."

Some suggest that an 8-2 triumph over the Phoenix Coyotes was Salo's most meaningful win. "In that one," says Botta, "Tommy twice made huge stops that were immediately followed by Islander odd-man rushes for goals."

Mike Milbury elaborates: "Those are what I call 'two-goal saves.' Tommy comes up big for us in our end, and we cash in right after. Those are the types of saves that win games."

For home town consumption, Salo's most impressive effort followed the Phoenix encounter. On this night he faced Wayne Gretzky and the New York Rangers. Tommy gave up an early goal and then was confronted with a five-on-three penalty kill. Over a period of one minute and 40 seconds, Salo stopped seven legitimately dangerous chances that thoroughly frustrated the Madison Square Garden crowd.

The performance enabled the Islanders to counterattack and eventually win the game 5-3. But the masterpiece save was executed with eight minutes remaining in the match and the Isles leading 5-2. "Salo made a save on Gretzky so stunning the Garden audio operator prematurely sounded the horn for a Rangers goal."

Salo won the goaltending job from Fichaud. Both coach Rick Bowness and Milbury agreed that Tommy was their man. Unfortunately for the Swede, he did not exactly have the most formidable team fronting for him. There were nights when he saved the Islanders singlehandedly, and there were others when he regressed to his earlier, less dependable form.

"Tommy has played well at every level," notes Islander legend Bob Nystrom. "What he needed most of all was to gain confidence in himself, knowing that he could play at the NHL level."

The Islanders surprised a number of teams with a strong run for a playoff berth in March and April 1997, although they slipped out of contention in the final week of the season. Salo was steady enough to rack up 58 games and was ranked 14th overall in *Goalies' World* magazine's 1996-97 final rankings.

"For me," says Salo, "the most important thing is that you have to like playing hockey. If you're just in the game for the money, that's no good. I love it when everyone is standing in my crease. I love the action. I love playing against the best players in the world. I love the challenges. I want to be in the NHL for a very long time."

Tommy still has memories of his first pro game in Denver; how he fell, got to his feet and won the hockey game.

The vignette just might symbolize the emergence of a star goaltender in the big show.

Chico's Skinny
On the Top 26 Current Goalies

Roy understands the butterfly style as well as any goaltender in the N.H.L. This is no surprise. What makes him so unique is that he understood it at age 19. His tremendous start back in 1986 as a rookie with the Montreal Canadians, reinforced his confidence and his belief in this style. After 86 Roy knew his butterfly would bring him success in the league. Typically, goaltenders take up to age 25 to get all the mechanics of the butterfly down to an art.

Roy will drop into a butterfly position on about 7 of 10 shots. Goaltending gurus predicted Roy would prove to be vulnerable to high shots and the opening of the five hole. This hasn't happened because Roy has two physical assets which enable him to compensate. One is his 6 foot 190 pound frame. Roy's torso seems longer than his height would indicate. This allows him to take away a lot of the top of the net. Second is the way his muscles and ligaments are attached to his skeletal structure. His legs fan out from one side of the net to the other. The flexibility in his knees permit him to position his upper leg and fan out his lower leg at almost a 90 degree angle. Visualize this as two capitol letter L's back to back. These two physical assets allow him to execute a near perfect butterfly. In addition, Roy technically executes four components of goaltending superbly; he challenges the shooter, he stays square to the puck, his stick is *always* in the correct position, and his stance is tight and compact. A compact stance means that pucks don't go between his arm and body or his skate and stick. If a puck is going to get by Roy, it will have to go around him rather than through him.

Roy's glove hand is tremendous. He sets himself up in the net so intelligently that a shooter believes he has to shoot to that side. Among all of Roy's armament his glove hand may be his most effective weapon.

Another of Patrick's assets is his mental toughness, something he acquired in the Quebec Junior League where he played for a weaker team. Roy got pounded night after night but he took the punishment...hung in there... improved his mental game and was battle-hardened by the time he was promoted to the Canadians. He was able to make the transition to the hotbed of hockey, Montreal, without any mental lapses.

To be a great goaltender there has to be a melding of mind and body. Roy is a great goaltender. In overtime during the 1993 Montreal vs. Los Angles Kings Stanley Cup Final, we saw an example of this mind-body meld.

Picture this. The puck was positioned behind Roy to the left halfway between the post and the corner of the rink. An LA forward quickly passed this puck to a teammate who was off Roy's right post about ten feet from the goal line. Most goalies in this situation would think " I'm vulnerable. I'm on the left post and I need to get to the right post, *quick* because that's where the shooter will try to score. So, I'll stretch out my leg and arm as far as I can towards the right post." When a goaltender stretches wide, he opens up the area in the middle of the net between his legs: the 5-hole. Remember great goalies seldom let pucks go through them. Roy held his tight position and butterflied laterally towards the right post. If the LA forward made the perfect shot he hoped to — just inside the post — it would be game over, but such a shot is difficult to make under pressure. So where does the forward hammer the puck? He shoots it right into the middle of the net. Because Patrick didn't panic and dessert his style, he wound up making a terrific clutch save. The save was spectacular but not in the way most people thought; the save was spectacular because Roy's style did not break down under pressure. That kind of play epitomizes what Roy is all about. He doesn't beat himself. He makes the shooter beat him.

It may be worth noting that Patrick.may be responsible for a league rule change. Roy was leader of a pack of goaltenders wearing oversized, illegal equipment. Some estimate that goalie pads had become one to two inches wider than the league rule. In the summer of '96 the league announced that oversized pads would cost goaltenders in the form of fine and suspension.

What's also interesting about Roy is that he doesn't have what you would call an impressive physique. His upper body is not defined or chiseled. As with most established superstars, Roy was allowed to run his own program as long as he was able to come through when the game was on the line. When the Canadians stumbled to start the 95-96 season, GM Serge Savard and coach Demers were fired, Patrick's situation changed. Not only did the Hab's bring in a new coach, Mario Tremblay, but one whose job it was as a radio hockey analyst to be at times critical or analytical of Roy's performance. Initially Tremblay walked in and the Canadians began to win. However behind the scenes there was a battle going on involving two different philosophies. The young coach Tremblay was trying to establish the team concept where everyone is treated the same. Roy's belief was that older, proven superstars need and have earned some special considerations, perhaps less training during a heavy schedule of games or having the option of being excused from a morning skate. The main area where players of Roy's caliber demand being cut some extra slack from a coach is in the area of criticism; especially in the media but even within the presence of the team. Right or wrong, it is generally recognized that older, established players do not get criticized in the same manner as rookies or role players. If there is one lesson an older, experienced, or probably fired coach has learned, it is that he must be more careful and sensitive to the needs of these players. Why? The reality is that these players more often determine the outcome of a game. Goaltenders in general, but especially Patrick Roy, fall into this category.

At the time of the Roy-Tremblay conflict perhaps Mario did not completely understand that a power shift from coaches to players has gradually occurred in the league. In today's game a coach can never allow the impression to be created that he is publicly trying to discipline his elite players. If he does the results can be explosive. Such was the case the night Detroit blew out the Canadians at home when Tremblay refused to pull Patrick and Roy stormed off the ice demanding to be traded.

I don't know if Tremblay was trying to make a point or not. It doesn't matter. What does matter is that Roy thought he was. That sad note ended the career in Montreal of one the greatest French Canadian goalies to ever pull on the venerable red, white, and blue CH.

The "dominator" as he is affectionately called dominated the NHL individual awards like no goalie has in the last 35 years. He was voted by the 26 general managers as the goaltender judged to be best at his position (Vezina Trophy). He was voted the NHL outstanding player as selected by the players of the league (The Lester B. Pearson Trophy). Most impressive was his win of the Hart Memorial Trophy for being named the MVP of the league. Quite a tribute to a goaltender whose style was considered so unorthodox when he first arrived in North America from Czechoslovakia that hockey people took one look and said, "this will never work in the NHL." Dominik's style is not likely to be taught in any hockey schools in North America. Dominik's forte between the pipes is his instinct and that's something you can't teach kids.

If you study Hasek's technique, you come away thinking he is different. For instance, he has one curious move on a breakaway. When a player skates in on Dominik's left — his glove side — and then cuts across in front of him to his blocker side, Dominik will go down and put the paddle of his stick on the ice. If the player elects to shoot, Dominik is in excellent position — standard goaltending technique to this point. However, if the shooter elects to continue across the crease towards the far post, most goalies will stretch out their arms hoping to make a desperation save with their hands. Hasek's response in this situation is quite unique. He rolls from his side into a position where his pads are now straight up in the air where his head would normally be and his head and shoulders are flat on the ice where his pads would normally be. This is a goalie who stands on his head to make a save.

Another of Hasek's assets is his ability to effectively challenge the shooter. Once he is convinced that the shooter is going to shoot, Dominik has the courage to be aggressive and take a quick step out toward the shooter to cut down a little more of the shooting angle. This seems like no big deal but even at the NHL level some goaltenders will loose their nerve and take a small step backwards. This small step opens up more shooting area.

Like most goalies who set up in a wide stance (skates two to three feet apart), Hasek is constantly challenged to "plug" the 5 hole (the opening above the stick and between the pads). Goalies who use the traditional wide butterfly stance like Patrick Roy, simply squeeze both knees together and drop to the ice as quickly as possible, hoping to beat the arrival of the puck. Hasek's "5 hole jam" is slightly different in that he quickly drops his right knee to the ice while his left knee is still a foot or so off the ice. He uses this move because the flexibility in his knees does not allow them to flare out in the same manner as Roy's do. Also, Hasek is what I call "right leg strong." In most situations there is slightly more of his weight on his right leg and most of his moves generate off of the slight "right leg dip" that characterizes his stance.

I once asked Dominik how his unique style developed. He explained that growing up he never had a goalie coach and most of what he learned was by trial and error. He would try a move and if it worked he stuck with it. If it did not, he would invent a new technique and experiment with it.

Hasek's glove hand is a case in point. He holds it higher than most goalies, especially when he goes down into his "right knee dip" position. It appears at times that he is going to be beaten with a high shot, but then, with a snap and a twist, the catching hand comes up and swallows the puck with a cobra-like quickness.

Another aspect of Dominik's game that makes him so good is his constant aggressiveness on the puck. He is always thinking, "Attack the puck. Go to the puck!" His mind is very aggressive that way and most times serves him well. There was a time when his aggression backfired on him. In Montreal, when he charged to the blue line chasing a lose puck, Hasek collided with an attacking forward and broke his ribs.

I especially appreciate his technique for watching the puck. He finds the puck, reads the shot or situation, and then he reacts. Other goalies will at times visualize what they think has just happened and then start reacting. Unfortunately many times this premature reaction is in the wrong direction. Hasek may at times anticipate, but his greatest asset is his ability to be patient and read the situation before reacting.

More and more, contemporary goalies are taking a leaf from Hall of Famer Johnny Bower's book and using the poke check as a weapon to intercept the puck. Hasek has a first-rate poke check which he uses as effectively as anyone in the league. It especially works well in tight quarters. A player may come out of the corner thinking he can stuff the puck, but Hasek's poke check will strike like the tongue of a rattlesnake; a move totally untelegraphed! As he is executing this lightening-quick poke check, Dominik is conscious of the fact that his legs most be low, ready to drop to the ice to shut off the middle of the net. He does this because if he misses the puck with the poke check, there is a lot of area low on the ice where the shooter can simply slide the puck into the middle of the net — a pretty easy shot. However, as mentioned earlier, Hasek has the ability to slam his pads together on the ice to take away the low middle of the net. The shooter is forced to carry the puck laterally and then lift it a foot over the goalie's pads not an easy shot.

Like every outstanding goalie, Dominik has played in extraordinary games. One of his best was the marathon playoff against the Devils in 1994. It was what I called an "Iron Man" game. It was an ultimate test of body and mind. Hasek passed this test with flying colors. He stayed strong and his saves never became sloppy or saggy. He maintained his aggressiveness throughout and showed that his mental toughness is as sharp as any goalie's in the league. Hasek reminds me of Gretzky in his ability to perform at a high level game after game. People keep expecting him to have an off night but it seldom happens.

Hasek has been challenged and has had to overcome obstacles his entire career. The 1996-1997 year should have been Dominik's most triumphant campaign. For most of the season, it was. Unfortunately during the post season play, a series of events unfolded that tarnished his golden season. The last season controversies will undoubtedly make Domink's 1997-1998 season his toughest challenge yet.

Grant Fuhr is one of the greatest goalies of all time. He combines style with a natural grace which turns stopping a puck into an art form. When a person watches Grant play goal, it seems as if he were born to play goal and the position was created just for him. Even when Grant is scored on he looks great. If I am teaching goaltending techniques to youngsters at a hockey school and want to show a technically correct glove save, I show them Grant Fuhr. If I want to show a technically correct stick save, I show Grant Fuhr. If I want to show a technically correct blocker save I show Grant Fuhr. If I want to show a technically correct way to play a two on one situation, I show Grant Fuhr. He is the goalie goalies love to watch, a "goalie's goalie"

Fuhr has won 5 Stanley Cups. He never won a Conn Smyth Trophy, the leagues MVP of the Stanley Cup Playoffs. During a couple of the Cup winning playoffs, he played as brilliantly as any goalie ever has. It's too bad. The fact is his competition for the award were high profile players named Kurri, Coffey, Messier, and Gretzky. Fuhr's unbelievable brilliance during the Oilers 1-0 shut out of the Islanders during game first game of the 1984 playoffs was in itself a Conn Smyth winning performance. Without it there's an excellent chance the Islanders may have won their 5th Cup rather than the Oilers winning their first. In the eyes of the media and fans Grant's significance to the Oilers success may have been underestimated by the fact he played with so many outstanding teammates. However his importance was never overlooked by his teammates. His teammates were acutely aware and appreciative of the opportunity given to them to play "run and gun hockey," knowing Grant could handle every situation that came his way. Those great Oiler teams gave up more break always, two on ones, three on two odd man situations than any other dynasty team in NHL history. It was fire wagon, daring, wide open hockey at its finest, and Grant Fuhr supplied the confidence for them to play that way.

As with any goaltender Fuhr is not perfect. He never has been able to grab pucks off the boards and shoot them with the force or accuracy of many of his peers. Fuhr also is not the greatest at using his stick to poke check or intercept centering passes. These are minor deficiencies. He may occasionally get beat through the 5 hole or have one stuffed in on him from in close.

One of Fuhr's greatest traits is that when he does give up a shaky-looking goal he rarely compounds the problem by making another mistake. More often he will rebound with a spectacular save that regains his and his teammates confidence and momentum.

In dance, particularly ballet, body control and balance is the key. This is also true in goaltending. Fuhr seldom gets caught with his weight on the wrong leg or off balance. This allows him not only to react and make the first save but keeps him in position for the second or third shot as well. Fuhr has the ability to make combination saves — two or more rapid fire shots — look natural. On the ice Grant never looks flustered or out of control. Off the ice he is much the same; easy going, downplaying his role, praising his teammates, and deflecting pressure as effectively as he deflects pucks.

Fuhr is a great team player. The atmosphere at a practice can get tense. Goalies may complain about a drill or a high shot. Half kidding, forwards will say "ah shut up and just stop the puck." I doubt that quote was ever directed at Grant Fuhr because

Fuhr is not a complainer. Not a man of many words, Fuhr does his talking with his play. Some players may be remembered for their humorous, fiery or controversial persona, Fuhr will be remembered for his stylish saves. Anyone who has seen Fuhr play a few times will have a mental recollection of his classic stretch and glove save where he ends it with a plop to the ice on his derriere; his stick save, his butterfly, the blocker, the "stack" — Grant does it all now and has done for many years.

Part of Grant's greatness is his resiliency in overcoming setbacks and challenges. In his second year with the Oilers he was sent to the minors. Vulnerable because his five hole was too wide, he worked hard to correct this weakness. As a natural athlete, the mechanics of goaltending came easily to Fuhr. This may have contributed to Grant not taking his summer training seriously. For a short period in the middle of his career during the summer months Grant focused more on golf than training for hockey. He even played a couple of summers on the Canadian Professional Golf Association tour. There were injuries, weight gain, and a suspension after admission of experimentation with drugs. With this came trades to Toronto, Buffalo and St. Louis. Today Grant is back at the top of his game. Starting with a year-round training routine, he has played over 130 games in the last two years, including stellar playoff performance in 1997. There is every reason to believe that Grant Fuhr will finish his great career with the same grace and respect with which it began. The greatest tribute I can give to Fuhr is this: After observing or playing with the great goalies of the 60's, 70's, 80's and 90's, with utmost respect to all of them, if I were pressured to chose only one in the prime of their careers, Grant Fuhr is a goaltender extraordinaire.

The word that best sums up the Ranger's last line of defense is "preparation." Richter has been preparing to play in the NHL ever since he was a kid. And the most remarkable thing about his development is that a lot of it began in what we considered a non-hockey environment around Philadelphia.

Richter told me that he credits much of his growth as a goaltender to the ball-hockey games they used to play in Pennsylvania. From the get-go, he trained very diligently and it shows in his play today. Mike is one of the best-conditioned athletes you'll ever see.

He has the most powerful legs of any NHL goalie and works hard to keep them strong. He runs and exercises before games which, by the way, is a bit unusual for a goalie.

He's also very intensely involved on the mental level. He's analyzing the game all of the time, studying other goalies to determine what techniques work and what ones do not.

Style-wise, Richter is what I call "butterfly-standup." He doesn't go down as readily as the strictly butterfly goalies. He waits — Mike's game revolves around patience — analyzing the situation. Then, it's either a butterfly or standup reaction.

His style is a product of his background. Growing up in the wake of the Cup-champion Flyers, he learned about Philadelphia's greatest goalie, Bernie Parent, who was an orthodox angle-player. When the 1980's came and styles changed, Richter adapted the butterfly to the classic angle style and now enjoys the best of both worlds.

MIKE RICHTER

The Richter Theory is to make shots beat him on the outside of his body. Mike concentrates on assuming a tight, compact posture so pucks won't go through him between his arm and body or between his legs. Every so often, he'll struggle and when that happens, he opens up holes by thinking ahead of the play. He's intelligent enough to figure out his mistakes and adjusts rather quickly. In terms of balance he ranks with the best.

As a rule, the modern goalies are more loose than those from the earlier eras. Richter isn't a ball of nerves before a game. He's able to turn the switch on when it's time to focus. He doesn't carry the burden that the older goalies carried on game day and after the game.

Those who saw Richter perform on the medal-winning American team in the 1996 World Cup will recall how effective he was with his glove hand and how sound he was technically.

If there is any "soft" aspect of Mike's repertoire, it is his puckhandling. He's not in the class of a Martin Brodeur or Ron Hextall when it comes to firing the puck up the ice. Richter will usually try to make a play to one of his teammates near the goal rather than fire the puck over everybody toward center ice. Mike keeps his stickhandling very basic and simple.

A very impressive element of Mike's goaltending development has been his ability to develop a strong mental component at every level . Richter has toughened his "head" to the point where I would rate him among the elite when it comes to mental toughness. That he was able to do so in a non-hockey environment makes that accomplishment all the more amazing.

When Richter was sharing the Rangers goalkeeping with John Vanbiesbrouck, there was talk that if New York were to trade John, Mike might wilt under the pressure. There's no doubt that Richter did make some mistakes and blew some big goals — that Ron Francis long shot in the playoffs of 1992-1993 season was the worst — but Mike made the best of them. Through those blunders he acquired mental strength. He suffered through adversity, but was able to convert the experiences into an asset that he has carried to this day.

How do you beat Richter? Unfortunately for shooters, when he is on his game, he does not have a weakness. Opponents have to hope to catch him in a down cycle. When that happens, he might overplay some shots. I remember one in the first game of the Devils-Rangers series during the 1997 playoffs. Scott Neidermayer of New Jersey took a wide angle shot from the right side that seemed very stoppable. Instead, it went right through Richter's legs. Occasionally he will overplay some shots and become too aggressive. In those instances, he'll allow some holes just as he did on Neidermayer's shot. But any opponent who expects that to happen on a regular basis is sadly mistaken.

Mike Richter has worked and developed his craft to the point where he is now recognized as one of the great goalies to have ever donned the "big pillows." And to think it all began playing street hockey on the roads of a Philadelphia suburb - a tremendous inspiration for all young hockey crazed "puckstoppers" everywhere!

Here we have a product of the Canadian prairie. Joseph attended the Norte Dame School in Wilcox, Saskatchewan which has produced some awfully good hockey players. From there he went on the University of Wisconsin at Madison, where he faced a lot of shots; which is good training for a developing goalie.

By the time he reached the NHL, Joseph had refined his butterfly style, relying on his reflexes, legs and an excellent pair of hands. He'll resort to the butterfly in almost any situation. In that sense he's very reminiscent of Patrick Roy although I find him more active than Roy, with more dramatic moves.

His game revolves around his challenging the shooter from a low compact crouch. When CuJo is at the top of his game, he is at the top of his crease. He actually seems to be going at the puck. When Joseph is struggling, he plays closer to the goal line inside his crease. It's a common problem for every goaltender who is struggling.

Technically, Joseph does everything pretty well. In addition to his excellent butterfly, he has the ability to ad lib with the best of them to make that second — or desperation — save. We saw that during the 1997 playoffs between Edmonton and Dallas. Curtis had lost his stick. He seemingly was trapped near the left post. On the right side of the net was Joe Nieuwenkyk with the puck and an open net in front of him. If ever there looked like a sure goal this was it. The save Joseph made was as good as you will ever see in the playoffs.

To begin with, Joseph knew exactly where his body was in relation to the crease and the net when Nieuwendyk got the puck. There comes a critical point when a goalie has to get himself across the net. At times goalies will just throw themselves, hoping to get hit by the shot. At other times they are completely aware of where they are as they go across the net.

CuJo was not moving instinctively or blindly. He was conscious of exactly what was taking place and what more was required. He knew that Nieuwenkyk was capable of getting the puck up high, so Joseph responded by getting his hands in position. He dove across the goal line, threw up the back of his blocker, and made a spectacular, momentum changing save. When CuJo is at the top of his game he has the ability to rely of that "sixth sense."

I have a saying: "Anybody who wears the big pads and the big gloves can be a goalkeeper; but only a few times can you get to be a goal-robber." On some nights, CuJo has the ability to almost will himself not to give up a critical goal. Occasionally, he will play deep in the goal and he'll suffer some poor games. Which goalies haven't? That happens, in part, because his style revolves so much around being aggressive, both mentally and physically. When Curtis is not in his zone, there may be some games where you might watch him and think, "Geez, he doesn't look so hot and he's not." But, when you examine those really important games — the times when so much is on the line — you won't see CuJo come up with anything but a strong game.

In terms of personality, I rate him with the new wave of goalies — along with Mike Richter and Martin Brodeur — stoppers who are real loose between games, after the games and even right up to the game. They have a roll and a flow while never getting overly tense. The new breed is working toward a lighter balance; concentrating, yes, but without making their game preparation too intense.

Since his style revolves around being aggressive, he might get into trouble when he's physically tired. He'll lack that necessary zip of wanting to go right at the puck. Instead, he almost hangs back, thinking, "I'll play a little deeper and give myself an extra second." But that doesn't work on a consistent basis for any goalie, especially Joseph. He's not the type who can stand up and get hit with the pucks. His natural bent is to play in a low crouch outside the crease and aggressively react to the puck. When Curtis is doing this he is one of the best and most exciting goalies in the NHL. A great disposition and his ability to be a team-player also mark him as outstanding. No wonder he is respected by both goalies and shooters.

There isn't anyone who looks better stopping the puck than this guy. He has both a flow and a flair. If he played the trumpet or piano in an orchestra, they would call Nikky "a musician's musician." And if he was in the ballet, they'd dub him "a dancer's dancer."

His butterfly is as tight and fluid and technically correct as that belonging to any goalie in the NHL. His hands move beautifully — not jerky and stiff, and help to wrap up the whole smooth package.

As a puckhandler, Habby is average; more of a disher than a flipper out of the zone. He is okay handling rebounds, but not among the best. He has to learn to control them and become more efficient after he stops the puck. He is learning to battle to find those rebounds and looks like a goalie hungry to improve.

Khabibulin reminds me of John Vanbiesbrouck in that everything flows to the puck. The difference between Habby and Beezer is that the Russian kid is more hyper, more energized, and as a result, he gives up more rebounds. But like so many Europeans, he is still acclimatizing himself to North American hockey, particularly handling pucks around the net. In Europe the attackers don't jam the net as much as they do here. They don't play around and try the wraparounds that NHL skaters do so often. That is an area in which Habby will have to improve — the in-tight, jamming, physical play of the NHL.

Among his strengths is his fluid skating which enables him to challenge the shooter so well. He glides a couple of feet outside the top of the crease. He's fearless that way and has confidence in his movements around the net.

His five-hole is not too much of a problem. When he moves laterally, he gets his knees together and plugs the five-hole quite well. Overall, his crease moves are smooth and sharp.

Nikki's reflexes — the arms and legs moving in synchronization — are razor-sharp which mean those mid-range 10 to 12 foot shots are not that difficult for him to handle.

Determination is everything for a goaltender. Habby knows that and is determined not to have any chinks in his armor; not to give up any bad goals. He was a bit soft in this area when he came over from Europe. Hockey is not the life-and-death game overseas the way it is here. They're more realized about the sport in Sweden, Russia, and Finland. Over here, every game, every period, and every shift is like life and death. A European goaltender might say after a game, "Yeah, I did my best and it didn't work out. I made a lot of saves even though I gave up that one bad goal." By contrast, the North American goalie would be much more determined about the "one bad goal" that went in rather than focusing on the bunch of great saves he made.

As he started playing pro hockey in North America, Khabibulin learned how desperate a goalie has to be to stop every puck. It's not acceptable to give up one bad goal, even if you have made ten great saves. For a goalie in the high stakes world of the NHL, the heat is always turned on high. Khabibulin is learning there can't be any "cooling" if you want to be number one in the NHL.

There is a similarity between Eddie "the Eagle" Belfour and Dominik "the Dominator" Hasek who were once teammates in Chicago. Teaching others to copy them is very difficult because their technique is so individualistic.

Where Belfour differs from Hasek is in personality. Eddie is what I describe as a risk taking type of a guy. In the off season you might find him car-racing or doing some other sort of daring activity. Not surprisingly, his goaltending shows that aspect of his personality.

An average goalie will be two or three steps outside the crease, but Belfour will at times be four or six steps out. That's taking much more of a challenging posture than most goaltenders would feel comfortable doing. Practically speaking, he's way out! Belfour goes down earlier that most goalies and he's unpredictable in some of his moves. As a higher strung person, Belfour explodes in the crease and I don't criticize him for that. A goalie plays to his personality; Belfour has to play that way.

What he's doing may defy certain percentages in goaltending, but his explosive energy and quickness compensate for any technical flaws he might have. The butterfly is a good example because, as butterflies go, it is weird. The base is very wide, too wide by the standards of goaltending purists.

Still, it's all right for Belfour because he has honed it to a sharpness he has made work. He's not overly big and crouches very low. When Eddie faces a shooter, he's saying "I'm taking away the bottom two thirds of the net, I defy you to beat me high."

The tendency would be to call him instinctive but actually, Belfour has a pattern to what he does. The pattern is unique in that it's dictated in large by his vast storehouse of energy. He needs to be very active in order to compensate for that distance he moves out, especially when he's guarding against a two-on-one. Eddie might be concentrating on the player with the puck on his right when suddenly the puck is passed across the ice to his left. That means Eddie has a long way to go in order to get back and cover the other side of the net. He has to fly across the crease to make that save.

When shooting against Belfour, players have to go high nine times out of 10. If they shoot high only two out of 10 times, Eddie will get the high ones. But when it gets to anywhere from seven to nine out of 10 times, the percentages will tell you that some will get by him and mess up his thinking.

The only time Belfour gets off his game plan is when he thinks the forwards are believing that he's vulnerable to the high shots. If they start shooting consistently high, he knows that he has to pull his legs in a little. That forced change, although it may seen insignificant, actually becomes significant — His basic style is forced into an alteration that also affects his thinking. In Belfour's case, he relies so much on that low crouch for his confidence — his" feel good position" that he's apt to lose some self assurance when he has to play a more upright game.

Belfour's glove is as good as anyone's in the league. He knows it and, as a result, he leans in a way that virtually lures the shooter to aim for the glove side.

But because his stance is so low, he has to make sure that his glove hand is held higher and becomes independent of his legs. Normally the glove is squeezed lightly against the top of the pad. Belfour's glove is held higher and separated from the pad. Likewise he keeps his blocker higher than the norm to cover the blocker side well.

On shots from in close there aren't many better than Belfour. He was one of the first goalies to use the paddle down on the ice during scrambles, wrap arounds, or close-in shots.

His puckhandling is less than great but acceptable and he handles rebounds very well. That is a must because he plays so far outside the crease.

It is apparent when Eddie is struggling when pucks go through his legs or he is being beaten high. For example when he is on his game, there are times when a shot appears to have beaten Belfour through his legs but because he is so fired up and explosive he is able to slam his pads to the ice and make a save. If he's lacking the emotion and energy that drives his game, those same shots will somehow sneak through his pads. Belfour's game revolves around emotion. In Chicago he would feed off of the crowd and Eddie uses the crowd's energy as well as any goalie. When the club moved to the new United Center, it wasn't the same. It could have very well been the atmosphere at the new, somewhat sterile building. It appeared that Eddie no longer could energize himself off the crowd the way he did in the more intimate Chicago Stadium.

The team chemistry began to change. Dirk Graham retired and Jeremy Roenick was traded early in the 96-97 season. Eddie and the team struggled. Pretty soon he found himself immersed in turmoil. Apparently he snapped and criticized his goaltending partner Jeff Hackett, publicly, something that is unacceptable to the Goaltenders' Union. I'm sure Eddie didn't mean it quite the way it came out in the press, but the damage was irreversible.

I remember seeing Belfour just before he got traded from Chicago to San Jose. He was sitting on a stationary bike in the hallway outside the dressing room. He seemed so removed from the team particularly with the curtain separating him from his teammates. I felt bad for him because there was once such a love affair between Belfour, his teammates, and the Chicago fans. Shortly after, not unexpectedly, he was on his way to California.

As we know, it didn't go all that well with the Sharks. There is now the question of what kind of team player Eddie is because of all the negative publicity that surfaced in Chicago. By the end of the 96-97 season, the Eagle seemed to be experiencing a free fall. Now he is with Dallas where it will be interesting to see how this stage in his career unfolds.

What we have to understand is, on the ice, Eddie is strung differently than say a Martin Brodeur or Guy Hebert. Eddie will likely always be a very tightly-wound goalie. When emotionally charged goalies like Belfour move into their 30's, they have to be refining and adjusting their system of play to adjust to their changing body and energy levels. Expending energy efficiently in most situations is the goal of all goaltenders. Belfour may be going through this process at this stage of his career.

How he'll do in Dallas will be partially dictated, as with most goalies, on how well the team plays. All indications are that Belfour will have one of the best teams he has ever had in front of him. I predict that Belfour will rebound in a big way. He has been kicked around the past year and a half. He will be hungry to prove that he is still one of the best NHL goalies on the ice in addition to being a positive influence in the locker room. With the Dallas Stars in front of him, Eddie the Eagle may soar to his greatest heights ever — a Stanley Cup.

Because of Sean's size, (6'4" 205 pounds), Sean Burke has had to make certain physical adjustments to play goal in today's game. On one side of the balance sheet, Sean has been given an edge because his natural body size covers more of the goal scoring areas; also his size gives him a longer reach with his arms and legs. On the other side of the balance sheet, his size can turn to a disadvantage because like all larger goalies, it takes more developmental time to learn how to maneuver a big body especially if he has to make shifts in style once in the NHL.

When Burke came to the New Jersey Devils as a 21 year old in 1988 he was essentially a stand-up goalie as were most of the top goalies of the time. His hot streak took the Devils to the playoffs on the final night of the season. He was on a roll. He didn't appear to have any weak spots and everything seemed under control. As with many rookies, he enjoyed his first year because he was talented and partially because he had no history with the shooters. It's interesting that even rookie goalies will know what to expect from forwards because they have seen them perform on television. But with a rookie goalie, the shooters have no idea what a new goalie's weaknesses are.

His second year was no bowl of cherries. The Devils missed the playoffs and Burke didn't look quite so invincible. Critics said he was suffering from the sophomore jinx. I don't believe that players are jinxed, though I acknowledge something frequently occurs often in the second season. I call it "sophomore syndrome." In Burke's case what he suffered from was a natural letdown form the first year high. Secondly, opponents began to learn his weaknesses and how to exploit them.

Burke, well aware of his own weaknesses as are all top goalies, began to work on them. It is important to bear in mind that Sean came into the league when the butterfly was taking over form the stand-up as the appropriate style to use. Burke looked awkward at times because as a tall, stand up goalie, he was trying to put those big pads together to plug the five hole and it put him off balance. As a student of the game, Burke recognized that he needed a butterfly component to cover the bottom of the net more efficiently. Whenever a goalie refines his technique it is common to see a small step backwards before you see the two steps forward. That small step backward during the tweaking period is why goalies, in this case Burke, often don't appear so invincible in the second season. Burke needed to adjust his style and he has.

When Burke starts to move his long legs, it doesn't take him long to reach the corners of the net and completely close them down. By the same token, the minute he starts to move those legs, he creates a really large, long high five hole. Interestingly, goalies like Burke are more conscious of the five-hole than anyone understands __ except fellow goaltenders themselves. Goalies know that not all goals through the five-hole are necessarily bad, although no one, coaches, teammates, fans, or the Press, believes that is true. It is always in the mind of Sean Burke not to let those shots go through his pads. A tall goalie can plug the problem of his larger five hole by utilizing an efficient butterfly. Early in his career with no effective butterfly, Sean plugged his five hole by sprawling and trying to jam his pads together. It's why he initially looked awkward. Again remember Burke was caught in the stand up to butterfly transitional period. Now that he has drastically improved his butterfly, his style has smoothed out.

In terms of fighting spirit, there is a touch of Ron Hextall in Sean Burke. Sean has had to develop this under trying times playing on weaker teams. Kudos to his perseverance, and effort.

There is more flow to Burke's game now than in the earlier stages of his career. He has a flair to his style and an excellent glove hand. He plays the puck pretty well and is strong mentally. As a goalie he is an excellent team leader and team player. I rate Sean in the upper edge of the middle of the goalie pack. He is in the top ten if not the top five in the league. Why I would pick Sean over some goalies with better stats is because of his leadership qualities as well as his strong goaltending.

Now that he has moved with the team down to Carolina, it will be interesting to see how they fair in a new environment where there will not be constant the turmoil that existed in Hartford.

Sean's problems are few, but if I had to name one it would be on shots that are low to his stick side. The refinements that he has added to his game have eliminated most of his weaknesses. He's now in a position to become a major force as a goalie, if his team improves.

Guy's forte is his inner strength. Among goaltenders, Herbert is one of the NHL's ultimate battlers and it's all rooted in his early development. He was not blessed with the God-given talent that enables his goaltending to look effortless. As a result, from Division Three collegiate hockey at Hamilton right up to the bigs, it has been a long difficult series of challenges for Guy. He has met them all admirably.

Technically, there is a lot that is correct about Hebert's style, it just isn't flawless. Guy has had to develop a style rather than have it simply come to him naturally. His butterfly isn't always smooth and fluid. Nor does it appear to flow naturally. He doesn't look like a Nikolai Khabibulin, who seems to be able to make smooth looking saves in his sleep. It is adequate and it is symbolic of the rest of his technical game.

One technical area in which Guy is more than adequate is when he uses his glove. His glove hand is excellent, at times outstanding.

Guy is not a great puck handler but he has given a lot of attention to that aspect of the game so that now he moves the puck better than he did earlier in his career. During times when he gets into trouble, he is playing a little deep in the net. Although he moves well laterally, when he is not feeling confident he falls back a bit to protect himself against cross ice passes. One might ask why any goalie moves back when he's in trouble? The answer is human nature. When one is in trouble one feels vulnerable and when that happens the tendency is too back off, or in a goaltender's case, back as far in the crease as humanly possible.

In Herbert's case he might not feel secure and quick in his lateral movement so he could be saying to himself "I won't venture out quite as far to challenge the shooter because if he passes, I don't think I will be able to get across the crease as smoothly or as quickly as I need to.

Intellectually, he will know that is the wrong approach, but it is difficult to overcome.

He may never move into that tiny, upper echelon of goalies but he will be right there in the next category and, at times, he will step up to be the NHL's hottest goalie.

If there were a contest to determine which goalies came from the best gene pool, Daren Puppa would be among the finalists. Puppa comes from a goaltending family. Both his father and brother were goalies. His father, Leo, attended the Detroit Red Wings training camp. He played minor pro hockey against Jacques Caron, former NHLer and the Devils goaltender coach. According to Caron, the elder Puppa had many of the same moves that have made his son famous. The only difference is that Leo caught with his left hand whereas Daren catches with his right.

Having a pro goalie as a father was a terrific boost for Daren's career, although Leo was never officially his coach. To this day Leo will point out certain things that his son might do to make his netminding better. When there are three goaltenders in one family there is sure to be plenty of talk about pucks around the dinner table. It also means that before others might have been doing so, Daren was developing that special goalie's "feel." In other words, the kid might see a spoon falling off the table and he would lunge and make the "save." Or he might be walking down the street and a ball would roll by from some kids game. Suddenly, Daren is kicking out his leg because he is always thinking like a goalie. It is wonderful that he was able to grow up in a total goaltending environment, always analyzing, always thinking about the next save. That is quite an asset.

It also means that before others might have been doing so, Daren was developing that special goalie's "feel." In other words, the kid might see a spoon falling off the table and he would lunge and make the "save." Or he might be walking down the street and a ball will be rolling by from some kids game. Suddenly, Daren is kicking out his leg because he is always thinking goalie. Daren's size (6-4, 204 pounds) has also been an asset. His strength is based both on his size and the fact that he has developed an excellent butterfly. He has a strong, flexible set of legs that flare out ideally. When he makes a glove save from the butterfly position, it looks classic. He has a natural ability to make glove saves look even more spectacular than they really are. It is not that Daren is showboating. It is just that his arms, hands, and body move with such flair and grace, that when he snaps up his glove, it is eye-catching. His glove hand is also a weapon because Daren is a lefty, so he catches with his right hand — remember forwards are patterned in their shooting strategy. With the glove in his right hand, Daren surprises shooters who actually think they are firing at his blocker. Left-handed goalies, just like baseball catchers, are more noticeable because there is something different about a left-hander. They hook their elbow a bit differently.

A big, stand-up goalie will occasionally have trouble with low shots because his size prevents him from positioning low. Puppa beats that problem because of his strong butterfly which enables him to hang lower in his stance. He's able to go down, jam the five-hole with his size, and take away the lower part of the net.

Puppa's skating and lateral movements are quite good for his size. You can't under-estimate how much more difficult it is for someone who stands 6'-4" to move around the crease compared to a goalie who is a six-footer. You have to remember that at 6'4", when he gets into his butterfly, his skates are naturally a little wider apart so he may not get the same strong push that some smaller guys get. Puppa is moving well when he's a little more upright than when he's hanging too low. A big goalie needs to be more upright to narrow his base to get that good glide. The tradeoff is this: because his legs are longer and his arms are longer, he doesn't have to move as far as a little guy.

His puckhandling is in the ordinary range. In that sense, he is more of a "dump-it-beats-the-first man in" puckhandler rather than a Ron Hextall clear-the-zone, make the long clearing pass type.

Daren's' assets, great butterfly, glove hand, and size mean that he has the ability to win the big games on his own. During the 1995-96 season, the Lightning ranked among teams destined to miss the playoffs — again. But Puppa played brilliantly down the stretch and they beat out the New Jersey Devils on the final weekend of the season.

Tampa Bay made the playoffs for the first time in franchise history and Puppa was the reason why. In addition, he was a finalist for the Vezina Trophy as the NHL's best goalie. (Jim Carey was the winner that year.)

Puppa has shown that he can be a *big* factor under optimum conditions. When the Lightning acquired him, he instantly became the number one and remained so as long as he stayed healthy. This was the first time in his career where he was the main man and had no competition to speak of and it seemed that he needed that. However, the health problem has intermittently plagued Puppa during his Tampa Bay career.

The 96-97 season was especially trying for both Daren Puppa and his coach, Terry Crisp. Crisp's team struggled and his number one stopper, Puppa, was injured for most of the year. When it seemed Puppa was recovered, ready, and fit to play, there would be a relapse and Daren's return would be delayed. Many people were speculating when he would be ready to return. An exasperated Crisp finally said, "Okay Daren, I don't want to hear it from the trainer and I don't want to hear it from your agent. When you are ready to play, you come and tell me and you're in."

He missed most of the 1996-97 with injury and not coincidentally the Lightning missed the playoffs. Still, the club had enough faith in him to give Daren a brand new contract. What his bosses have to worry about is his mental strength. When Daren weakens mentally, his style works against him. Then, he starts going down a little too early and he doesn't challenge quite as much. He seems to become unsure of himself and loses the positive aggressiveness that can work so well for a goaltender.

There are differences between quality goalies like Martin Brodeur and Puppa. When Marty is struggling, he is still able to hold his style together; it doesn't drastically change. Puppa, on the other hand, fluctuates during those down periods because his style is more integrated with his instincts and personality.

On game days, Daren is a little more uptight than your average goalie and very serious about his game. He has a game-day get-ready type of attitude; a throwback to the older goalies who were on edge most of the day of a game. Bill Smith the former New York Islander great, had a day of the game face like Puppa. His focus began at 10:00 AM rather than 5:30 PM. Not that it is right or wrong, but there is a distinct difference. Daren thinks more about his game and focuses earlier than a Mike Richter who turns it on about two hours before a game.

The bottom line is that Puppa is *the* guy for Tampa Bay and the players, in their heart of hearts, feel that he has to be in there if they are going to be winners. He was

the first and only true number one goalie in Lightning history. He has to be there —
and healthy — for them to win.

This is a goalie who has had to battle for whatever he has accomplished. Nothing has come easy for him, especially recognition. When he made it to the NHL as a rookie with Toronto, the Maple Leafs had a terrible team. This was a very difficult situation for a kid and it retarded his development for a while. Somehow, Kenny found a way to hang in there. For a while, it appeared as if his career was going in the wrong direction. But, he has hunger and he kept battling until something good came from his persistence.

He showed a lot of gumption in Philadelphia and even more so in Pittsburgh where he rescued the Penguins when Tom Barrasso was injured. Through it all, he has been tabbed by some as a perennial back-up, but I have seen enough of Kenny to put him in a number one category.

In terms of style, he is a throwback, almost unique. He stands up well, challenges but knows not to over-challenge. He is one of the few goaltenders who will go across the crease still standing up rather than go down to a butterfly. What he will do is drag his left — or right — leg the way Bernie Parent did when he was with Philadelphia. We call that a half-butterfly.

Wregget has an excellent glove and blocker and is more than adequate with his stick. To his credit, Kenny noticeably refined his game, adjusting to the new style of the 1990's without abandoning the traditional moves that worked so well for him. He was hungry and smart enough to change direction from mostly stand-up style moves that had been effective during his developmental years, the power hockey style of the 70's, to the more lateral flowing style of the 80's and 90's.

To me, the most impressive aspect of Wregget's development has been the ease with which he has handled tough situations, going back to that Game Seven against Pittsburgh when he pinch-hit for Ron Hextall and stoned Mario Lemieux and the Penguins.

Or, how he beat the Rangers — and Mike Richter — in the 1996 playoffs, making a save with his nose, of all things! And the way he singlehandedly saved the Penguins in that marathon affair with Washington — beating Olie Kolzig — that same year.

That tells you a lot about his ability, his heart and his perseverance. Any player who has ever had Kenny as a teammate will add that he is a wonderful guy to have in the room.

It's about time they stopped labelling him a back-up.

I can say without fear of contradiction that Ranford has made some of the greatest glove saves in National Hockey League history.

In most games he will be spectacular, acrobatic and whatnot but never boring. He's just a fun goaltender to watch but at the same time he can be erratic because he relies so heavily on his reflexes.

I call him "a spontaneous goalie" because he is always reacting to the play rather than anticipating.

I'm tempted to compare him with Dominik Hasek in this regard except for the fact that Hasek has a more of a game plan. By contrast, Billy is hard to figure from save to save. One time he will poke check and another time, in virtually the same situation, he won't. He might come out; he might stay back. He might make a two-pad slide or try something different on a similar play a few minutes later. That is a "spontaneous goalie."

Because of that pattern of not having a calculated system, he tends to be erratic. He gambles a lot but with a lot of energy to make the saves possible that would seem sure goals. Even when he is scored upon, Ranford seems to look good. He throws his leg up, tossing a blocker, causing commotion, even though he may have blown the shot.

But with all that, I have to say that he has had the talent to arrange and pull together his flamboyant behavior to form a reasonably coherent style that not only works but is respected around the league.

That and his attitude are special plusses for Billy. He battled his way up the NHL ladder, starting in Boston, going to Edmonton and always being the good team player, returning to the Bruins and then to Washington.

He has a positive personality, works hard in practice, challenges his teammates and always seems mentally fired up.

The one thing you have to remember is that no matter how off-beat Ranford might appear, he did win a Stanley Cup and he knows what it takes to be a champion.

Getting back to Billy's glove. He hangs low to the ice, keeping his catcher's mitt low, ready to fire out at a split-second's notice. When his glove comes up a lot of wind is displaced and his muscle-fibres are firing in all directions.

His movements in the crease are very quick. He comes across hard and will occasionally sprawl, appearing to be out of position yet making the save nonetheless. Billy can play on an underdog team and win games by himself even though he is up in years.

But when a goaltender reaches Ranford's age, there always is a question as to whether he will be able to maintain his top competitive level. When Billy was traded from Boston to Washington late in the 1996-97 season, the feeling was that he — along with Rick Tocchet and Adam Oates — would ease the Capitals into a playoff berth.

They didn't and there were whispers that Billy may have been off his game a bit. That's why you know Bill will be ready to start the 1997-98 season. To quiet the whispers and lead the Capitals to the playoffs.

One of the advantages of Marty's development is that the New Jersey Devils did not rush him into the National Hockey League. They let him mature for a couple of years in the minors and made sure that their goalie guru, Jacques Caron, monitored his progress and made suggestions to Brodeur along the way.

Interestingly, Marty was not one of those Quebec hotshots when he played Junior hockey. He was good, to be sure, but not a "can't-miss" type the way they have tabbed Roberto Luongo, who was picked fourth overall by the New York Islanders in 1997.

Marty has had to adjust and re-adjust and work at developing a style. This persistence — with the able assistance of Caron — has enabled him to mold a style whereby he now is one of the best in the business.

To his credit, Marty has not stopped there. He believes there are ways to become better and he is still working toward improvement.

The combination of Brodeur and Caron has enabled the Devils to deliver some of the most consistently first-rate goaltending any team has enjoyed. Caron is one of the best goalie coaches around and is superb at expressing his points not only to Martin but to others in the Devils' system.

What helped was the fact is that Brodeur is innately smart and able to absorb the teachings and then put them into play on the ice. That, plus his physical attributes, have put him up at the top of the pack.

Then there is the matter of blood lines. His father, Denis, was a Grade A goalie in Canada, played for his country's national team and would have made it to the NHL had there been a 26-team league when Denis was a pro.

Denis has had some influence on Marty, not only as a father but as an instructor as well. The result is that Marty has combined some of his dad's style from the 1950s. The kid can pokecheck the puck and he can throw that two-pad slide when necessary. Marty has also used elements from the 1970s in that he is reminiscent of the great "angle" goalies.

Some will say that Brodeur's prime asset is his puckhandling confidence. He will think nothing of firing the puck to his defensemen 50 feet away to clear the zone. Watch the ease with which he caroms the puck off the sideboards or makes passes to his teammates. Marty does it so well he has virtually become a third defenseman in addition to goaltender. You could also say he has been like a forward, too, especially after his scoring the goal in the open net against Montreal in the 1997 playoffs.

He has a good glove hand and is expert at setting himself up for an attack. As the enemy moves toward the Devils' zone, Marty prepares himself both mentally and physically to handle whatever play develops.

If, for example, the shot is off to his right, Marty will set his weight so he is covering the short side with his body, and so he can blast across to the far side, which is really the only place the shooter has to shoot. What he is saying is, "I'm taking away this one option, so if you shoot there, it's going to hit me. All I have to worry about is the side that's open and I set my weight and mind up so I'm ready to go for it." Marty does that as well as anybody.

Brodeur's size is something he uses to an advantage. He is an exceptionally hard worker in practices as well as the games. He prepares for a game as well as any goalie I know, and apart from his individual skills, his mental strength is his greatest asset. On the ice, his composure is rock solid. Simply put, he doesn't very often get rattled. We saw that during the 1997 playoff between the Canadiens and Devils. Marty is from Montreal so it was natural for him to be besieged by the Francophone media. Many players would shy away from all the interviews, or at best, do about five or ten minutes worth and then beg off. Not Marty; he hung out with the press as long as they wanted to talk, or at least until Mike Gilbert, Devil's PR director, would have to step in and say, "Let's go Marty."

That would be at the morning skate. Before the game, Marty is the same way. He would think nothing of doing an interview at 6:30PM for a game that starts at 7:30PM. Other goalies wouldn't even talk to the reporters in the morning, let alone at night.

Such behavior would lead some to think that Marty is not prepared, but the opposite is true. The trick is that Brodeur has the ability to get within himself in a hurry, to turn his focus on what he needs to do and then to do it. While his game preparation is tremendous, it doesn't take a lot out of him. He's loose and funny while at the same time, intense and focused. In other words, he channels his energy the right way.

I know other goalies seem to go into a relaxed mode — as if they are in a coma — but they come out of it too late. Marty comes out of it real quick. Part of that knack I attribute to his having grown up in a goaltending environment, thanks to his father. Denis Brodeur has a good sense of balance — always did when he played — and passed that on to his son.

Ironically, his mother has yet to see Marty play an NHL game. She watches him on television and holds a lucky bracelet he gave her when he broke into the game.

Brodeur's arrival in New Jersey was perfect timing. He had a few years in the minors and then came to a team that was well-suited to his style. Marty was what the Devils needed and the Devils were what Marty needed. He was in a situation where he could succeed early and, for him, that was the right kind of success.

Marty has told me that he doesn't feel comfortable unless the game is within one goal. He revels in the tight games when the so-called pressure is at its most intense level. You want a goaltender whose mind thinks that way. You certainly want a goalie who is and has been as consistent as Brodeur has since he entered the NHL.

Martin Brodeur has a healthy approach to goaltending and the world of a professional athlete. Like most elite athletes, he has been blessed with much. What makes Martin so special is his ability to share. He is always kind, generous with his time, approachable and accommodating. His warmth and sense of humor are already legendary among the press corp. As enjoyable as he is to watch on the ice, he is enjoyable to know as a person.

Talk about cool customers, there aren't many like Moog. An iceberg would seem hot compared to this guy. Part of it is due to his experience. Andy goes back to the earliest days of the Edmonton Oilers, even before Grant Fuhr joined the team. He played on Edmonton's first Stanley Cup winner in 1984 and has remained one of the quality stoppers ever since.

Durability is just one of his positive traits. Andy is smart and wise enough to have refined his technique as shooting styles have changed. In terms of what he has in his armament there isn't a goalie around who has polished his style better than Andy.

Of all the NHL goalies, few give themselves a better chance to be hit with the puck more than Moog. Every one of his moves is smooth and calculated. He has worked out the percentages in his head and follows through with the body mechanics to make saves. He has played that way ever since he was a rookie with the Oilers at the beginning of the 1980's. Consistency has been his hallmark. He says, "I'm going to do this in this situation every time and that is it." There is nothing flamboyant about Andy and consequently, he is noticed less than, say, a Bill Ranford . But Moog's efficiency without fuss or fanfare enables him to conserve energy. Which explains why at 37 he seems in mint condition.

Nevertheless, his age raises doubts from year to year. While he played well during 1996-1997 in what was an excellent regular season for the Dallas Stars, he was out-dueled in goal in the first playoff round by Curtis Joseph and the Stars were eliminated. In the off season the Stars acquired Ed Belfour which enabled Moog to sign with the Montreal Canadians. With the Habs he will be asked to stabilize what has been a shaky goaltending situation since Patrick Roy's departure. Whether that means stopping "la rondel" during games or helping with the development of the young Thibeault and Theodore, on and off the ice Andy Moog presence will be appreciated by the Montreal Canadiens new coach Alain Vigneault.

You won't find a keener student of the goaltending than Jeff Hackett. He is so serious about the business that during the summer of 1997 — after he had become the number one goalie on the Blackhawks — Jeff attended a goalie's school, but not as a teacher, as a student! Now *that* is dedication. That wasn't the first time Hackett has attended a goalie school as a student. For many years he was a pupil at Craig Billington's, the Colorado Avalanche goaltender, goalie school. Actually he and Craig are very good friends. They have a lot in common. They are excellent students of the game, instructors, and ambassadors for the goaltending profession. Their styles are similar. Basically they stand up, play the angles, while remaining technically sound in everything they do. When one observes them play, it becomes obvious they have spent some time working with each other.

Jeff has always been very thoughtful about stopping the puck. In fact, it had been said he was too studious about the profession when he turned pro in New York, although I'm not too sure one can ever be too inquisitive about analyzing goaltending.

It is, however, fair to say when he first arrived in the National Hockey League as an Islander prospect he didn't have a free flowing feel for stopping the puck. He appeared somewhat stiff and mechanical. At times Jeff appeared to play as if he were thinking that if every save were technically correct, he would be in position for every rebound as well. That was a mistake I made early in my own career. From a certain _____ing that was impossible to achieve. There is a _____ alyzing the mechanics of goaltending and let-_____ y.

_____ l every technical rule of playing goal correctly, _____ p the puck the way he would like, he may begin _____ s an old goaltending bromide that says "over _____ tt awhile to learn to how to find that balance. _____ rom thinking too mechanically, trying to do _____ up and going down every so often when nec- _____ ut a goalie who insists on standing up against _____ oals than one who butterflies. _____ easant one. He didn't make it on Long Island _____ ew team that gave up a lot of quality shots, in _____ Jeff was maturing and making progress which _____ ould remain a second string goaltender. But, _____ ots in San Jose were forcing him to be more _____ ame, the hotter the action the less time to be analytical. Nowadays, Jeff is getting down lower in close, putting his paddle down on the ice, and using the butterfly.

During his early struggles, what saved Jeff was his attitude. He is a terrific person, very positive, very much a team player who is willing to go with the flow. He proved that when he was back-up to Eddie Belfour in Chicago. Jeff knew that Eddie was the main man and accepted his role. He was a superior backup because of his teamsmanship. Coaches knew that they could throw Hackett in at any time, any place and they would get that good game out of him. He never rocked the boat.

the terms of the Rules and Regulations eposited/withdrawn. statement. FORMATION IS SHOWN BELOW. Transaction Receipt 111113/92

Even when Belfour apparently ridiculed him in the middle of the 1996-1997 season, Hackett just shrugged it off, without a whimper or complaint.

Jeff doesn't have a distinctive style. He handles the puck decently. He has a good glove, and has refined all the basics to play at a high level. During 1996-1997 season, Hackett created so positive a jump in his goaltending as well as in peoples' perception of his abilities, that the Blackhawks had enough faith in him to trade Belfour. What's noteworthy is that for the first time in his career, starting in the fall of 1997, Hackett was the unequivocal number one goalie on a high profile team. Blackhawk fans have always loved their goaltenders. They were only getting to know Hackett late in the 96-97 season. By the end of the 97-98 season, hopefully, there will be a full blown love affair at the United Center.

STEPHANE FISET

Stephane Fiset was a very promising goaltender when he graduated to the National Hockey League. He filled the net well, had some big league moves which he had developed in the Quebec Junior League, and was confident and aggressive. That is pretty good parley for an aspiring goalie.

When he was only nineteen, Fiset was doing everything well. After seeing him, I said to myself, "Whoa! He is going to continue to develop those good traits of his and that will only make him better. He is going to be a great one!"

As of this season, however, Stephane's play would be considered good, but not great. Perhaps part of what slowed down Stephane's development was that he wound up playing for the Quebec Nordiques at a time when they were not one of the best teams in the league. The team wasn't ready to win, yet he was asked to carry them. Then just when it seemed that he had arrived and the Nordiques were moving upwards, the Nordiques traded for Ron Hextall. That meant, of course, that Fiset wasn't number one anymore. Eventually Hextall was traded, but then he was challenged by the Nordiques number one draft pick, Jocelyn Thibeault. The Nordiques moved to Colorado and Fiset appeared ready to shine when the avalanche brought in Patrick Roy. Fiset was on the outside once again. Finally, when Stephane was traded to LA for the 96-97 season, he got another chance to be the top banana.

The trade from a Stanley Cup contender to a rebuilding team forced him to make a big time mental adjustment, if not a style adjustment. Now in LA, he sees a lot of quality shots and they just keep coming. On a team whose confidence is fragile, that makes mistakes at critical times, it is a real challenge for any goaltender to be consistent. Fiset's game that once appeared to have so much potential has not progressed in the manner I know Stephane would like.

The good news is, Fiset still has all of that natural skill. He simply needs to shore up a couple soft spots. His glove can be dynamite. He possesses a pair of quick, strong legs. He has size. He has terrific reflexes. He has a good attitude and is a team player. This is pretty much a complete package for any goaltender.

So why hasn't it all come together? First of all is the example I try to impress upon students at hockey schools. How consistent and effective you can become as a goalie rests entirely on the type of goals that get by you rather than on the saves you make. For example, I have watched and marveled at Fiset making good save after good save and then, *boom*, a puck squeezes through his arm. Then two or three great leg saves and, *poof*, a puck goes through the five hole. Stephane would hold good position for long stretches of the game and then he would over-challenge a situation and get burned. It has been this inconsistency which has plagued Fiset and held him back from reaching his potential.

For Fiset, some re-examination is in order. He needs to step back and look at all of his assets and understand precisely what he does well. He then has to isolate the weaknesses that make him inconsistent and get to work, tighten up his stance under pressure so that fewer pucks go through the arms and body, work to make his low position more air tight, that may mean a tighter squeeze of the knees on the butterfly; and mentally, Stephane needs to be more patient and not over-react in certain situations. When it comes to making changes, Stephane is no different than any other goalie. Where Stephane is different is that his potential is so incredible.

If Fiset can correct a few of the basics and eliminate the average shots that go through him while continuing to make the great saves that have characterized his career, he will become a premier goaltender in the National Hockey League.

FELIX POTVIN

A few years ago, Felix Potvin was rated a "can't-miss" kid who figured to be a Vezina Trophy winner __ or close to it __ by 1997. That has not happened. If Potvin's game has not regressed, it has stalled. When Glenn Healy was obtained as a free agent by the Maple Leafs in the summer of 1997, some Toronto newsmen said that it was to have someone who could "motivate" Felix. Assumption was that somehow, somewhere, the Cat got complacent in Toronto. The fact was that as the team in front of him deteriorated and his game went along with it.

His five hole, rarely exploited in the past, has become a problem. As action thickened around his net, and the Leaf defense fell apart, Potvin began playing deeper and deeper into the net. When any goalie does that, it is because he feels that he needs an extra second to see the puck and react to it. What actually happens is he loses what advantage he may have had because when he backs up, he opens up more net space.

Felix got himself into a vicious cycle. Though he had the wide five-hole stance when he was playing out of the net, it was okay. When he moved back, he knew that he had to cover the corner so he widened his five-hole a bit to try to hit those corners, but in the process he would open up with an even bigger five-hole.

The earlier-better Potvin came out of the crease and challenged. When he did that, he knew that he wasn't giving much room in the corners and could keep his legs a bit tighter.

Any goalie's confidence and style changes with a losing team. Potvin has faced more shots and been confronted with more pressure while hearing the constant murmur of trade talk. These elements weighed heavily on a young goalie, no matter how well he had played earlier.

It's important to remember that even though his game has slipped, he remains one of the National Hockey League's best goalies. He was one of the first to use the paddle; putting his stick down against the ice to block shots. He has a tremendous glove, which he relies on, and he is a fiery, well-prepared performer.

The key for him is for the Leafs to provide a bit more defense in front of him so that he can start winning some games and regain his confidence. He has to start winning the 2-1 games instead of losing them. He has to feel good about himself — and move farther out of the net.

JOHN VANBIESBROUCK

Nobody is better prepared for a game than Beezer. He can tell who is shooting at him by the label on the stick. He can look at the shaft and say, "Oh, that's Gretzky!" without evening seeing the player's face. Now that's preparation!

In most situations, Beezer is in position to give himself the best chance of either stopping the puck or being hit by just slightly moving his blocker or glove hand. John has made many smooth, great glove saves. He is so calculating when it comes to taking care of the little things in goaltending that the big things take care of themselves. I call his style "percentage-wise correct."

Since he is among the smaller puckstoppers, he realizes that it's vital for him to come out as far as possible to cut down the shooter's angle. He does that with expert precision. In so doing, he also understands that he's far from the net and may have to react laterally. Since his younger days, he has been refining this so that he now has one of the smoothest lateral motions in the game. He can slide across, and do the two-pad slide, or slide across and do the butterfly. It is a thing of beauty.

When it comes to intensity, nobody tops John. He's right up there with Ron Hextall. To them the crease is like their office. They want to get a good, honest day's work done and want things done right. Beezer has a tremendous work ethic, both mentally and physically, in a game or in practice.

John doesn't just go out there and try to get a sweat going, just try to stop some pucks. He is thinking all of the time — "am I doing enough to help the team win?"

There's an electricity about Beezer that's a function of his personality. He's got charisma, not only in terms of the crowd's reaction to him, but for his teammates as well. That trait gives his defensemen and forwards more confidence than they otherwise might have. Even when Beezer gets beaten, he never looks really bad. It's almost as if the puck just happened to sneak by him, not that he fanned on a shot. Few goalies have ever looked better missing shots than Vanbiesbrouck. Johnny is silky smooth, has confidence and class.

He has withstood the test of time as well as any goalie from the 1990's and proved how adaptable he can be after he was moved from his original team, the New York Rangers, to a brand new expansion club, the Florida Panthers. For Johnny, the motivation is the Stanley Cup. After he left New York, the Rangers won it and, of course, Beezer came within four wins of the championship in 1996. He might just feel now that he can never be considered one of the greatest unless he plays on a Cup-winner.

Right now, Beezer is at the top of his game. He carried his club to the Stanley Cup Finals in 1996 and came back with another strong season a year later. His challenge now is to continue that stellar play and continue to work as hard as he has for the past decade.

If you watched Tommy Salo in the Olympics or in the International League, you would come away assured that he would be a star in the National Hockey League. He is a perfect example of a Swedish goalie who patterned himself in the style of the late great Pelle Lindbergh, arguably the best Scandinavian goalie of all time.

When Lindbergh came to the Philadelphia Flyers, he studied under Hall of Famer, Bernie Parent. At first, Lindbergh used the butterfly which he learned from the Soviet ace, Vladislav Tretiak. When Parent got hold of him, Lindbergh switched from the deep butterfly to more of a standup style. He moved around more on his feet and avoided going down to his knees. When I watch Tommy move across the crease, staying on his feet a little more than the others, I was reminded of Pelle.

Like Lindbergh, it took Salo some time to acclimatize himself to the different sizes of the NHL rinks. In Europe, the rinks are Olympic size, which means that goalies see different types of shots than they do in the tighter North American rinks. In Europe, more shots are developed out of plays that are coming at you, whereas here shots come more quickly __ and more often from the corners and in bang-bang fashion. One second the goalie is hugging the post and then you have to be shifting your momentum to the far side as fast as possible.

His European credentials are excellent as was his minor league record in North America. He's one of the best goaltenders to come out of Scandinavia and has played on championship teams in the International League.

Salo has not had an easy time with his big league experience. His first attempt at making the grade with the New York Islanders was just short of a disaster. He was beating himself and seemed to wilt under pressure. When he was sent back to the "I," Salo became a whiz once again. The good news was that the Islanders kept the faith in him. They felt he needed more time to develop and mature and they were right. In his first two trips to the bigs, he didn't have a very good team in front of him. But the third time was different — and better.

During the 1996-97 season he beat out Eric Fichaud for the number one job and showed signs of turning into a solid goaltender. Although he had a very young defense in front of him, Tommy played well under pressure and proved himself to his team and to management.

What is most encouraging about Salo's maturation is that his teammates are sure he will no longer give up the easy goals. Meantime, management is happy because now he's able to handle all the hype that comes with his job. After suffering some self-doubt, Tommy has come to believe that he can do it in the NHL. He showed that self-assurance when he took over the top spot.

He still has work to do on some mechanics. Here's an example. The Islanders were playing New Jersey and Tommy was hugging the post when John MacLean came out of the corner. Salo prematurely moved away from the post and gave MacLean room that he shouldn't have given him. MacLean then beat him upstairs, inside. It was a play where Tommy didn't play the percentages as well as he might have.

His coach, Rick Bowness, has been supportive and stayed with Salo during his difficult periods. Tommy repaid the favor by improving his game to a point where he nearly helped the Islanders into the playoffs. Although they missed out in the last couple of weeks of the season, it was through no fault of the goaltending.

I believe Tommy has a bright NHL future and will continue improving to a point where he will be considered a latter-day Pelle Lindbergh.

Over the years there have been small goaltenders who were taken lightly by the media and fans, but who gained a lot of respect from the people in the hockey business. Jacques Cloutier, who played so well in Buffalo was one and Ron Tugnutt is another. Both have been admired because they were mentally strong, intense competitors.

Neither Cloutier nor Tugnutt were blessed with tremendous natural skills, but they managed to overcome any tangible weaknesses with guts and a feeling of invincibility, as well as innate intelligence.

Ronnie does everything imaginable to stop pucks and to win hockey games. He has figured out all the angles, the percentages which give him a chance to get hit by the puck. Anyone who watched him lead Ottawa down the stretch drive in the 1996-97 season felt that he would never beat himself. When Damian Rhodes faltered, Tugnutt stepped up and played the best goal of his life. What's more, for the most part, he did it very simply. He played his angles perfectly and would move a leg or arm ever so slightly to make a save. He did, however, make some excellent second effort saves.

Most of the time, his moves are subtle rather than glittery. Even when he makes a big save. you're not apt to shout, "Wow! What a move!" Tugnutt is living proof that a goalie does not have to look spectacular to be good. He has organized his skills in such a way that he produces consistently.

When he carried Ottawa into the playoffs, he wasn't so much sensational as he was solid and consistent game after game. He didn't allow the other team to win.

Yet when you examine his career, you find more downs than ups. He has faced considerable hardship, played for many inferior teams, but never quit on himself. Even after he was buried in the minors, he kept plugging away until Pierre Gauthier gave him a shot with the Senators.

He repaid Ottawa with that wonderful homestretch and then the seven game series with Buffalo. Unfortunately, that seventh game proved to be an agonizing finish to his great season. The Senators led 2-1 in the third period of the seventh game and then it slipped away. On the tying goal, Tugnutt got burned on one of the most unusual goals I have ever seen scored. As the face-off began, the sticks of the two opposing center icemen struck the puck exactly at the same time. This caused the puck to pop into the air shoulder high, slightly to the right of centerman, Alexi Yashin. As Yashin spun to find the airborne puck, his blade caught the disc and literally flung it high into the near side of the net. It was like a lacrosse shot which was why Tugnutt was confused. He saw the puck pop up, then the black puck was on the black tape. Meanwhile, Ronnie was giving up a little of the short side thinking the puck was going to the top of the circle which, of course, it never did. It was a goal that could shake even the most stable goaltender. Actually, Tugnutt and the Senators played great following the goal and could have won it in regulation time, but the other 96-

97 playoff goalie Cinderella, Sabres' Steve Shield, was playing sensationally well. The winning goal had come from outside the face-off circle on the right wing. It was one I know Ronnie feels he should have had. That was a goal in sudden death overtime, so there was no redemption. Actually, there was. The Senators were so happy with him, they gave Ronnie a brand, new contract — well deserved!

Trevor Kidd is one of the most active goalies ever to come into the National Hockey League. He is a ball of energy, movement and aggressiveness. At times he is like a small whirlwind between the pipes. He pivots, turns, dives from left to right. Trevor's trademark has always been his incredible quickness and reflexes. In Junior Hockey he was flamboyant and utterly fearless. Most of all, he was fun to watch. You might have seen him trapped out of position and were positive he were going to be scored upon, then swoosh! A glove, a leg, or his entire body would miraculously appear and Trevor Kidd would perform another goaltending gem. Trevor was so adept at covering any technical bad habits he may have developed up through his Junior career, that when they were exposed at the pro level, it was a surprise.

Trevor is going through the learning process that most young goalies must experience. Playing consistently well in the NHL is about balance and control and tight, compact movements that do not create shooting holes around the perimeter of the body. The old goaltending adage says, "It's not so much the ones that go by you that hurt, it is the shots that go through you that sting."

What Trevor needs to do to improve is tighten up his style and play in a more controlled fashion. This is not necessarily a major adjustment, but it does take a lot of concentration.

Kidd is now at the crossroads. Calgary missed the playoffs in 1996-97, the coach, Pierre Page, left and the Flames decided to trade for Rick Tabaracci who will compete with Kidd for number one. Understandably, Trevor was disappointed when he heard about the deal because he figured that it would stall his progression. Actually, it could help. Granted, Kidd may not play as much, but he can learn from Tabaracci who has gone through similar challenges as well and overcome them.

Tabaracci had been an inconsistent goalie when he was younger. He was flamboyant and overactive. He has since refined his play and is much more reliable. He may help Kidd learn to get over the hump in the same way. It's not a matter of making the spectacular saves, but being consistent enough to eliminate any clunkers.

Kidd has a lot of positive traits, foremost of which is his burning desire to play and improve. For him it's just a matter of arranging and adjusting a few moves and then he will be terrific.

MIKE VERNON

A big hurrah for this guy, winning his second Stanley Cup as well as the Conn Smythe Trophy for 1997! Mike definitely fooled a lot of people who figured him for washed-up, particularly since Chris Osgood had been the regular Detroit goalie heading into the homestretch. Vernon is a fascinating study for a lot of reasons, starting with his temperament which has been judged both an advantage and a detriment to his career.

The one factor that cannot be disputed is the instinct. Mike has been around the crease long enough to instinctively know when to do what. Oh, yes, he has a nice butterfly, an excellent glove, and he does come out to challenge intelligently, but so much of his success is based on instinct — an instinct that was sharpened when he was wearing the red and white colors with a flame on his chest rather than the winged wheel.

I remember when he was with Calgary during the 1980's. Edmonton had the Gretzky-Messier-Fuhr dynasty. The Flames would go up against the Oilers and in any given game, Vernon would make 15 great saves, but if he couldn't make the 16th, he would lose the game.

Playing against those tough Oiler teams all those years toughened up Vernon's strength and character. Eventually, he quarterbacked Calgary to the Stanley Cup in 1989 and that confirmed his status as a top-flight goalie.

I remember one outstanding save he made in the series against Vancouver. This was game seven of the Flames-Canucks series and Stan Smyl of the Canucks got the puck coming in off the wing. Stan was a terrific competitor and on this occasion he had a lot of room as he moved toward Vernon. His shot went to the short side __ the glove __ and Mike proved what a terrific glove hand he has. What looked like a goal-labeled shot wound up in his mitt. That grab saved the Flames and it enabled Calgary to come back and win the series and, eventually, the Cup.

Across the League — despite all his accomplishments — Vernon has had a mixed reputation. He is commended for some of his spectacular moves, but knocked for giving up the bad goal. Some of those who have been aware of Mike's loosey-goosey behavior off the ice have figured that he just didn't take the games seriously enough, assuming his easy going temperament affected his concentration.

To me that was a misrepresentation. I know that Mike Vernon takes his game very seriously and has studied it intensely and well. Anyone who questioned Mike's intensity got the answer in the late-season Colorado-Detroit game in 1997 when a brawl broke out and Vernon went toe-to-toe with Patrick Roy. If you saw the way Vernon handled his dukes in that one, you would know that the fire burns inside him as fiercely as any goalie.

Style-wise, Mike uses the blend of stand-up and butterfly. Through his years of experience, he has acquired the ability to read when to choose which stance. Mike plays the angles and reads attacks very well. He has never had trouble moving laterally around the crease. His glove can be lethal. He is not a big shooter, as far as goalies go, but he handles the puck with confidence. Vernon's game is a total package.

Reflecting back on Mike's career, it is interesting to note that at times (96-97 Cup), critics would rank Vernon among the elite. In other years, critics would rank him as just a good, solid goaltender.

It is my observation when he is ranked among the elite, pucks are rarely going through him. When he has been ranked among the solid goaltenders, you will find that pucks more often are sneaking through him. This point may seem too simplistic or obvious. The fact is, giving up those "through you" type of goals have a much greater negative effect than getting beat on a nicely executed clean goal. The pitfalls of a goal that goes through the goalie are many. The goaltender himself knows it was a shot he could have stopped, so his train of thought is like a negative stream — "All I had to do was to not move my arm away from my body… I can't believe my stick was partially off the ice… why did I let my butterfly get so wide that I got burned?" When teammates see shots going through the goalie, as opposed to shots that go around or even over, their thoughts too can turn negative. They become concerned about how strong the last line of defense is on that particular night. In addition there is the psyche of the other team. When they see that they can shoot just about anywhere in that four by six rectangle with the chance of the puck going "through the target" and into the net, they become encouraged and fired up. By contrast, nicely constructed goals or great shots in the corners do not have the same psychological impact.

Mike Vernon's impact on the Detroit Red Wing's Stanley Cup win was as much psychological as it was physical. Let's remember, going into the playoffs everyone recognized the Wings confidence was extremely fragile. A questionable goal at a critical time could send them and their fans into an "Oh no, here we go again," mindset! Vernon refused to let that happen. Under every kind of pressure and tension, Mike never wavered or gave up a sloppy goal. Mike's winning of the Conn Smythe trophy was as much about his unwavering consistency as brilliant saves.

I know Mike has tremendous respect and gratitude for Hockey Hall of Famer, Glen Hall, his coach and friend from his days in Calgary. It is obvious that Hall and Vernon have worked together on Mike's game. Mike's butterfly, which was Hall's strength, has improved from earlier in his career. Mental preoccupation, another of Hall's strengths, is an area where Vernon has never been stronger. The Hall-Vernon goaltending relationship is another example of why goaltending coaches are important. The Conn Smythe trophy was a fitting tribute to that relationship.

Mike's three years in Detroit have been unstable to say the least. His first year, the Wings spent the entire year trying to trade him. When they were unable, they gave him a chance to play in the playoffs, and he responded by helping the Wings reach the finals. When the Wings went down in four straight to the Devils, there were rumors once again that maybe Mike wasn't the man for the job. The Wings must have thought so as well. During Vernon's second playoff with Detroit, Chris Osgood, an excellent goaltender himself, carried the load. Coming into the 96-97 season there was no reason to believe Vernon's situation would drastically change. But, it did. It had taken Scott Bowman, Detroit's coach, a while to understand Vernon. Mike Vernon did two things that showed Scott Bowman and Detroit hockey fans the depth of his character. When he was pushed to the background during the grooming of Chris Osgood, he publicly kept his mouth shut, worked hard, and waited for his next opportunity. Secondly, down the stretch of the 96-97 season when the rivalry and bitterness between the Avalanche and Wings erupted, Vernon showed his gamesmanship by not backing down to superstar, Patrick Roy. That moment will forever be looked upon as the turning point to when the Red Wings became a team with enough grit to win the Stanley Cup. Mike Vernon became the catalyst that drove the Red Wing's engine to victory.

Despite this, at press time the Wings had traded Vernon to San Jose. He should fare well there.

The Canadiens loss to New Jersey in the spring of the 1997 Stanley Cup playoffs will be a turning point in young Jocelyn Thibault's career. Right or wrong, he was made the scapegoat for the Habs' loss to the Devils in five games. He lost the first three games before giving way to rookie, Jose Theodore, who won the fourth match, then lost the fifth game.

Thibault possesses the foundation materials for becoming an excellent NHL goaltender. Over all, his butterfly mechanics are sound. It is usually tight and low, with an effective flaring of the legs. One habit Jocelyn needs to improve upon is using his down on the ice butterfly in almost every situation. For example, when a shot comes from outside the top of the face-off circle, Jocelyn's first reaction is too often to drop to his knees into his butterfly. Even though he stops the puck, being down on his knees makes it very difficult to direct and control the rebound, especially on high shots.

Goalies with a more refined butterfly will hang in their crouch and drop down only if the shot is threatening to go through their legs. Otherwise, they will stop or direct the puck from this low standing crouch. Another example is when players come out of the corner with the puck, there are times when the best choice is to go down into a butterfly or paddle down on ice position. But not every time. Once a goaltender becomes predictable by dropping down onto the ice, the majority of the time he will surely be headed for trouble.

I believe this is the mechanical root of most of Thibault's problems. His hands are good. He moves well laterally. He does have an excellent butterfly to cover the scramble and low shots. It is just premature dropping to the ice on too many shots that is keeping Thibault from becoming more consistent.

Mentally it was a tough, but mind-strengthening year for Jocelyn. He struggled earlier in the season, but got it together down the stretch and was as responsible as any other Canadien for making the playoffs.

Then came the playoffs. Thibault struggled on a couple critical goals in the first and second games against the Devils. His team played well. Unfortunately, he did not. As someone who has been in his position, it was painful to watch.

Thibault is a terrific guy. He is respectful, caring, and approachable. He loves to play goal and wants desperately to be an asset to his team every time he pulls down his mask. No one felt worse than Jocelyn himself after game two. With the return to Montreal, many expected then Hab's coach, Mario Tremblay, to insert the other young excellent Montreal prospect, Jose Theodore. Instead, Tremblay, wanting to show his faith in Thibault, started him in game three.

The game went from bad to worse for the young Thibault and he suffered another demoralizing defeat. He just wasn't able to play at the level everyone believes he can. It was a sad ending to a productive season. He had played in a "fishbowl" all season. With goaltending legends like Jacques Plante, Bill Durnan, Ken Dryden, and Patrick Roy, the goaltending standards of Montreal are very high.

What Thibault, as well as Theodore, need is a mentor. Someone who plays a style of goal similar to theirs. Someone who has been through the wars, the pressure, and succeeded. Someone who has been a winner in every sense of the word. The Canadiens over the summer of 97 acquired just that person, Andy Moog.

I believe it is very hard not to succeed when you have skill, character, and experience. Thibault has skill. He has character. What he lacked was experience. We will see the reemergence of Jocelyn Thibault. This young man has too much natural talent and desire to allow one disappointing play off to sidetrack his career — chalk it up to needed experience.

You have to feel for this guy. In the eyes of many, Kirk has had an up and down career with periods where he was the best goalie in the NHL and stretches where he has been in the role of a backup, which was the case in parts of the 96-97 season. The fact that the Canucks as a team have been very inconsistent over the past ten years is the source of some of McLean's problem.

Overall, Kirk has had a very successful career with the Canucks. His performance during Vancouver's run for the Cup in '94 was near Conn Smyth material. In analyzing Kirk's game one would have to say that he has been the best "classic stand up" goaltender over the last ten years. Talk about a throw back to the 1970s. He expertly plays the angles. He moves around the crease on his feet as well as anyone. He makes great kick saves. Watching him use his glove and blocker to catch pucks is like a work of art. His stick work is solid. From a stand up style position, Kirk's reactions are tops.

Why the inconsistency? I believe if a goaltender doesn't play on great teams year after year his career will appear inconsistent. Secondly, Kirk choose to perfect a classic stand up style. It has served him well. Kirk grew up believing (remember his formative hockey years were during the stand up years) that he should stand up, play the angles, and play on your feet as much as possible. That is the way I was taught to play and Kirk came into the league as I was retiring. He is another goalie on the cusp of the transition to the predominately butterfly era. When is the last time you were in a hockey arena and the crowd yelled "don't go down or get back on your feet" at a goalie. This was a common crowd chant in the 70's and early 80's.

McLean's goaltending personality is easy going and well balanced. Another strong character trait of McLean is his ability to bounce back, whether it is from a game or a season. The 96-97 season was not a highlight year for either McLean or the Canucks. During the summer of 97 the Canucks signed Mark Messier. He will be a positive influence on the Canucks. If McLean rebounds the way he has in the past, the strongest positive influence could still come from between the pipes.

This is an interesting study, especially in light of the fact that he won the Vezina Trophy in 1996, at the budding age of twenty two. But first, let's go back. Carey came out of a New England prep school, went to the University of Wisconsin and enjoyed a lot of fanfare early in his pro goaltending career.

His path as a goaltender has been reminiscent of Mike Richter's. They are both American kids, both out of Eastern prep schools and have similar styles. Where they differ is that Richter is eight years older with four more years of NHL experience. In that time Richter has injected an element of carbonation and zip to his game while Carey has yet to do that and his game has remained somewhat flat.

When Carey first entered the NHL his style was crisp, clean, and textbook correct. He had the look that you would want to see in a goalie. Just right. Carey was square to the puck, his moves were well developed, and he never seemed to be out of position. Critics would have been hard pressed to say his play looked weak in any area.

There are two phases to goaltending maturity and development. A goalie needs to develop a style that is sound and efficient. In this area Jim had made tremendous strides. However, there comes a time when a goalie such as Carey has to add some flow and flair to his game.

For example, if you are a stand up goalie by nature, you may need to work hard to develop some aspects of the butterfly to enhance your repertoire. Conversely, if you are strictly a butterfly goaltender, you should work to become comfortable making saves on your feet. If you feel you are becoming too much of a technical goalie add some aggressiveness, play the puck more, or occasionally whack or shove an opposing forward. Each year a goaltender should strive to add a new tool to his toolbox, even if it appears that all the tools are accounted for.

In Washington, playing for a defense-oriented team like the Capitals may have made playing goal easier for Jim. This may have given Carey the impression that he would not have to change or develop much beyond the stage he was at. That sense was reinforced when he won the Vezina Trophy.

Not too many people would have guessed at the start of the season that Jim Carey would be voted the best goalie in the NHL for the 1995-96 season. Yet, there he was right at the top of the heap. And well deserved.

He won the Vezina partly because he had that solid defensive team in front of him. But also because he got on a roll which shot his confidence to a high level and it never dipped.

Goaltenders playing with teams so defensively adept as the Caps can subconsciously slide into thinking, "hey, I don't have to be flashy. I just need to make the first save and the defense will take care of the rest." And that how it worked. However, once he won the Vezina, everyone began scrutinizing his play. Expectations, quite naturally, grew higher than they had ever been.

Carey responded, as often goalies do, by wanting to improve to the point of perfection. But then the Capitals suffered a spate of injuries during the 1996-97 season. At that same Carey was struggling, too many pucks were going through him. The strange thing about it was that Carey still *looked* good. That is, he appeared to make the right moves and people in the press box would be saying, "Now, how did that go in?" I mean he was right there and appeared about to stop the puck. Then — poof! — it was in.

Carey had hit a wall. At that point he became too hard on himself. He became his own worst critic. The injuries never ceased in Washington and Carey never regained the form that won him the Vezina. Late in the season the Capital gave up on Jim and dealt him to the Bruins. By the time he arrived in Boston his confidence was nil. It now seemed obvious that he was thinking too much about how to make the save instead of just reacting and going with a natural flow. A goalie cannot be too thoroughly conscious of every move he is making. When he is thinking that intensely about each step into the save he is inhibiting his movement.

One play from the 96-97 season comes to mind. The Capitals were in overtime playing the Devils at New Jersey. The Devils created a two-on-one at center ice and quickly attacked the Washington net. Carey seemed in excellent position, challenging the Devil forward coming down his right side with the puck. The Devil forward made an early cross ice pass to the late charging Devil defenseman Scott Neidermayer. Scott, who was just inside the Caps blue line, straight out from the net, one-timed the pass toward the left corner of the net. Sure it was a nice shot, but everyone was surprised when Carey did not get far enough across to make the save. Whether he got a late start, the pass across surprised him, or he over-analyzed the play, it was an example of how Carey was not possessing a free flowing movement to his game.

When a goalie loses his confidence the way Carey did during the 96-97 season he starts to question everything he is doing. The most damaging aspect was that Carey was trying to answer these questions while trying to make the save. As he lost his confidence he moved deeper and deeper into his net and stopped challenging the shooter on a consistent basis. Every goaltender has been in this mental position. With Carey it was clearly mental. The physical skills were there but something was missing. Goaltending is made up of three ingredients. The physical, the mental, and the spiritual. Jim Carey has proven he can be sound and effective physically. Even though the 1996-97 season saw Carey struggle with the mental aspect, namely confidence, you do not win the Vezina and play as well as Jim has at times in the NHL without having the "right stuff." That only leaves the spiritual dimension. I am reminded of an interview I read on Martina Navratilova, one of the worlds greatest woman tennis players. Although she was always technically correct she was reciting how she learned to add spirit and emotion to her game. Early in her career she was a perfectionist. Winning a point, a game, a match, was often times not satisfying enough. If it was not done with perfection she would mentally criticize herself, which then would dampen the spirit, the thrill, the fun of her accomplishment. As she matured, she decided to change her thinking and say, "If I hit a winner, I don't care if the swing was not exactly perfect. I am just happy it's a winner even if it comes off the shaft of my racket." From that moment she felt free from the idea that every shot had to be executed technically correct. This change of thinking was a major addition to an already sound game. I believe most goaltenders have to come to the same sort of realization.

Jim Carey has accomplished so much in his young career. Remember when the 1997-1998 season ends he will just be reaching his 24th birthday. To say he is at a critical stage in his career may be a bit of an overstatement. The fact is he is now playing for a Boston team, a team in the process of rebuilding, who may need him to pull them out of the fire night after night.

This situation in Boston could add the sparkle and zest to Carey's already fundamentally sound style. Once this happens Jim Carey will have all the right stuff to "Carey" himself into the next century.

If there is one word that best describes Ron Hextall, it is intensity. It is a family trait. His grandfather, Bryan Hextall Sr., played for the New York Rangers when they won the 1940 Stanley Cup. Bryan Sr. was notorious for his hard-nosed style of hockey.

Ron's father, Bryan Jr., and his uncle Dennis also took the game very seriously and played a fierce game. Clearly, Ron Hextall grew up in a high-pressure hockey environment and started thinking *goalie* at the earliest possible age.

I remember Hexy telling me that in his pre-school years one of his favorite pastimes was standing at the bottom of the staircase with a rolled-up Pair of socks. He would throw the "puck" against the stairs and when it bounced off, he would try to make a glove save — or kick save, or a sprawling body save. That was his first introduction to the art of goaltending. When his father played for the Pittsburgh Penguins, Ron used to be allowed on the ice after the workouts and was allowed to play goal once the team left the ice. His dad would take shots at him.

In time, Ron played for his home team, the Brandon Wheat Kings of the Western Junior Hockey League. It was in Brandon where Ron developed his reputation as being a teammate who would fight for his crease as well as his teammates. He also proved that he was a first rate puckstopper.

His fighting nature is very reminiscent of my former teammate, Billy Smith. The same quality that made Battlin' Bill a winner is what did it for Hexy as well. Both of them felt that they wanted to be involved in *all* aspects of the game, not just blocking the puck.

"If a brawl breaks out, I want to be in the middle of it," Hexy says. If I were in a fox hole situation with Smitty on one side and Hexy on the other, I would know I'd walk out of there alive!

With this background, it isn't surprising that Hextall has done as well as he has during his career. His critics have said that Ron was too intense, but I can assure you that that is a fallacy. Hextall's intensity has never hurt his game any more than any other goalie. The myth had it that he would get so tight before a game that he would go wild and completely lose his focus. The truth is that Hexy is much more controlled than he led people to believe. There are many examples I can cite, but the one that immediately comes to mind was the classic Canadiens-Flyers playoff brawl that preceded the actual opening face-off. Hexy was the only player trapped in the locker room during that episode. Actually, Mike Keenan the coach, made a good move by locking the door before Ron could get out. When the brouhaha was over, Hexy was emotionally upset that he hadn't been able to help his teammates. It was the only time I had ever felt that he may have lost his focus before a game. So what does he do? He goes out and plays one of the best games of his entire career.

When I say Hexy is always under control, that is not to suggest that he still does-n't resent opponents camping around his crease; nor will I even hint that he doesn't get angry and doesn't want to whack the enemy. It just happens to be part of his game. Ronnie's style is built on explosiveness and raw energy.

Like Patrick Roy's jerking of his head, Hextall has his own physical idiosyn-crasies. His somewhat manic banging of the goalposts is an indication of how his mind is thinking. When the stick is banging, it's almost as if Hexy is telling himself to get that motor of his all revved up. Sometimes Ronnie does get a little over-revved and it can cause him a problem.

There are times when Hextall will miss a shot and fans will think he was too slow, but actually it's the other way around. He made the move too quick and over-played the shot.

One of his prime assets over the years has been his stickhandling. He was the first NHL goaltender to actually fire the puck down the ice and score and, he added new dimensions to trapping the puck the way he would come out of the net and field it along the boards. His ability to fire the puck out of his zone is unparalleled. Few goalies have ever moved the puck with greater purpose. His passes are accurate and his penalty-killing shots up the ice rank with the best the league has ever seen.

To many observers it has seemed that Ron's game is not as strong in some areas as it once was. As difficult as it is for me to say, I would have to agree. There are times when I notice Ron to be a little off balance. There were also a few shots during the '97 play-offs Ron would have never let in during the '87 play-offs. But Hey, most goalies experience and ebb and flow at certain points in their career. A lot of people thought Mike Vernon's game had slipped and *bam* he plays some of his greatest hockey ever.

I couldn't mention Hexy without mentioning his rookie year of 1986-87. It was my last year and I was fortunate to play on a great *Philadelphia Flyer* team. Problem was the Edmonton Oilers had an absolute power house and they won the Stanley Cup against the us in seven games. When the final series was over it wasn't Gretzky, Kurri Messier or Fuhr who won the MVP trophy. It was Ron Hextall. Hexy was spectacu-lar. It was a perfect example of an athlete succeeding under constant pressure. He was never out of position or off balance. He used every skill a goalie can possess to make one outstanding save after another.

The 1997 playoffs showed that Hexy can withstand pressure as well as ever. When Terry Murray called him off the bench after the Rangers had tied the series with Philadelphia at one apiece, Hextall took over at Madison Square Garden and reeled off three straight wins over New York to win the series. It was one of the most diffi-cult situations Ronnie had ever faced and he handled it without a problem.

Ron is a man of enormous pride and did not take kindly to the benching he received from coach Terry Murray at the start of the 1997 playoffs. More than any-thing, Hexy is a team player. He never complained and retained his composure. He is a terrific team guy.

The 96-97 finals were not fun for the Flyers or their goaltenders Hextall and Snow. Whenever a team looses 4 straight fingers are pointed… players get traded…

coaches fired. The 97-98 season will be very interesting for many of the Flyers, especially Ronnie. Regardless of what happens in the future, Ron has left his mark already in the history of the NHL. Winner of the Conn Smyth, first goal scored on a shot by a goaltender in the regular season, and in the play-offs, thousands of great saves and a couple of good scraps. More then all of that, Hexy is admired for his "team first" approach in all he has done. He is appreciated by all who have played with him, including myself. That was shown most vividly by Eric Lindros who came forward to publicly support Hexy when he was struggling at the end of the 96-97 season. It wasn't just words, it wasn't just said because that is what Captains are supposed to do. Eric did it with sincerity and passion. Exactly the way Hexy plays hockey and lives his life.

Johnny Bower (right) — *one of the great stand up goalies* — *frustrates Bobby Hull in the goal mouth. Most of today's goalies would be down at this point in the play.*

Roy "Shrimp" Worters was a goal-tending great from before World War II — note the absence of a catching glove and flat blocker.

The lightning glove of Terry Sawchuk. His 101 career shutouts is a record that has never been challenged.

Jacques Plante, holding one of his revolutionary contributions to the game, the goalie mask.

Glenn Hall, originator of the butterfly, makes a sweeping kick save against the Leafs. He filled the bottom two-thirds of the net more effectively than most goalies in his era.

*Martin Brodeur kicks out a threatening shot. One of a new breed of big,
mobile goalies, Brodeur is also an excellent puck handler.*

Grant Fuhr — the technically perfect modern goalie, and the inventor of a newer, easier-going pre-game attitude.

This picture clearly illustrates how Ken Dryden's size worked to his advantage — he literally fills the net!

Dominik Hasek, known as "The Dominator," displays his exciting and unorthodox style — here he is down and well out of position at the top of the slot. An error for most goalies, yet Hasek makes it work.

Patrick Roy, from his Montreal Canadien days, takes away the top of the net. Roy has proved to be among the greatest playoff goaltenders in hockey history.

Stars of Yesteryear

Glenn Hall

Georges Vezina

Jacques Plante

Terry Sawchuk

Bill Durnan

Turk Broda

Johnny Bower

Ken Dryden

Bill Smith

Frank Brimsek

Chuck Rayner

Gerry Cheevers

Roy Worters

Roger Crozier

Alex Connell

Gump Worsley

Bernie Parent

GLENN HALL (1952-71)

"Before every game, and sometimes between periods, I'd get sick to my stomach; I'd have to throw up. Sometimes it happened during a game and I'd have to fight it off until the whistle blew. I tried drinking tea between periods and that seemed to help. Nervousness is part of the game. It helped keep me sharp."

One can only imagine how stupendous a goaltender Glenn Hall would have been had he the luxury of a defense-oriented team or even one that occasionally concerned itself with back-checking.

But it was Mister Goalie's lot in life to front for a Chicago Blackhawks club whose pursuit of offense reached obsessive proportions, while amnesia took over whenever it came to protecting the goalkeeper.

With sharpshooters like Bobby Hull, Stan Mikita, and Ken Wharram, the Chicagoans could be excused for being mesmerized by red lights. Likewise, Hall could be forgiven for his inevitable bouts of stomach trouble preceding the hockey matches. The fact that he threw up before virtually every game suggested that he was afraid of his profession. It sounded good in the storytelling, but Hall later admitted that fear or dread of the puck was not why he vomited.

"It was the opposite. I was so excited to go out and play that it made me throw up. I thought of it as a strength. If I weren't up for a game enough to get sick before it, I felt I wouldn't play well. It was no big deal. I could have a glass of water and throw it up while it was still cool. A few years ago I was coaching a young guy who said, 'Gee, how could you toss your cookies before every game? I'm never nervous out there.' I told him, 'Yeah, but aren't you embarrassed that you play so horsebleep and you're not even nervous about it?' That wasn't the answer he was looking for."

He was nicknamed Mister Goalie because he was the best at a time when the National Hockey League boasted such legends as Terry Sawchuk, Gump Worsley, Jacques Plante, and Johnny Bower.

"You pretty much saw good goaltending every night," Hall says. "That was one of the great things about the old six-team league. You always wanted to force the guy in the other net to play well."

Hall broke in with the Detroit Red Wings in 1955, displacing Sawchuk as the Wings' regular goalie. He wasted little time carving his niche in the NHL, skating off with the Calder Trophy as the league's rookie of the year. After two campaigns in Detroit, Hall was traded to Chicago where he captured the heralded Vezina Trophy in 1963 and 1967 (he shared the latter with Denis DeJordy). In 1961, Hall led the Black Hawks to their first Stanley Cup since 1938, performing spectacularly as Chicago eliminated, ironically, his former mates from Detroit in the final round. The Hawks left him unprotected when expansion rolled around, and Mr. Goalie was drafted by the St. Louis Blues. While in Missouri, he won a third Vezina in 1969 (shared with Jacques Plante) and took home the

Conn Smythe Trophy in 1968. Additionally, Hall was an 11-time All-Star, and his seven First-Team berths are a record for his position.

More indicative, however, of the intensity of Hall's play — which is his greatest legacy — than any number of awards or remarkable numbers could ever be is an incident that occurred during a game between the Red Wings and the Boston Bruins in the semifinal round of the 1957 playoffs. While minding the net for Detroit, Hall suddenly found himself the only Red Wing around and, as such, the target of a straight-on rush by Boston's Vic Stasiuk. Stasiuk blazed in on the young goalie and shot a bullet that caught Hall on his unprotected face. He dropped to the ice out cold, blood flowing from his mouth. The crowd buzzed, and one writer noted that Hall, lying in a heap in his goal crease, "looked dead."

Taken from the ice on a stretcher, Hall regained consciousness in the trainer's room. Far from being impressed by the severity of his injury, his first words upon awakening were, "C'mon, doc, let's get this thing over with." The physician proceeded to weave 23 stitches into Hall's upper lip and mouth, which had been ripped into a war zone by the puck.

Implausibly, Hall emerged a half-hour later skating onto the ice, his eyes black, his face swollen and covered with bandages. As he took up his position in front of the goal, a Bruins player remarked, "I don't believe it. How do you stop this guy?" By that time the answer was clear: You didn't.

Resistant to change in his refusal to don a protective mask until late in his career, Hall was an innovator nonetheless. He is credited with being the forerunner in the development of the "butterfly" style of goaltending, the fanning out of the pads toward the goal posts while dropping to the knees to block shots. The butterfly technique, originally scoffed at as a perversion of the traditional stand-up goaltending style, eventually became the standard for goalkeepers from the late 1960s to the present.

A native of Humboldt, Saskatchewan, Glenn Hall was born the son of a railroad engineer in 1931. As a boy, he played center and captained his public-school hockey team. When he was 10, the club's goalie quit. "I picked someone to replace him, but he refused," Hall said. "So did the next 10 guys. As captain, I had no choice but to put on the pads myself. After a few years I actually got to like it."

The operative word is "actually." It implies that one needs an undefinable tenacity and grit to enjoy thwarting 100-miles-per-hour rockets. It also hints that one must have a screw or two loose to revel in hockey's job between the pipes. In light of his nausea-inducing butterflies, it was Hall's love-hate relationship with his profession which made his iron-man streak that much more remarkable.

Far from the raucous sounds of the hockey rink, Hall now spends most of his time on his farm, although he was once the goaltending coach for the late Colorado Rockies. The old master of puckstopping is hardly impressed with the direction of today's game and harks back to the good old days when defense was not yet against the law. Save for the neutral-zone trap, "we're seeing darn little defense, and I don't particularly like what I'm seeing," Mr. Goalie remarked.

From the beginning of his career, Glenn Hall was a defensive gem amidst a conglomerate of offensive specialists such as Howe and Delvecchio in Detroit and Hull and Mikita in Chicago. Nevertheless, Hall retired with a shining 2.51 goals against average to go with 84 shutouts in 906 career contests. He was inducted into the Hall of Fame in 1975.

Coiled in readiness in front of his cage, Hall's hair-trigger reflexes consistently kept him ahead of the most dangerous shooters in the NHL for close to two decades. For valiant service under fire with a steadiness unmatched by any other puckstopper, Glenn Hall deserves his place among hockey's great keepers.

GEORGES VEZINA (1917-26)

'In the stricken arena,'said one observer, 'all was silent as the limp form of the greatest of goalies was carried slowly from the ice.'

It's a pity his performances are not available on videotape.

Alas, we are only left with eyewitness reports of Georges Vezina's magnificence. That and the trophy named after him for excellence in puckstopping. But this much we do know: During his decade as a major-leaguer, Vezina was the titan of his time and position. He set a standard that would become a challenge for goaltenders in the National Hockey League's first major era of expansion.

The pity of it all is that Vezina's career ended so abruptly and before he could demonstrate his skills in the new NHL expansion cities of America, such as New York, Chicago, Detroit, and Boston. His life epitomized that of the tragic hero, yet his fatal flaw was not of his doing but of his misfortune. It told a tale that only Hollywood could conceive, save for the fact that it was reality.

Georges Vezina was born in January 1887 in Chicoutimi, Quebec, a city which sits on the edge of the dark Saguenay River and flows into the blue St. Lawrence at historic Tadoussac.

Although young Vezina established himself as a class-A goalie even as a youth in Chicoutimi, he had developed a habit of playing without skates. For some peculiar reason he found the idea of wearing skates a bother, and it wasn't until two years before he graduated to the Montreal Canadiens that he actually learned to wear skates while tending goal.

Conceivably, Les Canadiens never would have discovered Vezina were it not for a chance exhibition game between the Canadiens and the local Chicoutimi club on February 23, 1910. The match between the vaunted professionals from Montreal and the patchwork amateur outfit figured to be so one-sided that only a handful of fans turned out for it.

Chicoutimi hardly looked like a formidable foe except for the six-foot goalie, wearing a red-and-white *Habitant toque* on his head. Leaning against the goal post, the tall, lanky Vezina appeared almost too bored for words. But once the overpowering Canadiens sliced through the fragile Chicoutimi defense, he suddenly responded with a peripatetic style that thoroughly dumbfounded the pros. Try as they might, the Canadiens could not score. Chicoutimi won the game 2-0.

That was all the Habs high command had to know. They invited Vezina to Montreal, and he made his debut on December 31, 1910. Curiously, Georges never signed a contract with the Montrealers. He preferred a gentleman's handshake with his managers, first Joe Cattarinich and later Leo Dandurand.

The gangling six-footer guarded the Canadiens' nets when the team played in the National Hockey Association and later for the Habitants when the National Hockey League was organized.

In each milieu he excelled. Montreal won the NHA championship twice with Vezina

between the pipes and won three NHL championships and two Stanley Cups. He played a total of 373 consecutive games for Les Canadiens in an era when goaltenders' masks were unheard of and was nicknamed "The Chicoutimi Cucumber" for his birthplace and his cool under fire.

The father of 22 children, Vezina was virtually impregnable once he took his position in the goal crease. Once, during a game at Hamilton, Bert Corbeau smashed into him with such force that the goaltender's head was cut open and his nose broken. Vezina continued playing despite the wounds, his ability undiminished by pain.

According to hockey historians, Vezina was the author of several hockey classics, including the 1916 Stanley Cup final between Montreal and the Pacific Coast Hockey Association's Portland Rosebuds. The best-of-five series went the limit, the final game being played on March 30, 1916. With the score tied 1-1, Vezina defused the most explosive Portland offensives until Goldie Prodgers scored the winner for the Montrealers. Vezina and each of his Stanley Cup-winning teammates received $238 for taking the championship.

In the Roaring Twenties he was better than ever. During the 1923-24 season, he allowed only 48 goals in 24 games, including three shutouts for a 2.00 goals against average. He then blanked Ottawa, 1-0, in the NHL playoff opener and sparkled as Montreal swept the series. The Canadiens went on to rout Calgary and Vancouver for the Stanley Cup. Vezina's Stanley Cup record was six goals in six games — an even 1.00 average.

By this time Vezina's body was afflicted with the early symptoms of tuberculosis. A quiet man, Vezina continued to play although he was aware that his life was doomed. "Beads of perspiration formed on his forehead for no apparent reason," said Ron McAllister. "An expression of pain flitted momentarily across his face, but the Great Vezina invariably settled down to the business at hand, turning in his usual matchless performance."

During the 1924-25 season, despite the ailment, he came up with a 1.90 goals against average, easily the best in the league. But when he arrived at the Canadiens' training camp in the fall of 1925, he seemed unusually fatigued.

It has been said that not even those in his own family realized that Vezina was fighting for his life as he prepared for the 1925-26 season. This would be a particularly fascinating year for the worldly Vezina. The NHL was expanding into the United States more than ever. It had embraced a Boston franchise a year earlier, and now New York and Pittsburgh had been added, as well as a second Montreal team, the Maroons. The new Montreal squad would provide an English-speaking team as natural rivals for the Canadiens. Needless to say, the outstanding attraction in the American cities, among Montreal players, was the redoubtable Vezina.

Sadly, "The Chicoutimi Cucumber" donned the *bleu, blanc, et rouge* uniform for the last time in the season opener of the 1925-26 season. There were 6,000 spectators in the stands on that rainy night who had come to see the Great Vezina.

That November 28, his body racked with pain, Vezina skated out onto the ice of Mount Royal Arena to face the visiting Pittsburgh sextet. "No one knew," wrote author Ron McAllister, "that the greatest goaltender had struggled to the arena despite a temperature of 105 degrees."

"A deathlike chill settled over him; but with Pittsburgh forcing the play from the face-off, Vezina functioned throughout the first period with his usual dexterous ease, deflecting shot after shot." Few realized that, as he left the ice after a scoreless first period, he was bleeding from the mouth. "In the dressing room," wrote McAllister, "he suffered a severe arterial hemorrhage, but the opening of the second period found him at his accustomed place in goal."

Fighting desperately against the fatigue and fever that completely throttled his body, the great Vezina could no longer see the puck as it skimmed from one side of the rink to the other. Suddenly a collective gasp engulfed the arena. Vezina had collapsed in the goal crease. "In the stricken arena," said one observer, "all was silent as the limp form of the greatest of goalies was carried slowly from the ice."

It was the end of the trail for Georges, and he knew it. At his request, he was taken home to his native Chicoutimi where doctors diagnosed his case as advanced tuberculosis. On March 24, 1926, he passed away. An enormous funeral, held in the old cathedral in his hometown, saw players and fans from all parts of the country deliver their final tribute to the gallant goaltender. A year later the Canadiens owners donated a trophy in his honor.

The Vezina! How often we have heard the equation with goaltending excellence. The Vezina Trophy, from 1927-81, was awarded to the netminders who delivered the lowest goals against average. Since 1982, it has simply been given to the NHL's "outstanding goalie."

More than any National Hockey League prize, this one has the deepest meaning because Georges Vezina was a nonpareil athlete whose ability was matched only by his infinite sportsmanship He was the personification of courage and capability. When someone in hockey says, "The Vezina," he need say no more.

JACQUES PLANTE (1952-75)

The Montrealers had no spare goalie, and Plante refused to go back onto the ice without his mask. Blake had no choice but to oblige, and consequently, hockey history wove its way through the Garden that night. Plante wore the mask, won the game, and vowed to continue wearing the device as long as he played.

It is safe to say that Jacques Plante was the most revolutionary goaltender ever to take a paddle in his hands.

It was Plante who changed the entire manner in which the puckstopping profession was approached, not only defensively but offensively as well.

The revolution began when Plante decided to leave his crease and play the puck like a third defenseman. No goaltender ever had done that on a regular basis before.

The revolution continued when Plante decided to launch offensive counterattacks by skimming the puck to his forwards.

Then, of course, there was Plante's most revolutionary move of all: his decision to wear a facemask in every game despite nearly a century of tradition in which goaltenders confronted shots with unprotected skulls.

He was a winner. He was an expert. He was creative. He was durable. He was one of a kind. Plante may not have been the iron man that Glenn Hall was with the Chicago Blackhawks or the implacably perfect puckstopper that Georges Vezina had been during an earlier era with the Montreal Canadiens, but "Jake the Snake" *was* stupendous in his own right.

He won the Hart Trophy as the National Hockey League's most valuable player in 1962 and the Vezina Trophy as the top goalie from 1956 through 1960 and again in 1962 and 1969 (he shared this last hurrah with Glenn Hall). Plante was named to the First All-Star team in 1956, 1959, and 1962 and to the Second team in 1957, 1958, 1960, and 1971.

Unlike Terry Sawchuk, whose skills eroded with time, Plante was in mint condition at the age of 40 when he starred for the St. Louis Blues. Plante played for six Stanley Cup-winning teams and eight clubs that finished in first place. And, more than Sawchuk, Plante was the most innovative of the modern goaltenders. In fact, it would be safe to say that Jacques did more to revolutionize the modus operandi of puckstopping than anyone in the past 30 years. That Jacques Plante was the best his position ever saw is a statement that could be supported in some corners although not this one; that he was among the greats is an assertion few could challenge.

In addition to his goaltending prowess, Plante, plainly and simply, was a very interesting character. In his spare time, the "Snake" had a hobby of knitting toques, the French-Canadian wool caps worn by his ancestors. He was confident to the point of being cocky and betrayed a then-uncouth goaltending style that would soon be copied by other netminders around the league. Plante believed that he would be aiding his defensemen by roaming out of his cage, formerly a strict taboo, and behind the net when pucks were caromed off or wrapped around the boards. By leaving his crease, Plante was able to control the puck and pass it off to a teammate, in turn facilitating the breakout. He introduced the new technique when the Canadiens, then coached by Dick Irvin, were engaged in a thrilling semifinal playoff against the Chicago Black Hawks in 1953.

All this was well and good and uniquely fascinating, but for the adventurous and unconventional Plante to experiment during the playoffs with his Canadiens on the brink of elimination was something else! But Irvin had made a commitment to his young netminder, and it paid off — Jacques the Roamer went into the cage and stopped the Hawks cold. He foiled a breakaway early in the fifth game, and with that impetus Les Canadiens won two straight games and the first round. In the process, Plante won himself a job and helped the Habs to the Stanley Cup.

By the late 1950s, Montreal had the most formidable club of the decade — if not all time — with the defense of Doug Harvey and Tom Johnson available to thwart attackers. Unfortunately for Plante, times change and so do coaches. Toe Blake replaced Irvin as coach, and a coolness developed between the explosive coach and his enigmatic goaltender.

But Plante remained the National Hockey League's premier netminder, although he occasionally enraged spectators with his scrambles behind the net. When Plante botched the new technique — notwithstanding the fact that this rarely happened — and the disc crossed the goal line, he drew the ire of Blake and the passionate Forum fans alike. In November 1958, Plante's goals against average began climbing, which was matched by Blake's temper.

The Blake-Plante repartee was, perhaps, even more ominous than it sounded. Severe to a fault, the Canadiens taskmaster was down on his goaltender from the start; the relationship only became increasingly strained as the seasons progressed.

Not surprisingly, the Blake-Plante rift widened at the precise point when Jacques executed one of his most courageous acts. The date was November 2, 1959, and Plante was in the Canadiens' net facing the New York Rangers at Madison Square Garden. Rangers right wing Andy Bathgate, one of the league's hardest shooters, released a quick shot that struck the Habs netminder squarely in the nose, sending him bloodied to the ice. His face looking like a mashed potato laden with ketchup, Plante was helped to the dressing room where seven stitches were taken in his pulverized proboscis.

For a good while leading up to the game, Plante had been experimenting during practice sessions with a mask that had been molded to his facial contours. Blake, an old school hardliner, was irrevocably opposed to Jacques' wearing the face piece in a regular game but found himself in a bind on this occasion. The Montrealers had no spare goalie, and Plante refused to go back onto the ice without his mask. Blake had no choice but to oblige, and consequently, hockey history wove its way through the Garden that night. Plante wore the mask, won the game, and vowed to continue wearing the device as long as he played.

Blake, for one, was not the least enamored of the idea, although he publicly asserted that, as long as it helped Plante keep the pucks out of the net, it would be all right. For 1959-60, Plante's invention proved effective, and the Vezina Trophy placated his demanding coach for a time.

Alas, Toe Blake was a hard man to please, and his grievances against Plante simmered within him and, often, without. The breaking point came in 1963 when Plante was

dealt to the Rangers. Blake had wanted nothing less than an uncompromising attitude toward the game from his free-spirited goalie, the kind that marked other Canadiens, most notably Maurice Richard. This, however, was not Plante's way. He pursued his unorthodoxy while playing in Manhattan and, later, with the St. Louis Blues, Toronto Maple Leafs, and Boston Bruins.

Jacques Plante was born January 17, 1929, in Shawinigan Falls, Quebec, and like many a French-Canadian youngster, played his hockey on the outdoor rinks of *La Belle Province*. His goaltending excellence was unquestioned in the early 1950s, though the Canadiens originally did not give him serious thought as their potential starter because they already had a relatively young and quite efficient Gerry McNeil guarding the twines for them. Lo and behold Irvin took his dramatic gamble in 1953, and Plante rewarded him with the aforesaid clutch effort.

"Jake the Snake" concluded his NHL career with the Boston Bruins in April 1973, then became general manager-coach of the Quebec Nordiques in the World Hockey Association. This was another case of a superstar being unable to orchestrate from the sidelines as well as he had on the ice. A season later, at the age of 45, Plante returned to the nets with the WHA's Edmonton Oilers. He played commendably for the Oilers but finally retired for good at the conclusion of the campaign to become a part-time goaltending coach for the Philadelphia Flyers, a position he retained through the early 1980s when he became a netminding advisor for his former employers in Montreal.

During the course of his long career, Plante rubbed several people the wrong way, and many have never forgotten what they interpreted as an abrasive manner. But no follower with a sense of hockey history will ever forget the comprehensive contributions made by Jacques Plante or his consummate skill at blocking a puck.

There was nobody like him before, and there will not be anyone like him again. An original. A craftsman.

TERRY SAWCHUK (1950-70)

"I spend my summers in the hospital."

The first, best young goaltender developed in the post-World War II era was Terry Sawchuk who launched his big-league career with the Detroit Red Wings at the start of the 1950s.

Sawchuk was so good that when Detroit general manager Jack Adams promoted him from the Indianapolis farm team, he knocked Hall of Famer Harry Lumley right out of the Motor City lineup. This when Lumley was at the very top of his game.

Sawchuck was a definitive goaltender, and no less an authority than Emile Francis, a professional goaltender himself for more than 20 years, regards Terry Sawchuk as the greatest goalie of all time.

Were it not for a series of debilitating injuries and some erratic behavior rooted in personal problems, Sawchuk could be regarded as number one. But he lacked Glenn Hall's extraordinary durability, strength, and even temper. At times Sawchuk was his own worst enemy in a career marked by extreme peaks and valleys.

Terrance Gordon Sawchuk was born on December 28, 1929, in Winnipeg, Manitoba, and, from all indications, was physically unfit to be a goaltender before he reached his teens. Injuries plagued him ad infinitum, and while they could not stop his climb to the top, they doubtless hastened his premature descent.

His glory days — and the ones which helped mold his image of immortality — were spent with the dynastic Detroit Red Wings of the early 1950s. He was named rookie of the year in 1951 and won the Vezina Trophy in 1952, 1953, and 1955. As a Toronto Maple Leaf he shared the Vezina honors with Johnny Bower and fully earned half of the prize.

Creator of the crouch style of netminding, Sawchuk was named to the First All-Star team in 1951, 1952, and 1953 and was a Second team choice in 1954, 1955, 1959, and 1963. He played for four Stanley Cup winners and four first-place teams.

In the Motor City, he was fronted by an exceptionally gifted crew including Gordie Howe, Ted Lindsay, Red Kelly, Marcel Pronovost, and Alex Delvecchio, but he was as responsible as any for the club's success. He was an innovator, and his ability to cope with screened shots by use of the crouch was considered a great advance in goaltending technique in its day.

Sawchuk was the product of the Red Wings' farm system, which developed a remarkable string of Hall of Famers, starting with Harry Lumley and also including Glenn Hall. Lumley had starred on the Detroit 1950 Stanley Cup winner while Sawchuk was in the wings, playing superbly on the Indianapolis farm team.

In a terrific gamble, Red Wings manager Jack Adams dealt Lumley to Chicago and elected Sawchuk as his number one netminder, and Adams' gamble paid big dividends. Lumley was quickly forgotten, and by springtime, Sawchuk was the talk of the ice world.

The Red Wings annexed the Stanley Cup in eight games, during which Terry allowed but five goals for a 0.62 goals against average.

Nothing speaks more eloquently about Sawchuk's first five NHL seasons than his goals against average, which never rose higher than 1.98. Yet, despite the triumphs, there always was a shadow of gloom surrounding him. His right elbow, which had been dislocated in a childhood football accident, continued to bedevil him, and he underwent operations in the summers of 1950 and 1951 to have pieces of bone removed that had chipped off in the elbow.

Unfortunately for Sawchuk, the operations were unsuccessful, and surgery was ordered again in 1952, whereupon the surgeon removed 60 pieces of bone. Sawchuk believed his troubles were finally over; for the first time in 10 years he had almost complete movement in his right arm.

But complete health was never to be for the young goalie. The cumulative effect of all the hospitalization seemed to boomerang on Sawchuk both physically and mentally. His weight, which had consistently been around 205 pounds, dropped during the 1952-53 season to 168. Sawchuk was given exhaustive medical tests, but the results proved inconclusive and his condition became all the more perplexing.

Less than a month later, he was hospitalized for an appendectomy. Even Terry himself found humor in his woes. When a reporter asked him what he did during the off-season, he chortled: "I spend my summers in the hospital."

He wasn't kidding. He returned to the hospital in 1954 after an auto accident resulted in severe chest injuries. Once again he recovered to play more than competently for the Red Wings. But now — irony of ironies — Sawchuk's threat was the Detroit farm system. Jack Adams had another whiz goalie in Indianapolis named Glenn Hall, who could not be kept in the minors.

Once again the Red Wings' boss packaged a major deal involving his goalkeeper, this time sending Sawchuk to the Boston Bruins. What few skeptics there were questioned Terry's ability to play superior goal for a relatively weak team such as the Bruins, but his high standard of performance delighted Boston Garden fans and, for one season at least, the deal looked good.

Alas, his second year in Beantown was a disaster. He was stricken with infectious mononucleosis and spent 12 days in the hospital. When he returned to the ice — perhaps prematurely — he seemed almost skeletal, a shell of his former self.

He lost four of his next eight games, and the Boston press turned on him. His weight was now 166 pounds, and at age 27, he felt exasperated by his unfailing inability to regain his health. To the astonishment of teammates and foes alike, he announced that he was retiring. "I told them I thought it best to quit since my nerves were really shot."

It was suggested that much more was being concealed than reached print. Sawchuk, some noted, never did take to the Boston scene and yearned for his old stomping grounds in Detroit.

His "retirement" lasted until the beginning of the next season when Adams sweet-talked the Bruins into giving him the rights to Sawchuk, "because he's too good a goalie to remain out of hockey." That done, Adams dealt Hall to Chicago, and Sawchuk played seven more years for the Red Wings, often displaying preillness form.

Following the 1963-64 season, the Red Wings high command figured that Terry was washed up. Toronto Maple Leafs general manager Punch Imlach, always one to give a veteran a chance, signed Sawchuk, and Terry demonstrated that, yes, there was still some good goaltending left in him. The Leafs won the Stanley Cup, defeating Chicago and Montreal, and Sawchuk won six of Toronto's eight victories.

While one might have expected Terry to be a joyful man in Toronto, where he was receiving unanimous raves, the fact remained that he seemed to be an unhappy man. "He reminded you of a prisoner in a wartime concentration camp," said Toronto journalist Jim Hunt.

When the NHL expanded from six to 12 teams in 1967, Terry was obtained by the new Los Angeles Kings, played one season on the West coast, and then returned to the Red Wings in 1968-69. A year later he was signed by the Rangers, playing for Emile Francis, the man who had admired him so much.

By then it was clear that Sawchuk no longer considered the game anything more than a way of making a dollar, but every so often he would betray the beautiful part of his game — the one that moved Jack Adams to unload a superstar just to put Terry on his roster.

One can only wonder what Sawchuk's fate might have been had he not reported to the Red Wings' camp one season weighing a roly-poly 229 pounds. Adams was furious and ordered Terry to go on a strict diet.

Week by week, Sawchuk's weight dropped until he had lost 40 pounds. But at that point the weight loss was uncontrollable, and management was unnerved to say the least. He was ordered to a doctor, and the loss finally was stemmed, but Terry never was able to put any of it back on.

It has been theorized — and correctly so — that the pressure of his grueling job had also gotten to him. From that point on his emotional graph described a downward turn that bottomed out in Boston. He had left his wife and children back home in Detroit and lived in a rooming house.

While he did recover, it was always difficult for Terry to enjoy even the most intense moments of glee. One that should have brought him happiness was the Stanley Cup finale in 1967 when he and another veteran, Johnny Bower, guided the Leafs to the championship. While teammates exulted in the dressing room, sipping champagne, the goalies, as Jim Hunt observed, "sat in a corner by themselves, dragging deeply on cigarettes and grappling silently with the frayed nerves and many physical ailments that are an inescapable part of life for aging men."

Nevertheless, the Toronto experience was one that also provided some inner peace and satisfaction, particularly the Cup-winning effort. "I'd like to leave hockey like that," said the famed goaltender. "In style."

He didn't, of course. He played his last professional game on April 9, 1970, against a mighty Boston Bruins team in the Stanley Cup playoffs. The Rangers were beaten 5-3 and soon were eliminated from the Cup round.

Conceivably, Emile Francis might have invited Sawchuk back to the Rangers for the 1970-71 season as a goaltending coach and possible second goaltender. But three weeks after the Rangers were eliminated, Sawchuk, who shared a room in suburban Long Island with teammate Ron Stewart, had a row with his pal. The precise details

never have been fully pieced together, but Sawchuk was taken to the hospital to have intestinal injuries treated.

At first it seemed just a matter of weeks until he would be released but Terry's condition worsened dramatically, and finally, he was moved to a more sophisticated Manhattan hospital where emergency surgery was performed. It was all in vain — Terry Sawchuk died of a pulmonary embolism on May 31, 1970.

How to make sense of a roller-coaster career alternately laden with moments of immense triumph and frustrating setbacks? Sometimes you just don't — in Terry Sawchuk's case, it's best to marvel at his successes and leave his former troubles alone. Only then can he truly leave hockey "in style."

BILL DURNAN (1943-50)

Bill asked for the then huge sum of $4,200, and surprisingly enough to Bill, the Canadiens management agreed.

He became known as hockey's greatest 'holler guy.' With his deep voice booming, he advised, urged, and roared whenever the play was torrid around the Canadiens' end of the rink.

Ask a goaltending expert today to name the premier puckstopper in the world and the answer is apt to be anyone from Dominik Hasek to Mike Richter to Patrick Roy to Martin Brodeur. But in the mid-1940s' there was no problem producing an answer. Bill Durnan of the Montreal Canadiens was the very best. Period. No questions asked.

Durnan not only was clearly several cuts above other members of the goaltenders' union, he was unique in the business at the time.

Durnan was an ambidextrous goalie.

From minute to minute, throughout a game, Durnan would switch his goalie stick from right to left hand as the play dictated. He was the only goalie ever to wear identical gloves on each hand and the first netminder to be named captain of a Montreal team that featured such leaders as Rocket Richard, Toe Blake, and Butch Buchard.

Self-effacing, introspective, and extremely intense, Durnan was a William-come-lately to the National Hockey League, although that was more the fault of the Toronto Maple Leafs than Durnan himself, as our narrative will later relate. But once Les Canadiens found him, Durnan became a superstar as quickly as General Manager Tommy Gorman could flick a light switch.

He was hockey's version of Sandy Koufax. For the brief time he called the Montreal Forum home, his star shone as bright as a supernova. During the latter part of the World War II years, and through 1947, you could not find a hockey expert who believed there was a better goaltender playing than Bill Durnan.

Canadian sportswriter Vincent Lunny expressed the prevailing sentiment in 1948 when he wrote the following appraisal: "It would be superfluous to say that Bill Durnan is the greatest netminder of the last 20 years and probably the greatest of all time. We'll accept that as an established fact."

What prevents Durnan from attaining a higher ranking is his relatively brief big-league career. He was discovered late and played for the superb Montreal Canadiens during the 1940s with Rocket Richard. He joined the Habs in 1943 and, stricken with a nervous ailment, tearfully retired in the spring of 1950, although he had won his sixth Vezina Trophy. But during his seven seasons with Les Canadiens, Durnan set new standards for goalkeeping excellence.

Amazingly, Bill won the Vezina Trophy in 1944, 1945, 1946, 1947, 1949, and 1950. In the process, he also became the first player to win it four consecutive years, spanning 1944-47. Not surprisingly, he was named to the First Team All-Stars those same seasons.

During his tenure in Montreal, the Canadiens finished first four times and won the Stanley Cup twice, in the years 1943-44 and 1945-46.

The ability that made Durnan unique among goaltenders was his ambidexterity. Steve Faulkner, who coached him at Westmoreland United, taught him that trick, and it helped him become the best goaltender in the National Hockey League. Faulkner showed Bill how to use his hands instead of relying solely on his stick and pads to block shots, and his switch was so deceptively quick that it fooled the opposing forwards.

Durnan became known as hockey's greatest "holler guy." With his deep voice booming, he advised, urged, and roared whenever the play was torrid around the Canadiens' end of the rink.

Big Bill (six foot two, 200 pounds) had large hands and lightning reflexes. He possessed a keen analytical mind that simply soaked up hockey intelligence, although he made no conscious effort to study the styles of opposing forwards. Not coincidentally, few players scored hat tricks against Durnan.

He was one of the most popular Canadiens among his teammates, as is evidenced by the fact that his forwards were often willing to sacrifice their opportunity to score to help him. His fellow Canadiens often thought of him and his bids for records when they might not have given another goaltender a thought. If they were leading by three or four goals late in the third period, one of the players would often say to Coach Dick Irvin: "We've got enough goals to win now, Skipper. Is it all right if we just back-check and help Bill with his shutout?"

It was that kind of respect and reverence shown Durnan that enabled him a position few goaltenders ever had. Irvin gave his goaltender the heralded captaincy of the Montreal Canadiens.

William Durnan was born opposite a city dump in Toronto on January 22, 1915, the younger of two brothers. Bill was nine when he tried out for a hockey team of the Westmoreland United Church. The boys were grouped according to weight. Bill was a big kid, and the other players felt he was too heavy to compete with the fellows on the forward line, so he was moved into the nets. Westmoreland won five city championships in the six years that Durnan played in the nets for them.

In 1930-31, Bill joined the North Toronto Juniors, a farm club for the Junior Marlboros, which was a farm team for the Maple Leafs. Red Burnett, a hockey writer for the *Toronto Daily Star,* recommended Bill to the coach of the Sudbury, Ontario, Junior team. They invited him to play on their team the following year.

Big Bill was considered a hot prospect while he was playing in Sudbury, as he helped them win the Memorial Cup in 1931. The Leafs were impressed and signed an agreement with him. He was only 20 years old.

Before the start of the 1932 season, however, Bill and a friend were wrestling on Wasaga Beach, and the promising goalkeeper twisted a knee. This sidelined him for a season, and the Leafs dropped him as a prospect. His pride was really hurt by Toronto's treatment of him. "I was disillusioned and figured if that was the kind of treatment I was to get, then hell, I didn't want any part of it."

During the 1934-35 season, Durnan ended up playing in the T and Y Mercantile League in Toronto. In 1936 he took a job as a millwright in a gold-mining mill in Kirkland

Lake in northern Ontario and, between shifts, played with the Kirkland Lake Blue Devils; he stayed with the Blue Devils for four seasons. In 1940, Kirkland won the Allan Cup, emblematic of the Senior championship of Canada, with Bill as their goaltender.

After the success of the 1940 season, Durnan moved to Montreal to tend goal for the Montreal Royals, the top amateur club in the Quebec Senior League and a Canadiens farm operation. At this point, he was still smarting from the snub he received in Toronto and had no plans of becoming a professional hockey player.

Bill was a man of few illusions, and he would have been satisfied if he spent the rest of his career with the Royals. He was earning a comfortable living with his part-time job in the accounting department of the Canadian Car and Foundry. However, his boss was Len Peto, who was also a director of the Montreal Canadiens.

Peto began pressuring him into turning professional, but Durnan said no, the incident with Toronto still burning in his mind. He did not want to play pro hockey, but Peto insisted. Bill asked for the then huge sum of $4,200, and surprisingly enough to Bill, the Canadiens management agreed.

He tried out for the Canadiens in the autumn of 1943, and he was scheduled to be the goaltender in a preseason exhibition game. The average rookie would have been ecstatic to receive an opportunity such as this. However, Durnan was not your average rookie. He was 29 years old, and it didn't matter to him whether or not he played pro hockey.

His Montreal softball team was in the provincial finals, and Bill was their star pitcher. He turned down the Canadiens' net assignment, unconcerned that it might endanger his NHL career. At his own expense, Bill instead went back to Montreal and pitched his team to the Quebec championship.

Coach Irvin finally persuaded Durnan that his place was in goal. In 1943, his first season with the Flying Frenchmen, remembering the advice of Faulkner, he used his hands in his goaltending and seldom let a rebound escape. He emerged as the premier goaltender that year and won the Vezina Trophy, becoming the first rookie ever to win it. In the process he helped his team beat the Chicago Black Hawks in four straight games to win the Stanley Cup.

In 1944-45, the Montreal Canadiens placed five players on the First Team All-Stars, the first time that had ever happened. The team consisted of Emile Bouchard on defense; Elmer Lach, center; Maurice Richard, right wing; Tow Blake, left wing; and Bill Durnan as goaltender. Dick Irvin was named coach to form a sextet.

It was during the 1948-49 season that Bill set the NHL modern record for the longest shutout sequence by holding his opponents scoreless for 309 minutes and 21 seconds with four consecutive shutouts. That was the longest shutout sequence in 18 years. That year he had 10 shutouts in 60 games, and he was the runner-up to Sid Abel (Detroit Red Wings) in the voting for the Hart Trophy, awarded to the most valuable player in the league.

During his entire career, which spanned 383 regular season games, he registered 3 shutouts and had a 2.35 goals against average. In 45 playoff games, he shut out the opposition in two games and his goals against average was 2.20.

However, Bill had trouble with the fans in Montreal. The Canadiens were in a slump in 1947, and The Forum crowd began chanting: "We want Bibeault!" (Paul Bibeault was the Canadiens' goaltender before Durnan.) "They booed me and made me feel six inches

high," he said. All this despite the fact that he had won the Vezina Trophy every year since 1943-44. The 1947-48 season ended Durnan's Vezina streak, as Turk Broda of the Toronto Maple Leafs took home the heralded prize.

Nevertheless, Durnan rebounded and won the prize each of the next two years. The 1949-50 season, however, was the beginning of the end for him. There was little fun left for him in the game, for a lot of his friends were leaving — or had already gone. The old camaraderie was missing.

In January 1950, he told Dick Irvin he would be retiring at the end of the season. He felt his reflexes were slow and the grind of playing season after season in the fire that was, and remains, Montreal had worn on him.

Hockey had begun to get rough for him toward the end of the 1940s. Durnan had broken his hand earlier, and even though it had mended, his entire arm would ache whenever he caught the puck. He was going to be 35 years old in an era where the goalie played the entire season without an alternate, and with no mask for protection.

Moreover, the most he had ever made in a season was $10,500, despite the Vezinas, Stanley Cups, and the countless writers who had proclaimed him the best goalie ever. He wasn't educated, and he had two girls to raise. Bill Durnan began to worry.

The end came quickly. In March 1950, the Canadiens were to play the Rangers in the first round of the playoffs. Montreal had finished second, and the Rangers had finished fourth. Naturally, the Canadiens were favored. Quickly the Rangers won three games in a row from the Canadiens.

The nerves and pressures began building up, and it was then Big Bill Durnan decided to retire. Before the fourth game, Irvin asked him to go in and tell the players that it was Bill's decision to quit, not Irvin's. In a poignant scene in the dressing room, a tearful Bill Durnan handed young Gerry McNeil his stick. McNeil, the successor, took the stick from the master, crying as well. It was a very emotional scene to say the least.

The McNeil-led Canadiens went out and won the fourth game, but the Rangers won the fifth contest and took the series. "A lot of people thought it was a nervous breakdown," Bill said, "but it wasn't. To this day, people won't believe me. What the hell, I'm quitting and this is as good a time as any. If the kid goes in and wins, well great, it's a terrific start for him."

Durnan ended his professional career in the middle of the 1950 playoffs, a victim of frayed nerves. Although he played but seven seasons, his outstanding netminding was remembered and rewarded, as he was inducted into the Hockey Hall of Fame in 1964.

On October 31, 1972, in Toronto's North York General Hospital, Bill Durnan died at the age of 57. He had been in ill for some time, having been afflicted with arthritis for years. He left his wife, a son, and two daughters.

Durnan could pass for the greatest goaltender of all time had he endured the test of time and played more seasons. Still, in those seven seasons he raised the art of goaltending to new heights and, in doing so, solidified his place among hockey's best goaltenders of all time.

TURK BRODA (1936-52)

That night Maple Leaf Gardens was packed with 13,359 Turk fans, and when Broda skated out for the opening face-off, the Gardens' regimental band swung into "Happy Days Are Here Again" and followed it with a chorus of "She's Too Fat for Me.

From 1947 through 1951 the Toronto Maple Leafs won four Stanley Cups, including a run of three straight that ended in 1949. Not coincidentally, the goaltender on that dynastic team was Walter Broda — alias the Turk. It's also worth noting that this somewhat unlikely looking puckstopper also won a Stanley Cup in amazing fashion in April 1942; but that's another tale.

The Broda story is rather simple. During the six-team NHL, he was the quintessential clutch goalie, and the five Stanley Cup rings bestowed upon him merely underline the point. Of course, his saga is more complicated than that. A Hall of Famer, Broda was the centerpiece of one of big-league hockey's most fascinating clubs. He also became half of the first top-flight two-man goalie platoon to win the Vezina Trophy, along with his other half, Al Rollins.

The Turk was fat and funny. And maybe that is the reason why he often was bypassed when the cream of the goalkeeping fraternity was discussed.

Had he been a tragic figure like Terry Sawchuk, a worrier like Glenn Hall, or an eccentric such as Jacques Plante, Broda might have received more serious consideration. But the image of Toronto's fabulous fat man always was light and upbeat — except when it came to the big games.

While he is fondly remembered for winning his "Battle of the Bulge" campaign against excess poundage, Broda also is revered by historians for his impeccable ability to excel in the most critical moments.

As such, it is not surprising that he twice won the Vezina Trophy for having the best goals against average, was twice a First Team All-Star, was once a Second Team All-Star, and played for five Stanley Cup-winning teams.

Broda, along with center Syl Apps, formed the cornerstone of Manager Conn Smythe's rebuilding effort when Toronto began their ascent to dizzying heights in the 1940s. Their Cup win in 1942 was the first for Broda, whose career was interrupted by World War II. Following his military service, he returned in spectacular fashion to help Toronto win an unprecedented three consecutive Cups (1947, 1948, 1949) and still another in 1951.

Turk had the ideal disposition for a goaltender and was a superb team player on a club sprinkled with scintillating characters.

It could be said that Bill Durnan, who starred in goal for Montreal during the same era, was a better textbook goalie than Broda and produced superior averages, but Durnan couldn't match the Turk in Stanley Cups or longevity. Broda became a big-leaguer before Durnan arrived and outlasted him by two seasons.

The records indicate that Broda's best season — statistically — was 1940-41 when he

rang up a 2.06 goals against average. But the vintage Broda appeared during the 1942 playoffs when he starred in the seventh (Cup-winning) game of the finals and again in 1947-48 when he powered the Leafs to a first-place finish. In the process he took home the Vezina and then, surrounded by one of the most formidable teams in hockey history, annexed the Stanley Cup.

Yet many Torontonians prefer the memory of November 1949 when Smythe demanded that a number of his stars trim their waistlines in a hurry. The antifat edict made headlines throughout North America.

Smythe singled out defenseman Garth Boesch and forwards Howie Meeker, Harry Watson, Vic Lynn, and Sid Smith for his blasts, but the key target of his ire was his longtime goaltending stalwart, Broda.

Smythe's opening gun in the "Battle of the Bulge" was a demand that his players reduce their weight to specified limits. Broda, who weighed 197 pounds, was ordered to lose 7 pounds *within a week*. To underline the seriousness of his offensive, Smythe promptly called up reserve goalie Gil Mayer from his Pittsburgh farm team. It was Tuesday, and he was giving Turk until Saturday to fulfill the demand. "I'm taking Broda out of the nets," Smythe said, "and he's not going back until he shows some common sense."

Smythe's outburst reverberated across Canada and parts of the United States, and soon "The Battle of the Bulge" became a cause célèbre. Neutral observers regarded Turk's tussle with the scales as a huge joke, win or lose, but to the Toronto boss it was no joke. None of the Leafs were particularly amused, either.

After one day of severe dieting, Turk trimmed his weight from 197 to 193, and all of Canada seemed to breathe easier. Smythe had set the final weigh-in for Saturday afternoon, just before the evening match against the New York Rangers at Maple Leaf Gardens. He refused to divulge what specific action he would take against Broda or his compatriots if they did not pass muster, but he suggested that it would not be lenient. Turk moved forward and gingerly placed his feet on the platform. The numbers finally settled — just under 190 pounds! He had made it. Turk was delighted, and Smythe was doubly enthusiastic because he regarded his goaltender with paternal affection. "There may be better goalies around somewhere," said the manager, "but there's no greater sportsman than the Turkey. If the Rangers score on him tonight, I should walk out and hand him a malted milk, just to show I'm not trying to starve him to death."

That night Maple Leaf Gardens was packed with 13,359 Turk fans, and when Broda skated out for the opening face-off, the Gardens' regimental band swung into "Happy Days Are Here Again" and followed it with a chorus of "She's Too Fat for Me."

Referee George Gravel dropped the puck to start the game, and the Rangers immediately swarmed in on Broda. This time, however, he was the Turk of old. Broda's slimmer teammates couldn't push the rubber past goalie Chuck Rayner of the Rangers, however, and the first period ended with the teams tied 0-0. It was the same story in the second period, as each team desperately probed for an opening. The Rangers got their big break late in the middle period when Pentti Lund bisected the Toronto defense and moved within easy scoring distance of Broda. Lund found his opening and fired the puck mightily, but somehow Broda thrust his pad in the way and deflected the rubber out of danger. To a man, the fans rose and toasted Turk with a standing ovation, and when the second period ended, the contest remained a scoreless deadlock.

Early in the third period the Leafs were attempting a change in lines when Howie Meeker and Vic Lynn, two of the marked fat men, combined to feed a lead pass to Max Bentley, who normally wouldn't have been on the ice with them. Bentley moved through the Rangers' blueliners and unleashed a steaming shot that flew past Rayner. Later in the period another rotund fellow, Harry Watson, skimmed a pass to Bill Ezinicki, who also beat Rayner.

Now all eyes fixed themselves on the clock as it ticked toward the twenty-minute mark and the end of the game. With only a minute remaining, Broda still had a shutout, sans the malted milk. The countdown began: ten, nine, eight, seven, six, five — the crowd was roaring as if the Leafs had won the Stanley Cup — four, three, two, one. The game was over; Turk dove for the puck and gathered it in. It was his symbolic trophy for winning the "Battle of the Bulge."

Walter Broda was born on May 15, 1914, in the wheat country of western Canada. His hometown, Brandon, sent many a young hockey player to the professional ranks, but few appeared less likely to make it than the portly young netminder. Although his skating was poor and his reflexes lacked the spark of a thinner player, Broda earned a spot on the school team — by default. Luckily the principal began working privately with his student, teaching him the finer points of goaltending, until Broda's game began to improve. He soon caught on with a local club, the Brandon North Stars, and played goal for them in a one-game playoff with the Elmwood Millionaires. Broda's club lost 11-1! Despite his inauspicious start, he somehow managed to take over the goalkeeping for the Manitoba Hydros of the Brandon Commercial League in 1930-31. He played so capably in an intermediate league during that time that he was named to its All-Star team.

Turk got his break after trying out and failing his audition with the Brandon Native Sons, a top Junior entry. Although the manager had rejected him, the Native Sons' boss remembered Turk. He called on Broda that spring when the regular Native Sons' goaltender was ruled overage in a last-minute discovery, leaving the Junior club desperate for a goaltender.

Amused rather than annoyed at the sudden turnabout by the Native Sons, Turk accepted their offer to take over the goaltending during the Memorial Cup playoffs for the Junior championship of Canada.

Brandon swept the series, and Broda was at his best, as always would be the case, in the most excruciating moments. It was only a matter of time before he would make his way up the ranks to the pros. Conn Smythe signed him in 1936 for what turned out to be one of the best moves ever made by one of hockey's most insightful entrepreneurs.

After his playing career, Broda took a number of coaching jobs in both amateur and professional ranks, the last of which was with Quebec in the American Hockey League. Alas, Turk Broda died on October 17, 1972, much too soon, at the age of 58.

The Turk will always be remembered as a happy performer, and his serious-yet-comical victory in the "Battle of the Bulge" will forever remain one of the most entertaining episodes in hockey lore. Most of all, however, Broda should be recalled for his impeccable play when the game — sometimes the season — was on the line.

JOHNNY BOWER (1953-70)

"When hockey's no longer fun, it's time to quit."

In a sense, John Bower's career was semitragic. He had proven himself a competent National Hockey League goalie during the 1953-54 season, his rookie year with the New York Rangers. His goals against average with a team that didn't even make the playoffs was a handsome 2.60. It appeared that at the age of 29, Bower would enjoy a lengthy big-league career.

Instead — inexplicably — Rangers general manager Frank Boucher dispatched Bower back to the minors and replaced him with Lorne (Gump) Worsley. For four seasons Bower languished in the minors, although it was generally accepted in the hockey fraternity that he was as good as — or better than — some of those netminders who were regarded as big-leaguers.

That's why Bower's 25-year career is so remarkable. He didn't become a full-time NHL goalie again until he was rescued from the American Hockey League by the Toronto Maple Leafs in 1958 at the age of 33. From there Bower remained a first-string goaltender well into his 40s.

Goaltending has driven younger men into early retirement, and by normal athletic standards, Bower should have been well past his prime when he guided the Leafs to their last Stanley Cup in 1966-67. But his was a unique career driven by a body that could withstand punishments that would bury lesser men.

Many felt that without Bower in the nets, the resurgence of the Leafs may never have taken place. He joined the club when it was in last place in 1958 and was the key to its ensuing success. After taking over between the pipes, Bower's Leafs appeared in the playoffs for nine straight years from 1958 to 1967, and again in 1968-69. During that span the Torontonians took home Lord Stanley's Cup four times.

Johnny played with some fine players, including Red Kelly, Tim Horton, Carl Brewer, and Frank Mahovlich, but the team's netminder was the essential cog on the Cup-winning teams.

Bower was born in Prince Albert, Saskatchewan, supposedly on November 8, 1924. His actual date of birth has long been debated, though. On three different occasions when hospitalized with hockey-related injuries, he gave three different birthdays. "I've lied about my age so often that I've forgotten how old I really am," he joked.

Regardless of how old he really was, Bower was a wonder in the world of hockey. He was still sprawling to stop shots, kicking deftly at pucks, always alert and agile. Remarkably enough, he had the reflexes of a much younger man.

Growing up in the middle of the Depression, John William Bower knew what it meant to be poor. His first pair of goalie pads were fashioned from an old mattress, and his stick was cut from a branch with a suitable bend.

Bower received his first pair of skates from a player on a senior team. He was 10 years old at the time, and the skates were much too big for him. Glad to even have a pair of skates, he noted, "I worshipped those skates even if I couldn't get used to them." Bower ended up playing in the nets because it was the one position in hockey where you didn't have to have blades.

He spent two years with the Canadian army during World War II and, upon receiving his medical discharge, returned to Canada in 1943. He was still eligible for Junior hockey and played for Prince Albert that year. Other teams in the league questioned how a man who served two years overseas could still be of Junior age. Unfortunately for them, his birth certificate could not be found, and he was allowed to finish the season.

Bower turned pro in 1945, signing with the Cleveland Barons of the American Hockey League. He played well for eight seasons but in relative obscurity. At that time, there were only six goalie jobs in the NHL, and it was difficult to rise quickly from the minors.

In 1953 Johnny Bower got his chance as the New York Rangers obtained him. Gump Worsley, then the Rangers' goalie, said later, "We thought he was an old man then, and that was 15 years ago." The Gumper had been rookie of the year the season before, but Bower won the job away from him.

The Blueshirts failed to make the playoffs that year, through no fault of Bower. He had five shutouts to go with the aforementioned 2.60 goals allowed per game. Still, the next season Bower was replaced by Worsley and shipped off to Vancouver of the Western Hockey League. From British Columbia he was sent off to Providence of the American Hockey League and finally wound up back in Cleveland in 1957.

While at Providence, Johnny's club won the Calder Cup, and he was chosen for the AHL's All-Star team. Additionally, he was named Athlete of the Year, which he considered one of the highlights of his career. In fact, he won the AHL's Most Valuable Player Award three times along with the Outstanding Goalie Award once. He was also named best goalie the one season he played in the WHL.

Bower might have remained in the minors indefinitely had it not been for Lady Luck. The Maple Leafs finished in last place during the 1957-58 season for the first time in the history of the storied club, and Billy Reay, the coach at that time, was searching for a new goalkeeper. He was set to sign Al Rollins (who was playing for Calgary in the WHL), but on the night that he was scouting the netminder, Rollins had an off night. Reay opted for Bower instead and bought Johnny for $10,000 and a Junior player.

Still, Bower was undecided whether he wanted to go to Toronto or not. He was very happy in Cleveland and didn't think he could help the Leafs. However, the Torontonians offered him a large, two-year contract, and he was persuaded to sign. Johnny Bower was nearly 34 years old when he was rescued from the veil of the minor leagues. He battled goalie Ed Chadwick for the starting job for a few months and claimed victory when Chadwick was banished to the minors.

Ironically, Reay never saw the benefits of signing Bower — he was fired before he could take credit; in the end, Punch Imlach looked like the genius.

The Maple Leafs soared from last place to make the playoffs in 1958-59 only to lose in the finals to Montreal. In the 1959-60 season, they again made the finals and again fell to the Flying Frenchmen. But in 1961-62, Ontario's finest took home the Stanley Cup for

the first time in 11 years. In fact, while Bower guarded the net for the Leafs, they won the Cup four times — in 1961-62, 1962-63 (finishing first), 1963-64, and 1966-67.

Bower was such a superb competitor that he never complained over the many injuries he endured. He suffered broken ribs when he was shoved into the iron goal posts; a skate blade gashed against his jaw, ripping out a tooth and requiring 32 stitches; all of his teeth were knocked out at one time or another; and once, while diving for a puck, a stick wedged under his tongue. Injuries would not stop him.

Standing five feet nine inches and weighing 188 pounds, Johnny's face was carved with lines — some curved, some jagged — all healed scars from cuts inflicted by skates, sticks, and pucks. He estimated that he had received over 200 stitches on his face alone just to close facial cuts.

In 1960-61, he played 58 games, had two shutouts, and ended the year with a strong 2.50 goals against average. He was elected to the First-Team All-Stars that year and subsequently won the Vezina Trophy.

Bower continued his fine play in the 1964-65 season when he played in 34 games and had three shutouts to go with a 2.38 average. That year he also won the Vezina, this time sharing it with his teammate Terry Sawchuk. The Leafs had acquired Sawchuk earlier that year to share the goaltending chores with Johnny. Most athletes, with their enormous egos, would have taken deep offense if their team picked up a player of Sawchuk's caliber. Johnny Bower was unlike most athletes. "I just can't play 70 games," he said very pragmatically. "We need two goalies, and Terry is a great one. I'm glad he's with us."

In 1966 Bower played in only 27 games due to injuries, especially pulled muscles. "Of course I get tired during those two-a-day workouts," he admitted, "but I know if I'm tired then I've been working hard. That's how I stay in shape."

After the 1966-67 season, Bower had to face the threat of expansion and the fact that Toronto might not protect him. Nevertheless, he was not yet ready to retire. Fortuitously, the Leafs kept him, letting Sawchuk go to the Los Angeles Kings.

"When hockey's no longer fun, it's time to quit," Bower once remarked. The fun at long last went out of it for Johnny when constant injuries made him feel "painful muscles that I didn't know I had." In 1970 he retired.

Johnny Bower played 13 seasons during which he played 552 games. He totaled 37 shutouts for a 2.52 career average. His playoff statistics included 74 games (five shutouts) with a 2.54 average.

After leaving the ice he joined the Leafs' scouting staff as their chief eastern scout and went on to coach their goaltenders. Johnny was also a co-owner of a resort hotel in Prince Albert, having bought it with the money he had made from his thriving hamburger business.

In 1976 he received hockey's greatest acclamation: induction into the Hall of Fame. King Clancy remarked, "Of all the people who are in the Hall of Fame, there is none more worthy than Johnny Bower. He is one of the most honest and conscientious hockey players I've ever met. He is in a class by himself as a person. During my 54 years of association with the game, I have seen few better hockey players."

Johnny Bower was a fiercely competitive man who often played wracked with pain. He went all-out whether it was workouts, games, or Stanley Cup competition. Bower was agile and ageless, and he enjoyed a career of incredible accomplishments. Whether he was 46 or 50 when he retired, it did not matter. Clancy's words ring as true today as they did then; John Bower was a gem of a player and the epitome of a class act.

KEN DRYDEN (1971-73; 1974-79)

"I told Sam Pollack when he took Dryden from us he had just assured himself of a Stanley Cup. He was that good."

—Floyd Curry

As long as hockey is played with a rubber puck and steel blades, there will be debate as to precisely how good — or even great — Ken Dryden was as a major-league goaltender.

The pro-Dryden contingent claims that six Stanley Cups and Hall of Fame acclamation reaffirms his greatness.

The anti-Dryden contingent asserts that the erudite puckstopper was carried by one of the best defensive quartets in history, not to mention three forward lines which paid as much attention to checking as they did to scoring.

The answer is somewhere in-between. Dryden — much admired by his Habs coach Scotty Bowman — did what he had to do with the team in front of him. He was stoically calm, insightfully sharp, and good for four Vezina Trophies, three of which were shared with Michel Larocque. In a city which invariably placed its goaltenders under a critical microscope.

In the late 1960s and early '70s, Montreal was far from a likely setting for a rookie goaltender to make a spectacular entrance into the National Hockey League. Les Habitants were stockpiled with talent to the envy of the rest of the league. Accordingly, it was standard operating procedure within the fabled organization for freshmen netminders to serve a lengthy apprenticeship before being thrown into the lion's den. The Habs didn't count on Kenneth Wayne Dryden. After being called up from the Montreal Voyageurs of the American Hockey League in the spring of 1971, Dryden made proponents of the "sit before you skate" theory blush.

Born on August 8, 1947, in Hamilton, Ontario, Dryden's unique career began as it ended: with a Stanley Cup in tow. After watching his first game from the press box, the lanky puckstopper played six regular season games and was impressive in allowing only nine goals. Many in the league thought the Canadiens were merely brewing Dryden a cup of coffee — a couple of games of NHL experience — as they ran through the end of their schedule. With the playoffs lurking just around the corner, few believed they would ever go with a rookie at such a crucial point; in the experts' eyes, Rogie Vachon was going to be the man.

One man thought otherwise. Voyageurs coach Floyd Curry was that man, and he recalled a conversation with Sam Pollack. "I told [Sam] when he took Dryden from us that he had just assured himself of the Stanley Cup. He was that good." Curry proved sage that spring.

Notwithstanding his minor-league skipper's praises, the Habs' choice to go with their rookie in the opening round against the defending Cup champion Boston Bruins rocked the hockey world. Many believed throwing a 24-year-old rookie against the Orr- and Esposito-led Bruins was akin to sending David with one arm tied behind his back to fight

Goliath. It was not long, however, before it became obvious that this rookie played with the composure of a hardened veteran.

More than anything else, this "coolness under pressure" epitomized the man. The pose was the person. Above all, Ken Dryden will be vividly remembered most for his posture in the crease when the hail of enemy shots had desisted. Big number 29 would dig the tip of his stick into the ice and fold his arms across the knob, coolly relaxing until the action resumed. Uncharacteristic of the nervous and beleaguered sort of goalie a la Glenn Hall, Dryden was as cool and confident inside as he appeared on the outside.

Such poise helped carry the Canadiens to victory in a seesaw, seven-game series versus the Beantowners that spring. Save after spectacular save left the Bruins slamming their sticks against the boards and glancing toward the heavens in hope of some sort of divine intervention. Woe unto Beantown, for apparently God was not a Bruins fan that year.

Propelled by their mammoth upset of their rivals to the Southeast, the Canadiens dispatched the Minnesota North Stars in six and the Chicago Black Hawks in seven games to annex the Cup. In retrospect, it is hard to believe any of it could have been possible without the standout performance of Dryden. Through 20 playoff games, he compiled a 3.00 goals against average and was awarded the Conn Smythe Trophy as the most valuable player of the playoffs. This, with merely six games of NHL experience under his pads.

Expectedly, the experts began comparing Dryden to past goaltending greats. At six feet four inches, he reminded observers of another tall Canadian goalie of the 1940s — the expertly ambidextrous Bill Durnan. "The way Ken gets in front of shots to make impossible saves," said team captain Henri Richard, "he's a lot like Durnan used to be. Dryden murders you with surprise moves from seemingly impossible positions. It's great for a defenseman or a forward to know he's behind you."

As impressive as Dryden's playoff record was in 1971, his 3.00 goals against average was to be the most permissive digit of his career, regular season or playoffs. In 1971-72, the big fellow became the workhorse in the Montreal nets by playing 64 games with a 2.24 goals against, good enough to earn him the Calder Trophy as outstanding rookie of the year. Dryden thus became the first player ever to be named MVP of the playoffs before proving himself the best rookie of the league!

He became a model of consistency the following year by working 54 games between the pipes, compiling a 2.25 goals against average and walking away with his third major award in less than three seasons, this time the Vezina Trophy for the best goals against average.

In addition to performing at the top of his sport, Ken Dryden was never a one-dimensional jock type. Wire-rimmed spectacles, long hair, and mod style of dress separated the young star from his peers almost as much as his semi-intellectual personality. A graduate of Cornell University and McGill Law School, Dryden was as unpredictable in his career decisions as he was predictably magnificent in the Montreal nets.

By 1973 it appeared as though the sky would be the limit for the young netminder. He had reached the peak of his game and seemed a fixture at The Forum. But then he dropped his bombshell. Prior to the 1973-74 season, Dryden announced that, at the age of 26, he was retiring from hockey to accept a job "articling" for the Toronto law firm of Osler, Hoskin and Harcourt for the sniveling salary of $7,500 a year. At this, the collective jaw of Montreal dropped in amazement.

Dryden had never been secretive of his desires to pursue a career in law, and if worst came to worst, had been prepared to sacrifice hockey for the rigors of the courtroom. With the Canadiens, Dryden had been earning a modest salary despite his enormous appeal and proven ability. He believed he deserved more money, a salary equal to his standing as one of the best goalies in the NHL.

However, management would not budge, and Dryden departed. For that season the Habs struggled with three goaltenders to no avail; the Flying Frenchmen crash-landed in the playoffs, being bounced by the Rangers in the first round. A few hundred miles west of The Forum, Dryden worked diligently at his profession and enrolled with an industrial team as a defenseman.

After considerable haggling and finally some give and take by both parties, Dryden and the Canadiens came to terms. He rejoined the team for the 1974-75 campaign and found that kicking around the industrial league had done little to keep him on top of his game. He struggled some and wound up with what would be his highest regular season goals against average of his career, 2.69. The Canadiens again did not reach the Cup finals, and the masses buzzed with speculation over the future of their once-prized goaltender. It was the last time Dryden ended his season with a loss.

From the 1975-76 season until his retirement in 1979, Ken Dryden was absolutely outstanding, a goaltender nonpareil in the NHL. His personal statistics, in addition to the fact that the Canadiens earned four consecutive Stanley Cups during that period, is testament to the excellence of both the team and its goaltender.

In those four years of Dryden's dominance, his goals against average never climbed higher than 1978-79's 2.30, and in 1975-76 it reached its minuscule low of 2.03. Between those years he enjoyed his finest season, playing in 56 games during 1976-77 and turning in 10 shutouts and a 2.14 goals against average for the regular season. In the playoffs he appeared in 14 contests and logged 4 shutouts and an almost-invisible 1.56 goals against average.

During his remarkable career, in addition to the Calder, Vezina, and Smythe Trophies, he was named First Team All-Star five times and Second Team All-Star on one occasion. As an example of Dryden's exceptional ability to handle the puck after making the save, he accumulated 19 regular season and four playoff assists.

Again proving unpredictable, Dryden suddenly called it quits — this time for good — after the 1979 season; this while apparently at the top of his game. Just four years later, he was named to the Hockey Hall of Fame.

In a brief and enigmatic career, Dryden helped the Canadiens to six championships. His mettle in the clutch separated him from his peers more than his exceptional size and personality. The pose truly was the person. This combination of all his abilities made him distinctive enough to be ranked here as one of the finest goaltenders ever to roam the crease in the NHL.

In another surprising move, Ken Dryden accepted the presidency of the Toronto Maple Leafs in May 1997, 18 years after withdrawing from hockey altogether.

BILL SMITH (1971-1983)

*"The off-ice Bill Smith I saw was hardly the hateful guy
I had clashed with an hour earlier."*

— Kevin Lowe, Edmonton Oilers

On the ice Bill Smith was as dislikeable as they come. Dislikeable, that is, unless you happened to be a New York Islanders fan.

Hunched in the net for Al Arbour's dynastic Stanley Cup team that won a record 19 consecutive playoff series, Smith often seemed more warrior than goaltender.

He would think nothing of swinging his stick at an opponent — as Wayne Gretzky painfully learned — nor would he shy away from actual fisticuffs. Once, in a playoff game against Boston, Smitty and goalie Gerry Cheevers of the Bruins went toe-to-toe like Mike Tyson and Evander Holyfield.

"Smith's antics had bothered us for years," says Kevin Lowe, the veteran Edmonton defenseman, "but on the other hand we respected the way he played goal."

The Smith goaltending technique was nothing to write a manual about. At times he appeared awkward, without style, and more lucky than good. It was, however, a deception.

Like Hall of Famer Tony Esposito and other formless — but expert — puckblockers, Smitty accomplished the primary task as well as anyone. Which meant keeping the biscuit on the right side of the goal line.

"He was as good a clutch goalie as you'll ever see," says Chico Resch. "Maybe the best ever when the chips were down."

There is ample evidence to support Chico's case.

Exhibit A would be the 1975 Rangers-Islanders playoff series. Extreme underdogs heading into the series, the Isles managed to force a decisive rubber game. Smith continually repelled the Broadway Blueshirts until the Isles won in sudden-death overtime.

Exhibit B was the decisive sixth game of the Stanley Cup finals between the Islanders and Flyers. After blowing a two-goal lead in the third period, the Isles were in disorderly retreat before a Philadelphia onslaught. Smith did everything but stand on his head preserving the tie until Bob Nystrom won the game — and the Cup — for New York in overtime.

Exhibit C was arguably the best example of clutch goaltending one could imagine. The setting was Northlands Coliseum, 1983, Game One of the finals between Edmonton and the three-time champion Islanders. Smith was up against Wayne Gretzky, Mark Messier, Paul Coffey, Glen Anderson, and Jari Kurri, among other Oilers sharpshooters. The Islanders best scorer, Mike Bossy, was sidelined with tonsillitis.

From the opening face-off the Oilers poured through the Islanders defense, sending volley after volley at Smith. From the blue line, from in close, one-on-one, two-on-one, Smitty was brilliant and challenging. The bottom line: He would not be beaten.

Armed with Duane Sutter's first-period goal, Smith seemed to grow bigger and bigger in the nets — at least in the Oilers' eyes — so that it seemed impossible to beat him. Which it was. Thanks to an open-netter near the end, New York won 2-0.

"That game proved that two factors — excellent goaltending and patient, disciplined checking — can save a vastly overwhelmed team from defeat," said Lowe. "We came at the Islanders in offensive waves. Not one line or two lines — but everyone, and Bill Smith was out of his mind."

Not only did he stop pucks, but he antagonized the Oilers with his threatening stick. Once he cut down Edmonton forward Glenn Anderson by slashing his ankles. Smitty took two minutes for that but was nonplussed.

"That one was special," says Smith. "I guess I played my heart out. It's a great feeling. But to be honest, they missed a few. It was a wonderful way to start a playoff series."

When someone asked Smith whether he was concerned about Anderson, he shot back, "I thought his funeral was today!"

The Oilers' funeral was conducted after the fourth game. Edmonton went down, one-two-three-four, over and out. Smith was awarded the Conn Smythe Trophy as most valuable playoff performer by NHL president John Ziegler. "I couldn't show this around some parts of Canada," he chuckled. "I'd be shot."

As much as the Oilers loathed the stick-swinging Smitty, they allowed that he wasn't such a bad guy once the uniform was removed and the paddle put back on the rack.

Lowe: "I remember seeing Smitty after a hard-fought game in which he had swung his big goalie stick at a few guys. But the off-ice Bill Smith I saw was hardly the hateful guy I had clashed with an hour earlier. He had had a couple of beers in the dressing room, was completely relaxed, and as he walked past us, he turned and said, 'Hi, fellas, how are you doing?' as if he were our buddy. As he left to meet his wife at the van, he made some comment about the rain and then took off. I said to myself, 'This can't be the same guy who was just on the ice.'"

The passage of time would emphasize Smith's claim to a place in the pantheon of puckstoppers. In addition to the Smythe, he won the Vezina Trophy in 1981-82 and shared the Jennings Trophy with Roland Melanson in 1982-83.

None of these laurels were particularly apparent when Smitty played Junior hockey in Cornall. A native of Perth, Ontario, Smith benefited from the NHL expansion of 1967, although it wasn't until 1971 that it had tangible results.

The Los Angeles Kings needed a promising, young netminder and promoted Smith to the NHL in 1971-72. He played five games and had a 1-3-1 record with an eminently unimpressive 4.60 goals against average. He spent most of that season with Springfield of the American League.

When the Islanders entered the NHL for the 1972-73 season, Smith was obtained in the Expansion Draft and managed 37 games for a club that was routinely described as "hapless." Smith's 7-24-3 (4.16 goals against average) record hardly informs us about his goaltending. He fought opponents as well as the puck and impressed Coach Al Arbour and General Manager Bill Torrey enough to remain with the team.

In time Smith and Chico Resch became a one-two — or two-one as the case may be — combination. Despite their divergent personalities, Smitty and Chico understood one another and blended as well as any goaltending tandem could as teammates and competitors alike.

Against some teams such as Pittsburgh, Resch would get the playoff nod, while against others, such as the Rangers, it would be Smith. The difference between the two was in the area of truculence. Chico minded his business when he was in the crease while Smitty minded everybody else's business, including his own.

Bill also took umbrage with opponents who had prima donna tendencies, especially ascending superstar Wayne Gretzky. The most discussed episode involving the two exploded at Nassau Coliseum. The Great One, as was his wont, moved behind the net with the puck, whereupon Smith swung his stick horizontally and connected with Gretzky's left leg.

Suddenly, the Oilers ace collapsed. More than three minutes were required to revive him, but he later returned to take a normal shift. The Islanders claim that the sharpshooter had exaggerated the injury. Whatever the case, it marked the beginning of a career-long Smith-Gretzky feud.

"It wasn't intentional," Smith maintained. "I do that all the time. I don't even look. I try to knock the puck off his stick or knock his stick hard enough to make him lose the puck.

"What's his biggest move? Stuffing the puck. I can't baby him. I hate to see a guy like that get hurt. I think he's good for hockey. But I'm not going to go out of my way to let him score three or four goals because I babied him."

The incident drew huge headlines both in New York and Edmonton, but Smitty also attracted attention for an even stranger accomplishment. He actually "scored" a goal. That is, scored in the technical sense if not the actual sense. It all happened during a game against Colorado on November 28, 1979. Rockies defenseman Rob Ramage mistakenly shot the puck down the ice and into his own empty net while his club was on a delayed penalty. Smith received credit for the goal because of geography; he was the last Islander to touch the puck!

But there was his name in the box score. "Third Period — NYI, Smith, 1, 4:50."

Smitty remained an Islander for his entire career, retiring after the 1988-89 season much to the delight of Gretzky, et al.

His goaltending reflected a transitional style, linking the 1970s with a newer mode of accentuated butterfly play introduced by the likes of Patrick Roy in the late 1980s.

"Say what you will about his style," concludes Resch, "but you can't argue with his intensity, his four Cup rings, and the fact that nobody was better at what he did when the chips were down. Bottom line: Smitty was a *big* winner."

FRANK BRIMSEK (1938-50)

"Tiny was such a great goaltender I had to be good or they would have chased me right out of Boston."

When USA Hockey — the national organization representing the amateur ice game in America — picked Uncle Sam's all-time team in 1997, there was no hesitation in naming Minnesota-born Frank Brimsek as the best netminder ever produced in the good old U.S.A.

One can only surmise how much better Brimsek might have been had his career not been interrupted at its very prime by the guns of World War II. From the late 1930s until the months after Pearl Harbor, Eveleth's gift to the Boston Bruins was very simply the best puckstopper in the bigs.

If you don't believe it, check his nickname — "Mister Zero." That's "Zero" as in shutouts which, for a time, came as easily to Brimsek as exhaling. But perhaps we're getting ahead of ourselves. Let's start with the very beginning and a theme — carpe diem, "seize the day" — which says a lot about the Brimsek saga.

Sometimes the day seizes you, as was the case with Francis Charles Brimsek. Born on September 26, 1915, in Eveleth, Minnesota, the man who came to be known as "Mister Zero" found his way into hockey fame quite accidentally. His older brother John was the second-string goaltender on the Eveleth High School team, but what he really wanted to be was a defenseman. The Fates were kind, for seniority prevailed: John moved up to the blue line, and brother Frank took over in the nets. Thus began one of the greatest goaltending careers the game has ever known.

After playing at Eveleth High, Brimsek tended goal for a short time at St. Cloud Teachers College. Brimsek next decided to give the pros a shot, and in 1935 he traveled to Baltimore for a tryout with the city's Eastern Amateur Hockey League franchise. He gambled everything he had, including his savings, on making the club; he failed.

Diem carpe; the day seized Brimsek. Hitchhiking back home to Minnesota, depressed and disappointed, Frank once again landed in hockey by accident. Running out of cash while in Pittsburgh, Frankie stopped off at the old Duquesne Arena to see if he could borrow money for food. Lady Luck shone brightly on the Minnesotan, for the Pittsburgh Yellow Jackets of the Eastern League needed a goaltender and Frankie got the job. For two years Brimsek tended goal for the club.

In the fall of 1937, famed Bruins general manager Art Ross signed Brimsek to a pro contract without ever seeing the young man play. Assigned to the Providence Reds, Boston's American League farm club, Frankie waited in the minors. In 1938, Brimsek, barely one year out of the amateurs, became Boston's goalie.

Brimsek's break into the majors was quite sensational. At the time, Boston's goaltender was none other than Tiny Thompson, known to the hockey world as "the goalie without a weakness." Thompson was the best in the business, a four-time Vezina Trophy winner. Prospects didn't look good for the American kid buried in the minors.

Appropriately, it was quite by accident that Brimsek got his first chance to play in a big-league game. Thompson developed an eye infection, and Ross sent for Brimsek. Understandably, Frank was nervous. It was tough enough to fill in for any goalie, but the pressure was colossal, considering the kid was being asked to fill the nets for the great Tiny Thompson.

Frank's jitters vanished once the game started. Then only 23 years old, Brimsek won his NHL debut by a score of 3-2. Three nights later, with the kid in the nets again, the Bruins beat the Detroit Red Wings.

Thompson recovered, and Frankie was sent back to Providence. But Ross had liked what he had seen and now had a dilemma on his hands. Popular with the fans, Thompson was great and had been Boston's solid rock for 10 years. At 33 he would have several more outstanding seasons.

Trading Thompson would not go over well with the multitude of Bruins supporters, especially if Tiny's replacement failed. Accordingly, Ross journeyed to Providence to take another look at Frankie, who turned in a couple of shutouts while Ross scouted him. On November 28, 1938, Tiny Thompson was dealt to the Red Wings for $15,000.

On December 1, 1938, in a game against the Montreal Canadiens, Frankie Brimsek entered the crease for the first time, not as Thompson's replacement, but as the Boston Bruin's regular goalie. Even though the game was played at the Montreal Forum, Brimsek was aware of the critical eyes watching his every move.

The night did little to dispel the naysayers. The Canadiens, who had won only once in their eight previous contests, beat Boston 2-0. In Detroit, the exiled Thompson beat Chicago 4-1. It left little reason to doubt that Ross had made a mistake.

Frankie Brimsek was down but not out. It took only the next seven games for him to become a hockey legend. Playing the next game against the Chicago Black Hawks, Brimsek recorded his first ever NHL shutout, as Boston beat Chicago by a 5-0 count.

However, the fans were not yet warming to him, and Frankie did little to improve his image. He had an idiosyncrasy of wearing red hockey pants instead of the team's (then) gold, brown, and white colors, and his footwork left much to be desired. Nevertheless, his glove was quick and his confidence enormous; the Boston fans would be in for a surprise.

Two nights later, the same teams met in Boston. In Frankie's first appearance before the hostile home crowd, he scored a 2-0 shutout.

Frankie's next game was against the New York Rangers. Although the Rangers belted him with 33 shots on goal, Brimsek stopped them all; Boston won 3-0. When the final buzzer sounded, he had 192 minutes and 40 seconds of scoreless goaltending. Thompson's modern record of 224 minutes and 47 seconds was in sight.

By then even the Boston fans were wildly supporting Brimsek. The Bruins were so confident of Frankie's ability that they often sent five men into enemy territory, leaving Brimsek to fend for himself. The next game was against Montreal at the Boston Garden. The Beantowners jumped to a 2-0 lead in the first period, while Frank held Montreal scoreless. The amazing string of scoreless puckstopping ran to 212 minutes and 40 seconds.

At the 12-minute mark of the second period, the tension in the Garden grew. At 12 minutes and eight seconds the arena went wild! In only his fifth game as the Bruins' regular goalie, the young phenom had erased Tiny Thompson's scoreless record. Alas, with less

than a minute to go in the second period, four Bruins were caught down ice; Herb Cain took a pass from George Brown and dumped the puck in the Boston goal. Brimsek's marvelous streak had ended at 231 minutes and 54 seconds. Boston went on to win the game 3-2.

Thanks largely to the talents of their young American goalie, the Bruins sat atop the standings. Brimsek next shut out Montreal 1-0. Next was Detroit and the first face-to-face meeting with Thompson. Both goalies played well, but Boston won 2-0. Frankie cut down the New York Americans next, by a score of 3-0. It was his third straight shutout and his sixth in seven games.

Brimsek went after his own record in the next game against the Rangers. He held New York scoreless during the first period. During the second session, Phil Watson put the puck in the net for the first goal on Brimsek in 220 minutes and 24 seconds of hockey. When Frankie reached down to retrieve the puck, the fans gave him a standing ovation. Frankie Brimsek had done the impossible — he had won over the Boston fans and made them forget Tiny Thompson.

Looking back on his inaugural season, Frankie said, "Tiny was such a great goaltender I had to be good or they would have chased me right out of Boston."

Brimsek finished the spectacular campaign with a brilliant 1.59 goals against average to go with 10 shutouts. He had given up only 70 goals in 44 games and was rightfully awarded both the Calder Trophy and the Vezina Trophy.

That year Brimsek also was voted to the First All-Star team. He repeated as the Vezina winner in 1942 and was the First All-Star team goalie again that year. Six times Brimsek was named to the Second All-Star team during his Boston career. With Mr. Zero in the nets, the Bruins won the Stanley Cup twice and three times finished first during the regular season.

After the Great War, Frankie gave the National Hockey League another try. This time he rode against happenstance's variable tides. He played four more seasons for the Bruins, but his comeback was a great disappointment. He had lost his edge. The Bees management kept waiting and hoping for the magic to come back, but their patience was in vain. He was never the same player.

Eventually, Boston traded Frankie to the dismal Chicago Black Hawks in 1949. Brimsek bombed terribly in the Windy City, and he retired after one season. After his career ended, he settled in Virginia, Minnesota, a small town only five miles from Eveleth. There he became an engineer for the Canadian National Railroad, guiding freight trains between the various cities in Canada. Truly, a sudden and ignominious end to one of hockey's greatest goaltending careers.

Brimsek left the game at the relatively young age of 34. He had been the best, and he had been unique: an American-born, American-trained goaltender who excelled at his profession. He played on Stanley Cup winners and for a time stood alone on hockey's mountaintop as the finest at his profession.

There was never one before, and there will never be one again. Frank Brimsek was the original, and after him they threw away the mold. One would be hard pressed to find an American-born player who made a more emphatic impact upon the sport. Were it not for World War II, Brimsek might well have emerged as the greatest exponent of goaltending we have ever known. It was in some ways fitting that Frankie Brimsek's career ended just as it had begun — with circumstances entirely out of his control, with the day seizing him.

CHUCK RAYNER (1940-53)

He left his net and charged down the ice. His opponents were so surprised that they simply stopped in their tracks. Rayner skated within a few feet of the goal and shot. The opposing goaltender was dumbfounded and lunged to make the save, but the puck sailed right into the net.

You had to see Charlie Rayner in action to believe him.

When he did the splits — the 1940s version of the butterfly — it often seemed as if Rayner's left skate extended to the left boards and his right skate extended to the right boards.

Exaggeration notwithstanding, Rayner was big in physique, bigger in talent, and not bad at innovation to boot.

Although Jacques Plante justifiably gained renown as a wandering goalie, more than a decade earlier Rayner actually was brought up to his blue line on New York Rangers power plays.

He also indulged in an interesting experiment in which he shared goaltending with partner Sugar Jim Henry as part of the National Hockey League's first one-two netminding combination. But in this case, Rayner and Henry moved in and out of the net as part of line changes. Incredible but true.

Like an old romantic tune, the one phrase that best sums up Rayner's career is "To think what might have been." It is mind-boggling to imagine what dizzying heights Chuck Rayner might have reached had he enjoyed the luxury of playing for a genuinely powerful hockey team. But such was not "Bonnie Prince Charlie's" fate. The bushy-browed goaltender made his debut with the subterranean New York (Brooklyn) Americans and finished his valorous puckblocking career with a weak, if not pathetic, New York Rangers aggregation.

In between he demonstrated that he was either the very best or certainly among the top three goalies in the world, despite the fact that he never had a first-place team or a Stanley Cup championship to show for his efforts. Nobly, his hard-fought reputation spoke for itself.

Rayner made a permanent impression on the NHL and earned his way into the Hockey Hall of Fame. Beyond the pale that separated the Rangers from the league's elite, Rayner was also an innovator. He was among the very first to participate in what was then a revolutionary two-goalie experiment, sharing time with his longtime sidekick and pal, James (Sugar Jim) Henry.

Incredibly, he was and remains the only goaltender ever to have scored a goal by *skating* the length of the rink in an organized hockey game (although not in the NHL). Such a feat makes Martin Brodeur, et al, look like mincemeat. Additionally, Rayner's goal was the first of its kind, skating or otherwise.

Playing for the All-Star Royal Canadian Army team during World War II, Chuck was guarding the twine when a 10-man scramble occurred behind his net. He saw the puck

squirt free, with no one between him and the frozen disc. The temptation was too much for him to resist.

He left his net and charged down the ice. His opponents were so surprised that they simply stopped in their tracks. Rayner skated within a few feet of the goal and shot. The opposing goaltender was dumbfounded and lunged to make the save, but the puck sailed right into the net.

The 1949-50 season was in many ways the high point of Rayner's career, as he single handedly led the Rangers to the Stanley Cup finals a la John Davidson, circa 1979. It is a measure of the man's ability that he won the Hart Trophy — to that point the second goaltender in history to do so — as the NHL's most valuable player for the 1949-50 campaign.

Playing for a mediocre Ranger team that never finished higher than fourth, Bonnie Prince Charlie led the Rangers to an upset win over the Canadiens in the 1950 playoffs. They went on to the final round against the Detroit Red Wings. Without setting foot on home ice, they surprised the entire league with a strong and gutsy bid, only to lose the seventh game in dramatic fashion — in an electrifying, double-overtime affair.

When he won the Hart Trophy that season, it was one of the most popular announcements in the annals of the game, as he was one of the nicest guys in the sport. Oddly enough, that same year he finished fourth in the race for the Vezina Trophy.

However, his remarkable performance in the 1950 playoffs compensated for the oversight. He was nearly unstoppable during the championship round, as he stopped shot after seemingly netting-bound shot. Although the Rangers' quest for the Stanley Cup was stopped, the results of the voting for the Hart Trophy were a credit to the sportsmanship of hockey when the tall goaltender's name was announced.

Rayner received 36 out of a possible 54 points for a 13-point lead over Ted Kennedy of the Toronto Maple Leafs. The great Maurice Richard of the Montreal Canadiens finished third in the balloting with 18 points.

Claude Earl Rayner was born in the small town of Sutherland, Saskatchewan, on August 11, 1920. Like all of the youngsters of that locale, he went down to the local skating rinks to play the national pastime. Chuck always wanted to be a goaltender. When Chuck was 16 years old, he played goal for the Saskatoon Wesleys, leading his team to the Junior playoffs against the Winnipeg Monarchs. Later in the 1936 season, he went into the goal for the Kenora Thistles.

At the end of the 1939-40 season, Chuck progressed to the New York Americans' farm club, the Springfield Indians. Rayner had only played seven games for the Indians when the big team's starting goaltender, Earl Robertson, suffered a head injury, leaving open a berth in the nets.

Rayner was called up to take over Robertson's place, and so, in 1940, the young man from Sutherland was playing in the NHL at the fledgling age of 20.

Chuck played in the goal for the Americans throughout the 1942 season. He then went home and joined the Royal Canadian Armed Forces. Unlike some contemporaries like Frank Brimsek, the war did not stagnate his progress. Discharged from the service in 1945, Chuck Rayner returned to hockey to discover that the Americans had disbanded and that all members of the team were to be part of a raffle for the other NHL teams.

Rayner's name was pulled out by Lester Patrick of the New York Rangers and thus began one of the oddest stories in sport. Patrick had already hired a goalie, Sugar Jim Henry. Ultimately, Chuck won the Ranger goalkeeping job permanently.

He made the Second Team All-Stars three times, in 1948-49, 1949-50, and 1950-51. In his eight seasons with the New York Rangers, he played in 424 games and spun 24 shutouts. He added one more in the playoffs.

Injuries forced Rayner to retire after the 1952-53 season. He had damaged the cartilage in his knee. An operation temporarily held the knee together, but again, the knee weakened to the point where he felt he couldn't do the job any longer.

After his retirement as a player, Chuck returned to western Canada where he coached the Nelson Leafs. After two years there, he went to Alberta and coached the Edmonton Flyers. He then did some work for the Rangers before moving on to employment with the Detroit Red Wings organization and his friend Sid Abel.

By the mid-'60s, he had been coaching nine years, but he didn't enjoy it. Chuck didn't like having to tell a kid that he was traded. Bonnie Prince Charlie left the sport completely, and by 1979, he had been away from hockey for almost 10 years.

Chuck was a courageous man who often played black and blue. He was the kind of man who played when a lesser athlete would have sat out. To say it was unfortunate that such a nice guy with his capabilities never played on a Stanley Cup winner is an understatement. Even still, no one will ever forget the heroics Rayner accomplished during the exciting 1950 playoffs with the Cinderella Rangers. He is well deserving of his spot among hockey's greatest goalies.

GERRY CHEEVERS (1961-80)

"He was one of the all-time greats when it came to money games."
—Phil Esposito

He was Billy Smith before the Islanders wild man came along. Among the long list of feisty big-league goalies, Gerry Cheevers ranks right up there with such fist-flailing stoppers as Harry Lumley, Legs Frazier, and Ron Hextall.

Not that it was a problem for the man called Cheesey, but he did play for a team whose theme was go-go-go into the opposition end and let defense take the hind post.

Bobby Orr's Big Bad Bruins were the perfect match for Cheevers' Big Bad Behavior.

But it should never be forgotten that behind Cheevers' bombast was a superbly competitive athlete.

It was almost impossible to define Gerry Cheevers' style because there really was none. Occasionally flopping, sometimes diving, and often trying to punch an oncoming forward in the mouth, Cheevers usually found a way to stop the puck and acquired a couple of Stanley Cup titles to prove it.

Like the Islanders' Smith, at his best Cheevers represented the combative goalie of the 1970s and 1980s. He was as innovative as he was pugnacious and is best remembered for introducing painted scars on his white, plastic facemask to indicate where he might have required stitches had the puck actually ripped into his skin instead of the face covering.

On a Bruins squad dominated by the likes of Orr and Phil Esposito, Cheevers was almost an afterthought to the Boston media but hardly to opponents. His above-average goaltending not only spanned thirteen NHL years but also graced the World Hockey Association to which Cheevers emigrated in 1972. By that time Gerry had clearly established himself as one of the most arresting characters in pro hockey.

An interesting blend of healthy truculence, daring inventiveness, superior intelligence, and amazing agility — even when he appeared overweight in his declining years — made Cheevers unusual and placed him several cuts (no pun intended) above most of his goaltending peers.

Born on December 7, 1940, in St. Catherines, Ontario, Gerald Michael Cheevers seemed destined for a career with the Toronto Maple Leafs, which owned his rights during the early 1960s. He was obtained by the Bruins in 1965 and, after a few trips to the minors, made it to stay in the NHL in 1967. His arrival coincided with Boston's escalation to the top of the league.

Pugnacious almost to a fault, Cheevers more than anything proved himself a winner. He shared the goaltending with Eddie Johnston on the Beantown Bruins' last two Stanley Cup championship teams in 1970 and 1972. Not surprisingly, fans were soon hanging banners over the Boston Garden balcony: WE'RE BELIEVERS IN GERRY CHEEVERS.

However, the following season he left Boston for the Cleveland Crusaders of the World Hockey Association. He was voted the league's best goaltender that year and remained in Ohio until 1976. He was the number one goalie for Team Canada in 1974, during the series against the Soviet All-Stars, and was durable enough to span two decades as a professional. In America's bicentennial year, Cheevers returned to the Hub sextet. It was no coincidence that Cheever's return marked another upturn in the Bruins' fortunes. His habit of pursuing and stickhandling the puck delighted Boston Garden fans, and he frequently displayed the form that had endeared him to the fans several years earlier.

Few could match Cheevers' competitive zeal. His policy was strict and honest: When you lose it's like being shot on the battlefield, so don't go shaking hands with the enemy for that! Such was the case in 1971 when goalie Ken Dryden and the Montreal Canadiens upset his Bruins. At game's end the teams lined up for the traditional handshaking ceremonies, but Cheevers had already made a quick exit to his dressing room.

"I wanted to tell Dryden when it was all over that he'd done a big, big job, but I didn't," said Cheevers. "When the teams met in a straggly line at center and shook hands, I wasn't among those present. I've never congratulated a guy for beating me. I sure as hell didn't feel like gripping Mahovlich's paw, and Harper's, and Lemaire's. They put lumps on me and took my money. Why should I applaud them?"

Later, Cheevers called over Jacques Beauchamp, a Montreal journalist who was heading back to the plane that would carry the victorious Canadiens — and Dryden — back to Montreal. "Jacques," he said, "when you get on the plane, tell that giraffe (Dryden) he had one hell of a series. Tell him congratulations for me, Jacques."

Still, congratulations had enveloped Cheevers many times during a career that included 418 regular season National Hockey League games and 88 playoff matches. His goals against average was 2.89 for the regular campaigns and 2.69 for the playoffs.

In a sense, the figures were deceptive because Gerry goaled for a Bruins club that invariably accented offense — Phil Esposito, Bobby Orr, Ken Hodge were the big guns — and ignored defense. Which meant that Cheevers was pretty much on his own.

Nicknamed "Cheesey," Cheevers set an NHL record during the 1971-72 season when he played goal through 32 unbeaten games. "He was one of the all-time greats when it came to money games," said his longtime teammate, Phil Esposito.

Gerry remained a Bruins goalie until his retirement after the 1979-80 campaign, when he was named the Bruins coach. The transition from the nets to the bench was not an easy one. "It was," said Cheevers, "a tremendous learning experience."

Bruins general manager Harry Sinden nevertheless expressed confidence in Cheevers. "He acquired an excellent grasp of the coaching technique," said Sinden, who retained Gerry as head coach through 1985, in which the Bruins displayed a marked improvement. With Cheevers behind the bench the Bruins remained the class of the Adams Division, finishing first in the 1982-83 and 1983-84 seasons.

However, as one press box critic noted, Cheevers the coach was always at a disadvantage, "because he didn't have Gerry Cheevers in the net!"

ROY WORTERS (1926-37)

"When Roy quit the game, few players or fans remained untouched by his tremendous contribution to the game."

— *Ron McAllister*

When the National Hockey League expanded for the first time into the United States, it targeted New York City as the site which it most wanted to exploit for new fans.

To do so, the Big Apple's original team, the Americans, had to offer a number of star attractions, especially a goalie.

It was the good fortune of NHL ownership that the Americans first puckstopper of repute not only was an anomaly but also a goaltender with Hall of Famer written all over him. Ironically, Roy Worters looked like the antithesis of the perfect puckstopper. Even in the mid-1920s, hockey scouts preferred large goaltenders who could fill as much of the six-feet-wide by four-feet-high entrance to the net. Some of the greatest netminders, from Georges Vezina to Ken Dryden, were big men who filled much of the air space leading to the coarse twine. All of which helps explain why Roy Worters was such a marvel at his profession.

Worters measured only five feet three inches and weighed 130 pounds, yet his stature, compared to other notables who guarded the crease, remains immense to this day. The fact that he generally played for inferior clubs, such as the New York Americans, only adds to his glitter.

His size notwithstanding, Roy was the Hart Trophy winner in 1929 as the National Hockey League's most valuable player, the Vezina Trophy winner in 1931, and twice voted to the Second All-Star team (1932, 1934).

Worters is best remembered for his heroic performances with the Americans, but he actually broke into the majors as a member of the Pittsburgh Pirates, which joined the NHL in the fall of 1925. After a salary dispute with the Bucs, Worters was traded to the Amerks for the then unheard of sum of $25,000 *plus* two players.

At first the deal was the bane of Worters' hockey life. Hard-nosed galleryites at Madison Square Garden taunted him with catcalls. "So, you're worth 25 grand, eh? Worters, you're not worth twenty-five cents!"

Initially, Worters was distressed by the catcalls. He had inevitably become known as "Shrimp" to the Garden faithful. But he gradually pulled his game together and captured the imagination of these very same naysayers, and after one match, the "Shrimp" even received a standing ovation.

Shortly thereafter Worters had the distinction of losing a game to the Montreal Canadiens *without a goal being scored against him*. It was a 0-0 tie late in the match when the Habs' Howie Morenz broke into the clear for a shot against Worters. Roy stopped the blistering drive, deflecting it into the corner. But when Morenz unleashed his shot, Bullet Joe Simpson of the Americans had tossed his stick at the puck. In those days the stick-throwing foul was punishable with an automatic goal. Montreal won the game 1-0.

"Although Roy never saw the Stanley Cup awarded to his team," said Ron

McAllister, "he won every individual honor that a goalkeeper could possibly earn, and more. The thought of what he might have achieved with a winning team before him makes him a man of mystery in the record books."

Worters could have gained entrance into the Hockey Hall of Fame on guts alone. He suffered 216 stitches *in his face alone* and continued playing despite the pain of cracked ribs, a broken kneecap, three broken toes, and countless lesser injuries, including the loss of eight teeth.

He was born on October 19, 1900, in Toronto, Ontario, the son of a trolley car motorman. When he was old enough to carry a load, Roy began delivering milk for his uncle's dairy. In return Roy received free milk. "The future goalkeeper knew the lesson of work before he learned the meaning of life," said a friend.

Roy began his hockey career as a forward and remained up front until he was 17. At that point, his team, the goaltending-weak Toronto Riverdales, was searching for someone to tend the twine. Roy volunteered, and the Riverdales suddenly began winning games. Eventually, he moved up the Junior ranks to the Toronto Canoe Club.

The Canoe Club, with Worters performing uncanny feats in goal, marched to the Memorial Cup, the symbol of Junior hockey supremacy in Canada. One of Roy's most formidable opponents was a young whiz named Howie Morenz, who later would ripen as a superstar with the Montreal Canadiens. "Morenz," remarked Worters, "is some wild wind, that number 7 of Canadiens. To me, he's just a blur — 77777!"

To a man, Worters was like a wall in front of the uprights, despite his minuscule frame. Over a span of 488 games, Worters' goals allowed average was 2.36; uncanny considering the feeble defense in front of him.

Worters also was an innovator. He was the first netminder to direct rebounds into the corners of the rink with the back of his gloves and, needless to say, demonstrated that a smallish goalie could be as good as a big man with the pads.

At the age of 37, he was still blocking shots for the Americans when he suffered a hernia and was hospitalized. Red Dutton, who had become manager of the team, believed him capable of a comeback and offered Worters a sizeable sum to return to the ice. Alas, the goalie declined and returned to his native Toronto to begin his life after hockey.

"When Roy quit the game," said McAllister, "few players or fans remained untouched by his tremendous contribution to the game."

A foe who had been frustrated by Worters for several seasons said later: "For years after Roy left the game, it was hard to realize that he had been gone from the NHL for good."

He stayed close to the sport he loved so much and worked with the NHL Oldtimers Association as well as local charities. He was inducted into the Hockey Hall of Fame in 1969, 12 years after he had died of throat cancer. He was a David among Goliaths.

ROGER CROZIER (1963-77)

"I like everything about hockey: the traveling, the friends I've met, the interviews. Everything but the games. They're pure torture."

The National Hockey League has been blessed with top-flight little goalies ever since Roy (Shrimp) Worters toiled for the New York Americans in the mid-1920s. One of the best of all-time was Roger Crozier who broke in with the Detroit Red Wings during the six-team NHL when every club was well fixed between the pipes. Roger followed a great line of Detroit goaltenders, including the likes of Johnny Mowers, Harry Lumley, and Terry Sawchuk. As the numbers indicate, he was more than capable of continuing the tradition.

After a brief stint as a big-leaguer in the 1963-64 season, Crozier arrived to stay in the NHL the following season as a 22-year-old. "The Dodger," as he became known, played extremely well and won the Calder Trophy as the best newcomer in the league. Detroit finished first that year with Crozier in the nets.

The mid-1960s was a time when the "butterfly" technique was being introduced and popularized by Chicago Blackhawks Hall of Famer Glenn Hall. At the time, the art of goaltending was undergoing a major metamorphosis, and Crozier was a virtual clone of Hall, if not even more acrobatic.

While he lacked Hall's size, Crozier matched Glenn — and just about any other net-minder — when it came to heart. Afflicted with chronic pancreatitis, Crozier often performed in the nets while his body was racked with pain. Despite this handicap, his small size, and his nervous demeanor, he survived 14 seasons in the NHL. Unfortunately for Roger, he played most of his career on mediocre teams, namely the declining Detroit Red Wings and later the expansion Buffalo Sabres and Washington Capitals.

A compulsive worrier, Crozier developed an ulcer at age 17. Many times he could not eat before a game or afterward. Irrespective of the many troubles that faced Roger — the illness, the nerves, or the mediocre clubs that he played on — he was an outstanding goalie during his long career.

He was the goalie for the First All-Star team in 1965, an honor he richly deserved. In the 1966 Stanley Cup finals, Crozier won the Conn Smythe Trophy as the MVP for his team in the playoffs, despite the fact that the Wings blew a two-games-to-none lead, losing to the Montreal Canadiens.

When Roger played in the minors, critics were dubious about Crozier's durability because of his size (5-8), and they doubted that his sprawling style could succeed in the NHL. After spending the 1963-64 season with Pittsburgh, Crozier was summoned to the big club in the fall of 1964. Experts be damned: Detroit coach Sid Abel had faith in him, and he repaid with airtight performances.

During the 1966 championship round, Crozier "stole" Games One and Two at The Forum. Jacques Laperriere, the fine Canadiens defenseman, remembered it like this: "We were just as good (as Detroit), maybe better. What won those first two games for them was their goalie, Roger Crozier. He was making all the saves, and it looked like we could never get the puck past him."

Montreal rebounded to tie the series at Detroit and then took the fifth game in Montreal. Leading 3 games to 2 in the series, the Habs went back to Detroit to try and wrap it up.

The Canadiens got started when Jean Beliveau scored a goal in the first period. In the second, Montreal's Leon Rochefort put the puck past Roger, and Norm Ullman scored for Detroit to make it 2-1. Floyd Smith tied it in the third period, and the game went into overtime.

With two minutes gone in the extra session, a rush was mounted toward the Detroit goal, with Henri Richard heading for the slot. Just as the "Pocket Rocket" tried to get his stick on the puck, Detroit defenseman Gary Bergman knocked him to the ice.

Laperriere said, "Richard fell to the ice on his stomach, and I remember him sliding I don't know how many feet toward the goal. The puck was against his arm or his body, and Crozier was hugging the post as Henri slid toward him. It looked like he had it covered. But somehow the puck slid with Richard, and as he went past the post, the puck slid past Crozier — there couldn't have been more than four inches of opening — and across the goal line. There it stopped."

An unusual ending to say the least, but nonetheless the Canadiens were hockey's champions. The most valuable player? Roger Crozier, whose play had been spectacular as he held off the Chicago Blackhawks in Round One and who played so well against Montreal.

Roger Allan Crozier was born March 16, 1942, in Bracebridge, Ontario. Born to a family of 14 children, Roger began playing goal at six years of age. When he was 14, he was still in the nets and by that time was playing goal on an intermediate team with men twice his age. It was then that Bob Wilson, the scout who discovered Bobby Hull, spotted Roger. The only difference was that Wilson immediately knew Hull would be a star. Conversely, he figured Crozier was too small to ever make it to the National Hockey League. But the Blackhawks were in desperate need of a goalie for their Junior team in St. Catherines, so Wilson signed Crozier.

Roger got his ulcer when he was 17 while manning the crease for St. Catherines, and he was never again 100 percent healthy. The years of pro hockey only made him more nervous and neurotic. However, nerves were not his only ailment. One morning after the 1964-65 season, he woke up with a massive pain in his stomach. He was rushed to the hospital where doctors diagnosed his condition as pancreatitis. The infection of the pancreas gave him only a 50-50 chance for survival. For four days Roger hovered near death as he was treated with drugs and fed intravenously. Ultimately, he recovered, but when he reported to training camp for the 1965-66 season, his weight had dropped 20 pounds and his skin coloring had a yellowish hue.

After excelling at St. Catherines, Crozier moved up to St. Louis of the Central Pro League for the 1962-63 season. "I never even thought about the NHL then," he said later.

Little did Crozier know what was in his hockey future. The antics of tempestuous defenseman Howie Young had been grating on the Detroit Red Wings' high command. They finally decided to unload him — for any offer. They sent Young to Chicago of the American Hockey League in exchange for Crozier and a minor-league defenseman. Roger

then spent the 1963-64 season playing for Pittsburgh and did such a good job that Abel decided he belonged in the NHL.

As a big-league rookie, Crozier was remarkably durable. He was the only goaltender in the NHL to play all of his team's games, appearing in 70. He had an average of 2.42 goals per game and led the NHL in shutouts that year with six. Detroit finished in first place, thanks in part to the excellent goaltending of Crozier. He made the First All-Star team and won the Calder Trophy as rookie of the year. He lost the battle for the Vezina Trophy on the final day of the season to the Toronto duo of Terry Sawchuk and Johnny Bower.

The young Red Wing went home that year with $9,000 worth of bonus money and the proof that he belonged in the NHL. Although his self-confidence should have been growing, Roger worried more than ever. "The only time I really forget about my problems is after a game when we've won," Roger said. "But by the next morning I'll be worrying again."

Traded to Buffalo in 1970, Roger played several injury-plagued seasons with the Sabres. He had five pancreas attacks that hospitalized him for over nine months. When Crozier returned to Buffalo after almost a year of illness, he was scheduled to start against Toronto. During the warmups, he was hit on the right side of his neck, just above the unprotected collarbone by a drive from defenseman Jerry Korab. Roger was knocked unconscious by the powerful blow.

When Roger returned to action he still was not in the best of health. On a bad day he felt weak and nauseous. And even on the good days he wasn't feeling well. "I never feel 100 percent, and I never will again; I just have to accept it," he concluded.

Despite all the hardship, Crozier left an indelible imprint on the NHL. For one thing, he was one of the first modern goalies — having perfected the butterfly style. He was a stylist and an interesting goalie to watch. "I like everything about hockey: the traveling, the friends I've met, the interviews. Everything but the games. They're pure torture," he once said.

In June 1970, Crozier was traded from Detroit to Buffalo for Tom Webster. He remained with the Sabres through the 1975-76 season. Playing under Punch Imlack in Buffalo, Crozier had some of his best years. During the 1974-75 playoffs — alternating with Gerry Desjardins — Crozier helped the Sabres to the Stanley Cup final. He finished the playoffs with a 2.88 goals against average.

In 1977, he was sold to Washington by Buffalo and played three games for the Capitals. His 1.17 goals against average was impressive, but his health wasn't. He retired but remained with the Capitals' organization as the assistant general manager until he was relieved of his duties in a club shake-up.

Crozier finished his career with a respectable goals against average of 3.04 and had 30 lifetime shutouts. Despite his recurring illness, Roger played in 518 pro games.

Had he not been besieged by health problems through out his career, there is no question that Crozier would have ranked with the best goaltenders of all time. As it was, he was one of the best of his era.

ALEX CONNELL (1924-37)

"Alex was the only hockey player to cause the police riot squad to be called out in New York City."

—*Bill Roche*

For a goaltender to survive more than a decade in the pre-World War II maskless era, he would have to be an exceptional talent as well as a doughty warrior. Alex Connell, whose career spanned 1924-37, was just such a performer.

He earned his epaulets first with the Ottawa Senators and later confirmed his stature as a premier puckstopper with Detroit (Falcons) and Montreal (Maroons), respectively. During that time the NHL was graced with such notable Hall of Famers as Georges Vezina, Roy Worters, Charlie Gardiner, and Davie Kerr.

Connell was born on February 8, 1902, in Ottawa, Ontario. Canada's capital city but seemed destined for a career as either a lacrosse or baseball player. Instead, he turned to professional hockey with the Senators in 1924 and played for Ottawa until 1932 when he had a brief fling in the Motor City. It was during his stint with the Falcons that Connell became famous for a more dubious reason. "Alex," said Bill Roche, "was the only hockey player to cause the police riot squad to be called out in New York City."

The episode took place in 1932 at the old Madison Square Garden on Eighth Avenue and Fiftieth Street when the New York Americans were hosting Detroit in a game that would decide whether or not the Amerks would go into the playoffs later that spring. At the time, the New York club was owned by the infamous Bill Dwyer, reputed mob boss and undisputed King of the Bootleggers in the Empire state and several others.

The game was tied at the end of regulation time, 1-1, and the two teams went into a 10-minute overtime period. With about five minutes left in the period, Detroit received a penalty, giving the Amerks the much-needed advantage in manpower. New York players realized it was their opportunity to take the initiative and win the game. With no recourse but victory, it was a must situation.

The red-, white-, and blue-clad Americans bore down and administered intense pressure on the Falcons. Red Dutton, then a battling defenseman for New York, took a blistering shot that, according to the goal judge, eluded Connell and ricocheted in and — just as quickly — out of the net. The red light went on, and the Amerks celebrated their "win." But trouble was brewing: The referee, George Mallinson, disallowed the goal. He claimed he had a perfect view of the play and believed the puck never went in. Connell agreed.

During the melee that ensued, the goal judge berated the shocked goaltender with a string of the vilest profanities he had ever heard. Alex was not about to stand for that kind of abuse. He skated around back of the net and, taking advantage of the man's nose which was sticking through the mesh, bopped the harasser directly and resoundingly on his protruding proboscis. This sent the surprised and infuriated goal judge reeling in his own blood and started a panic among the security force at the Garden who knew the man to be a "high official in Billy Dwyer's mob."

Alex Connell had unknowingly put his own life in grave danger with one well-placed, ill-timed punch. But Connell was more concerned with the game, and after play resumed (the goal was nullified), he held the New Yorkers scoreless, and the duel ended in a 1-1 deadlock.

As Alex left the ice he noticed for the first time that there were policemen lining the walkway. Everywhere he looked he saw the boys in blue in great force blocking the spectators from approaching the players. When he got into the dressing room and began peeling off his sweaty uniform, two plainclothes detectives walked up, identified themselves to him, and then stood on either side of him with their guns drawn. It was explained to him that the man he had punched out was Dwyer's second-in-command and that there might be some serious ramifications if proper precautions were not taken.

Connell undressed quickly and was shuffled into a waiting taxi. Along with a police escort he was driven to the hotel where the Falcons were staying. Policemen combed the lobby for shady characters before bringing in the befuddled Alex Connell. He was then given strict instructions not to leave his room for the remainder of the evening.

Connell recalls how the rest of the evening went: "An old friend was visiting with me that night, and after we had talked about the strange goings-on, we decided to leave the hotel to get some sandwiches before I went to bed.

"We went out the front door and had only walked about 10 feet when I remembered the cop's warning. Then I noticed there were some people standing around us, and one big, mean-looking guy looked right at me and came toward us. We ducked into a diner and seated ourselves at separate counters. The large man came in and ordered me to go over to him for questioning. I paid no attention to him, so he repeated his order, adding that if I knew what was good for me I'd do what I was told.

"Then I walked over to him. He demanded, 'Aren't you Alex Connell, goalkeeper with the Detroit Falcons?' I replied that I not only did not know who Alex Connell was, but that I'd never heard of any Detroit Falcons.

"After a couple of minutes of him repeating the question and me repeating my answer, he apologized for bothering me and left."

When the cops heard about the incident from the hotel night manager, they decided to stand guard outside Connell's room for the rest of the night.

The next day Connell learned that his quick thinking and fast talking had probably saved him from a one-way "ride" with the gunslinging hoodlums.

Connell finished his career in 1937 with the Montreal Maroons. In those 13 years, he fashioned a career-record 1.99 goals against average; astonishing under any circumstances. Playing for Ottawa in 1927-28, he set a league record of *six consecutive shutouts*. Like his Ottawa neighbor, Clint Benedict, he played on Stanley Cup-winning teams in two different cities — for the Ottawa Senators and the Montreal Maroons.

After helping the Senators win the Stanley Cup in 1927, he amassed 15 shutouts the following seasons to go along with a goals against average of 1.30. In that extraordinary year Connell permitted but 57 goals in 44 games. His record-breaking shutout run spanned 446 minutes and 9 seconds.

Even at the age of 36 in his final season, Connell produced a nifty 2.37 goals against average. After the 1936 campaign he retired. Alex Connell died on May 10, 1958 at the age of fifty-six.

GUMP WORSLEY (1952-74)

"I used to feel like a duck in a shooting gallery."

It was hard to tell which he did better; stop pucks or tell jokes.

Even with the worst of teams — the 1952-53 New York Rangers — he excelled both in the nets and with his wit.

Playing for the decrepit Broadway Blueshirts, Worsley was an instant star and winner of the Calder Trophy. When a magazine writer interviewed him about his profession, Worsley was asked which National Hockey League team gave him the most trouble.

With the rapidity of a kick save, Worsley blurted, "The Rangers!"

A man who goaled to his own drummer, Worsley would feud with any coach who happened to get in his way, especially if that coach was named Phil Watson.

When Watson coached the Rangers, he accused Worsley of having a "beer-barrel belly."

"It shows you how much that guy knows," barked Gump. "I don't drink beer — only Johnny Walker Red."

In his later years, he looked more like a beer salesman who enjoyed tasting his product than a hockey goaltender. His potbelly made it seem like a herculean task for him to even wave at, let alone nab, the swiftly flying rubber disc. His lack of height gave one the impression that he never could see the shooters, what with the bigger men blocking his view like mammoth offensive linemen in front of a stumpy quarterback. Nevertheless, Gump Worsley proved to be one of the best at his trade, not to mention one of the most courageous and unorthodox as well.

Lorne Worsley was born May 14, 1929, in Montreal. As a kid, Worsley liked Davey Kerr, the hero of the Rangers' 1940 Stanley Cup championship team. He got his first break after winning a tryout with the Verdun Cyclones, a Junior team from a Montreal suburb, while playing for a second commercial-league club.

In 1949 he was invited to the Rangers' training camp and was assigned to their farm team, the New York Rovers of the old Eastern League. He played well and drank well, too. "We ran from bar to bar in those days," Worsley confessed, "and you know how many bars there are in New York. About 10,000. After most games we'd go out drinking and stay out until the joints closed at four in the morning. We were always there for the last call."

Despite the booze, Worsley continued the upward climb: from the Rovers to the New Haven Ramblers of the American League, with stopovers at St. Paul and Saskatoon before reaching the big club on Broadway.

Worsley won the rookie of the year prize in 1953, but the Rangers had bought Johnny Bower, a highly regarded minor-leaguer, and installed him in net the following season ahead of Gump. Worsley hit the minors but returned to stay the following year and remained a New Yorker until he was dealt to the Canadiens. After a squabble with the Habs in 1970, he was picked up by the Minnesota North Stars and concluded his career in April 1974.

Nicknamed Gump because, as a kid, he resembled the cartoon character Andy Gump, Worsley played his 860th regular-season NHL game against the Philadelphia Flyers on April 2, 1974. The final goal — he allowed 2,432 in his NHL career — was scored by Dave Schultz, who was born the year Worsley played his first pro game in 1949.

"That made me feel old," said Worsley. "Too old to consider another comeback."

There have been few first-rate netminders more durable than Worsley. He turned pro in 1952 when the National Hockey League embraced but six teams and retired when there were more than twice that number. He was a goalie on four Stanley Cup-winning Montreal Canadiens sextets but is best known for his escapades as a member of the Rangers between 1952 and 1963.

The New Yorkers often seemed mired in a subterranean section of the NHL, yet Worsley always seemed to be performing like Horatio at the bridge. New York fans appreciated the roly-poly goalie, but his coach, the volatile Phil Watson, was less enthused. Watson constantly singled out Worsley for criticism in one form or another. Despite the skipper's harangues, Worsley played splendid goal for the Rangers in the late 1950s, but then the team began to decline.

In his autobiography, *They Call Me Gump*, Worsley admitted that he turned to the bottle to ease the anguish. "I was using the bottle to chase all of those bad games and bad goals. I used to feel like a duck in a shooting gallery."

Worsley's Manhattan miseries ended on June 4, 1963, when he was traded to the Montreal Canadiens. As Gump succinctly put it, "That was the day I got out of the Ranger jailhouse."

Playing for the Canadiens was not exactly utopia for Worsley at first, but there was no question he would be an asset. He proved it in the spring of 1965 during the Stanley Cup finals versus the Chicago Black Hawks.

After playing the first two games of the series, Gump tore a thigh muscle in Game Three and had to be replaced. The series went down to a seventh and deciding game, with the teams knotted at three games apiece. Gump had been taking injections for his injury and was improving but doubted that he would play in the seventh match.

Prior to the game Worsley was sitting in The Forum lounge when Larry Aubout, the Canadiens' trainer, walked in and told him that he *was* playing. "I glanced at my wife, Doreen, as she ordered a rye and ginger ale — for herself. I could have used one too, but instead I headed for our dressing room to get ready for the game. Was I nervous? Here I'd been playing pro hockey for 15 years and finally was getting the big opportunity. This was it. The final game for the Stanley Cup championship. You bet your ass I was nervous."

Almost immediately after the opening face-off, Chicago's Camille Henry skated in alone on the Gumper. "My legs were knocking," Worsley admitted. But he made the save and went on to blank the Hawks 4-0.

"Nothing," said Worsley, "has ever matched that thrill. The first Cup victory is always the biggest moment in a hockey player's life. I was the luckiest guy in the world." And he did it with a *torn muscle in his leg*!

If that didn't show enough about his courage, then nothing will say more about the man's heart than the fact that he was the very last quality goaltender to play between the pipes without a protective facemask. His Yogi Berraesque physique belied a tremendous ability that led to his winning the Calder Trophy as rookie of the year in 1953 and the Vezina Trophy as top goaltender in 1966 and 1968 (the latter of which was shared with Charlie Hodge).

After retiring, Gump became a scout for the Minnesota North Stars, a position he retained through the mid-1980s. In September 1980, Worsley's career reached its zenith when he was formally inducted into the Hockey Hall of Fame.

Never did the Gump look like much, but he did know how to stop the puck. His longevity and championship rings attest to the fact that he did his job better than most. For this he merits inclusion with hockey's greatest goaltenders.

BERNIE PARENT (1965-79)

"I watched Jacques Plante play and watched everything he did, how he handled himself on shots. Whatever he was doing, I tried to do."

Bernie Parent was the Dominik Hasek of his day. As goaltender for two Stanley Cup-winning Philadelphia Flyers teams in 1974 and 1975, the French-Canadian stopper carried a club that had virtually no stars and relatively little scoring.

As in Hasek's case, there were so many times when Parent single-handedly won games for the Broad Street Bullies that it seemed implausible that he could compete in 73 out of his club's 78 regular season games in 1973-74. But he did and came out of it with a stingy 1.89 goals against average.

Not surprisingly, Parent won the Conn Smythe Trophy as the playoffs' MVP when Philly won each of its Stanley Cups. "Bernie," said Flyers captain Bobby Clarke, "is the most valuable player in all of hockey."

Parent's evolution as a superlative goaltender hardly came as a surprise. When he burst into the National Hockey League as a Boston Bruins rookie in 1965-66, Bernie was hailed as a future phenom. When expansion came in 1967, Parent was drafted by the Flyers and made the Bruins sorry they had left him unprotected.

A stand-up goalie in the tradition of Jacques Plante and Terry Sawchuk, Parent gave the brand-new expansion team instant respectability. Philadelphia won the divisional title in its first season, while Bernie excelled with a 2.48 goals against average.

At the time, the Flyers also employed another young netminder named Doug Favell, who also showed considerable promise. In the middle of the 1970-71 season, the Flyers took a major gamble, trading Parent to Toronto as part of a blockbuster deal.

For Bernie it was a fortuitous move. His companion goalie in Toronto was the legendary Plante, who took Parent under his wing and taught him elements of goaltending that he had overlooked before.

"We had pretty much the same styles," said Parent, "but Plante was 44 years old at the time. I watched him play, and I watched everything he did, how he handled himself on shots. Whatever he was doing, I tried to do."

When the World Hockey Association was born in 1972, Parent signed on with a team called the Miami Screaming Eagles. Bernie was the only player signed by the Florida club which soon folded. Parent then moved up to the WHA's Philadelphia Blazers and remained with them for one season.

He returned to the Flyers for the 1973-74 campaign and immediately asserted his excellence and durability. At season's end, Parent had played more minutes (4,314), had more wins (47), had more shutouts (12), and had a better goals against average (1.89) than any goalie in the league.

Bernie's finest hour would come in the playoffs. While the Flyers did have a successful season, they were not expected to seriously challenge for the Stanley Cup. Up until that year, no expansion team had ever won the championship, and the Flyers, lacking a Bobby Orr or Phil Esposito, certainly weren't believed capable of beating the Big Bad Bruins in the finals.

Astonishingly, the Philadelphians managed to throttle Orr and Esposito for a three-games-to-two lead in the tournament. Game Six was played at The Spectrum amid great expectations among the hometown fans, and Parent did not disappoint them.

Fortified with a one-goal lead on a Rick MacLeish first-period blast, Parent stoned Boston for the entire 60 minutes as the Flyers captured their first Stanley Cup.

Curiously, the 1975 final round between Philadelphia and Buffalo also went to a sixth contest with the Flyers ahead, 3 games to 2. Once again, Parent cemented the championship with a shutout (2-0) and Broad Street enjoyed its second straight victory parade.

"When I was a boy," Parent remembered, "I used to watch so many great Montreal teams win the Cup. In my mind I would try to figure out what the feeling would be like to win it. Now I know. It's wonderful!"

It is entirely possible that the Flyers would have established a dynasty by winning a third consecutive Cup in 1975-76 had Parent been in goal for them. But a damaged disc in his neck allowed him to play only 11 regular season games.

Philadelphia again reached the finals but not Bernie. His injury forced him to give way to second-stringer Wayne Stephenson, who played well, but he was no Parent. The Flyers lost four straight games to the Canadiens, and their Cup run was over.

Fully recovered in 1976-77, Parent returned to the Philadelphia nets and in 61 games recorded a respectable 2.71 goals against average. In 1978, Parent proved his recovery was complete by posting a 2.22 average in 49 games.

Tragedy struck the unlucky goalie again when, in the middle of the 1978-79 season, Parent was accidentally struck in the right eye by a New York Ranger stick in a bizarre incident in front of the net. The stick actually found its way through the tiny opening in Parent's mask.

Bernie, who knew immediately that he was in trouble, was rushed to the hospital, where he spent the next 10 days with both eyes bandaged. With an injury to the retina and a dislocation of the lens, observers feared Parent's days as a netminder were over. At the conclusion of the 1978-79 season, the popular goalie announced his retirement.

Up until the time of the accident, Parent had secured himself in the minds of hockey experts as a future Hall of Famer. He, of course, later was enshrined, but had he not been injured — and his brilliant career not curtailed — it is quite likely that his name would have been revered along with Terry Sawchuk, Glenn Hall, and Georges Vezina as one of the best ever!

Developing
an NHL Goalie

HOW TO DEVELOP A NO. 1 GOALIE IN THE NHL

7 KEY INGREDIENTS!

1 - TALENT

Obviously, it takes a great deal of talent to play in the NHL, even as a backup. Picking the right goaltender is one thing, but to bring him all the way to NHL stardom is another. Some first-round draft choices never made it like Jimmy Waite, Gord Laxton, and Ray Martiniuk. Successful NHL goalies drafted very low include Nikolai Khabibulin (204), Dominik Hasek (199), Guy Hebert (159), Andy Moog (132), and Ron Hextall (119). Ed Belfour and Curtis Joseph didn't even get drafted. All of these late bloomers, except for Moog, came from Europe or college hockey.

2 - DOMINATION IN THE MINOR LEAGUES

Confidence is the fuel for excellence and confidence comes with domination. No matter how talented a goaltender is, if he doesn't dominate, his confidence will suffer and it might kill his career. Few successful NHL goaltenders made it without dominating in the minor professional leagues or international levels.

Tom Barrasso, Grant Fuhr, Bill Ranford, and Stephane Fiset jumped right out of high school or Juniors into the NHL. Barrasso and Fuhr were so good that they became stars right away. They are the exceptions. Ranford and Fiset had to go back to the minors. After a full NHL season, Ranford played his second professional season in the AHL, where he dominated before being traded to Edmonton. He eventually became a star goalie.

Fiset went up and down and up and down. To make things more difficult, the Quebec Nordiques were a poor team. Fiset missed four key ingredients in his NHL career, so it's no wonder his difficult route has been a series of ups and downs. In fact, it's a wonder he is still in the NHL.

3 - PLAYING WITH A DECENT TEAM

One other difference between Bill Ranford and Stephane Fiset is the quality of the team they ended up with. While the Bruins were decent, the Nordiques were brutal. Among the current group of NHL goalies, John Vanbiesbrouck and Kirk McLean are the only goaltenders who eventually became All-Stars after starting their careers with poor teams.

4 - IS VETERAN GOALIE AROUND?

This is a very important and often underestimated aspect in developing goalies. A young goalie needs a veteran with him, a mature person who will help him to deal with the pressure of being an NHL goaltender. Andy Moog lacked this partner in Edmonton and it slowed his development. Actually he became a real No. 1 in Boston after splitting time with an excellent veteran, Reggie Lemelin. Other goalies who missed that partner in their first two seasons are Stephane Fiset, Guy Hebert, and Damian Rhodes.

5 - SUPPORT FROM MANAGEMENT

There is just no way someone can become a No. 1 goalie in the NHL if his own organization doesn't support him. Andy Moog, Guy Hebert, Bill Ranford, Damian Rhodes, and Dominik Hasek all became established No. 1 goalies with their second NHL team. They didn't get the support with their first teams who preferred, respectively, Grant Fuhr, Curtis Joseph, Doug Keans, Felix Potvin, and Ed Belfour.

It is also the management's responsibility to pick the right guy and to develop him. You just can't develop two goalies at the same time and hope that they will both become stars. For 12 years, the Montreal Canadiens had Patrick Roy. There was just no room to develop another No. 1 goalie with the Canadiens except at the minor-league level.

6 - SMART MANAGEMENT

Management has to make sure that the goaltender makes it step by step. They have to provide him with the right environment. They have to be patient and clever enough to realize they can't develop two top-notch goaltenders at the same time. The Boston Bruins have the bad habit of bringing up a young kid and giving him the No. 1 job right away. They are going too fast.

In exceptional cases, you might end up with a good duo like the Rangers did with Vanbiesbrouck and Richter, but a good duo is never as good as one great goaltender. To have great goaltending you need a clear No. 1 and also a clear future No. 1.

7 - GOALIE COACH

This is a relatively new criteria. In the old days, goaltenders learned from their mistakes. Today, they are taught at a young age, and now, almost every NHL team has a goalie coach. The first team which used a goalie coach was the Philadelphia Flyers when they hired Jacques Plante in the late 1970s.

Bernie Parent took over as the goalie coach in the early 1980s, and they started to produce goalies at an incredible rate. Within seven years, they managed to graduate five NHL goalies in Pete Peeters, Rick St. Croix, Bob Froese, Pelle Lindbergh, and Ron Hextall. When you have a good one, he can last for 10 years or more. For that reason, the Flyers haven't produced many goaltenders since the first NHL game of Ron Hextall. The same is true in Montreal where Patrick Roy took all the space.

Of course we are biased, but there is no question that the goaltender is the most important player on a hockey team. If an NHL team wants to develop a top goaltender, this means they are going to have to pay him at least one million dollars a year when he reaches maturity.

To pay a qualified goalie coach $70,000 or $100,000 a year seems to be a smart investment. The goalie coach not only helps the goaltender, he can also help management to make the right decisions. He should also be involved in the goalie scouting process.

WHY QUEBEC GOALIES HAVE SUCCESS

Quebec goalies have had a lot of success in recent years and there is a young generation coming out that will really stand out. I will tell you why Quebec goalies have success.

FEWER MOVES AND MORE SKATING

When you look at the young Quebec goalies and compare them with goalies from other provinces or countries, you find out two major things: Quebec goalies are more systematic and they are better skaters. They use fewer moves, favoring the butterfly, while elsewhere, they still teach the poke check, the two-pad stack and the skate save.

REACH THE NHL FASTER WITH THE QUEBEC STYLE

The Quebec style may not be the only way to reach the NHL. Anyone who has the talent will reach the big league. The difference is that when a goaltender has a very precise system, his chances of making the NHL at a younger age are better. The guy can make it at 20-21-22 instead of 23-24-25. That's the difference between one and two contracts. That may also be the difference between a career as a No. 1 goalie or as a backup. When you consider the longevity and quality, the difference, moneywity, can be very important.

INSPIRED BY PATRICK ROY

The reason why so many good goalies come out of Quebec is not only the style. I think more good athletes decided to become goalies because of Patrick Roy. Every time an athlete has some success, 100, 200, maybe 300 kids decide they want to be like him. This year, Patrick Lalime probably inspired 400 or 500 kids.

THE QUEBEC STYLE, ALL OVER QUEBEC

There are more goalie coaches and more goalie schools today in Quebec. The style taught is pretty much the same everywhere. Guys like Frederic Chabot and Patrick Lalime have learned that style and now teach in the summer in Drummondville. Andre Rocicot and Jean-Claude Bergeron have their schools up north, my brother Benoit has his, I have mine and many others have copied that style, too.

It is much easier today to teach. When kids come to your school, they know how to do a butterfly. This wasn't the case 15 years ago.

THE QUEBEC STYLE IN JAPAN

I don't really see the Quebec style taking hold everywhere, except maybe in Japan. I have been teaching in Japan for five years now and the goalies there have adopted that style. In 1991, they had no common style, and today, they all look the same. It is a country where they like to have a system. Their goalies will have success in Asian hockey as well as in the B pool.

THE YOUNGER THE BETTER

You may be only 10 years old and play like an NHL goalie. There are some 12 year old goalies who are excellent technicians. The younger you adopt a style, the better. If you are talented and play a good style, all you will have to do is to adapt to the speed of the game when moving up in caliber. If you start changing your style every two or three years, you will run into problems.

THE DEVELOPMENT CHANNEL

No matter how talented you are, if you want to make it to the NHL, you have to go through proper channels, which is playing AA, AAA Midget, and Major Junior. There are some exceptions to this rule but they are very few. When you get to the NHL, the type of team you get on is important. Goalies like Patrick Roy, Martin Brodeur, and Felix Potvin all started their career with good defensive teams. That is a big, big help.

WILL THE QUEBEC STYLE WILL LAST?

There have been many studies over the years on the type of shots in hockey. The studies all say that 65-70 percent of the shots go in the lowest foot of the net. That number keeps on increasing, which makes an even better case for the butterfly, or if you want, the Quebec style.

SIZE AND GOALTENDING

Is size overrated when it comes to goaltending? A close look at the top 50 goalies in the NHL last season suggests that it might be, although goalies who are six foot two or taller, do seem to have a slight edge. But on the other hand, small goalies do not seem to have a handicap when compared to average-size goaltenders who are under 6' 2".

When hockey coaches select a player, size is almost always taken into consideration, even with goaltenders. It seems that everyone likes to play with a huge goaltender on their team. If you look at the open net area behind a big guy like Sean Burke, for example, there is little to shoot at, and it is intimidating for a shooter.

Furthermore, big goalies have a distinct advantage when the play gets physical near the goalmouth because they are tougher to move.

On the other hand, big goalies are often slower at moving across the crease. They have less mobility than small goalies because they do not take off as quickly due to their size. Also, when they open up their legs to move laterally, the holes are larger. The plus is that they can stretch further, make more desperate saves, and reach more loose pucks. They also have more power when shooting the puck themselves.

The key for big goalies is thus to develop leg power and good technique so they can get across their crease fast without opening up too much.

Yes, there is less to shoot at when a huge guy is in goal, but there is one question that should not be overlooked though and it is: "If a pass is made through the slot, will the big goalie get there fast enough and will he end up in a good position?"

There is no doubt that with all other things being equal, a big goalie, with great reflexes, great lateral motion, and great style, will be better in the long run than a small goalie with great reflexes, great lateral motion and great style.

The key here is "all other things being equal." Any coach can tell you who is larger between two goaltenders but unfortunately, not all coaches can tell you who has more potential, desire, hockey sense, technique, anticipation, and mental toughness.

Many coaches often make the assumption that all other things are equal when they select a goaltender. It is not always the case and this can be a big mistake.

The 1995-96 NHL regular season goaltending statistics tend to demonstrate the fact that big goalies perform better overall, but not all that much better.

Very tall goalies (6' 2" or taller) stopped 902 of 1,000 shots. Tall, average, and small goalies stopped 898 of 1,000 shots. That means four goals for 1,000 shots or roughly four goals every 33 games.

On a standard NHL team, which gives up 30 shots per game, a very tall goaltender (6' 2" or taller) is likely to have a 2.97 GAA. Tall (6' and 6' 1") and average size (5' 10" and 5' 11") goaltenders will have a 3.09 GAA, while small goaltenders (5' 9" or below) will have a 3.12 GAA.

Now if you figure that your No. 1 goaltender will play an average of 66 games in a season, the tallest goaltender will give up 196 goals, the tall and average size goalie will give up 204 goals, while the shortest goaltenders will give up 206.

A two-goal difference between tall, average size, and short goalies does not mean much. Whether your goaltender is 5' 8" or 6' 1" hardly matters statistically.

But the big guys do have a very slight edge, it appears. According to our study, they will give up eight goals less than the tall and average size goaltenders and 10 goals less than the very short goalies.

What do 10 goals mean over 66 games? Certainly not 10 more wins. Of course, not every goal makes the difference between a loss and a tie or a win and a tie. But throughout a season, the difference could mean two, three, four, or five points, who knows?

The point is that the difference is minimal and this shows how hazardous it is to pick a goaltender based on size. There are more meaningful criteria, but it often takes a goaltending expert to evaluate them.

A big goalie with natural ability and great desire to excel is a very interesting project for a goalie coach who knows what he is doing, but bear in mind that size will never replace talent. Over the long run, a short goaltender with lots of talent will be more valuable than a huge goaltender with average ability.

That being said, five foot eight is probably the smallest frame acceptable for NHL standards.

CHICO RESCH ON THE EVOLUTION OF GOALTENDING IN THE NHL

When the National Hockey League was created in 1917 goaltending was just breaking out of its primitive stages.

Cricket pads, which had been used by the earliest goalies, were now being replaced by pads that were designed specifically for ice hockey. But goaltenders on the original NHL teams hardly were equipped like today's netminders, nor did they play much like them.

In the earliest days goalies were expected to stand up and, for a time, there even was a penalty if a goalie fell to the ice to make a save.

Goalie gloves were simple and much like those worn by forwards and defensemen while other protective equipment was minimal, to say the least.

This was not a problem during the 1920s and 1930s. Attackers used only two basic types of shots — the forehand (wrist) shot and the backhand. While they could be propelled relatively fast, they had none of the speed generated by today's high-tech sticks.

For that reason none of the goalies wore masks. In fact the only time a puckstopper wore any protective face covering was when Montreal Maroons goalie Clint Benedict broke a bone in his face and wore a makeshift leather device that allowed him to see and breathe but managed to cover his wound.

By the start of World War II improvements were evident. Chest protectors were worn under the jersey as well as shoulder pads and improved leg pads, most of which were hand-made by a fellow in Hamilton, Ontario named Pop Kenesky.

Gloves began growing in size but the blocker, as we know it today, didn't come into being until after World War II when Emile ("The Cat") Francis got the idea of adding more protection to his stick-hand glove.

In terms of style, basic stand-up was the order of the day. Lester Patrick, manager of the New York Rangers, authored a book on hockey-playing and stated unequivocally that a goaltender who falls to the ice was vulnerable to shooters. Patrick's advice was simple: *stay on your skates.*

To stop shots that were headed for the corners, some goalies mastered the spread-eagle — or split — which essentially enabled them to cover the six feet from post to post. Charlie Rayner of the Rangers was one of the foremost exponents of the split.

The most significant event that spurred major improvements in both style and protection of goaltending came about at the start of the 1950s. That's when Bernie (Boom Boom) Geoffrion of the Montreal Canadiens introduced the slapshot to the NHL.

At first other players frowned on the slapshot. They considered it awkward and uncontrollably wild. But Geoffrion demonstrated that the slapshot could be tamed and, with practice, could be almost as accurate as a wrist shot.

In addition, Geoffrion's slapshot was much faster than the fastest wrist shots and proved extremely difficult to detect because of its velocity. Goaltending was difficult enough before the slapshot but now Geoffrion was turning the job into one filled with migraines — if not broken jaws.

In the mid-1950s teams also were applying a strategy that also confounded goalies. They would station forwards in the line of the netminder's vision and "screen" the stopper from seeing the puck until it was too late for him to nab it.

An antidote was necessary to cope with the screened shot. It was developed by Terry Sawchuk of the Detroit Red Wings. Instead of facing the shots with a normal stance, Sawchuk would go into an exceptionally low crouch and, in effect, peer through the legs of players in front of him in order to view the puck.

Sawchuk's method worked, as his excellent record more than proved. In time, other goalies such as Glenn Hall — who followed Sawchuk in Detroit — and Roger Crozier would embellish the original Sawchuk moves.

Yet another revolutionary move was introduced shortly after the advent of Geoffrion's slapshot when his Canadiens' teammate, goalie Jacques Plante, replaced Gerry McNeil as Montreal's number one netminder in the early 1950s.

Plante was the first of the modern, post-World War II goalies to have a real, new system. He analyzed the game more carefully than any other members of the fraternity and had a reason for everything he did as a goalie.

Jacques believed that a goalie's weight should be a bit on one leg or another. (Any athlete knows that you can't kick out the leg that your weight is on, so you divide the ice right down the middle facing the other goalie. Anything to the right of that line — the near post — is called the short side. And what Jacques would say is, "Have your weight a little bit more on the short side."

He would say "Take away the short side with your body." Then you have eliminated one option. The enemy knows that if he shoots for the short side, it's going to hit the goalie's body with his weight a little more on the right leg.

If the shooter aims for the far side — which he will because Plante has exposed it by covering the short side so much — then Plante is able to make a quick move across and fill the opening. He is able to do this because he has set up his weight distribution accordingly to kick out or push across with ease. Basically, his weight was on the short side leg, meaning the leg closest to the goal post. He takes away the short side and then is set if the shot does go to the far side. As such, he sets up the shooter.

Another thing Plante did when a played moved laterally to the top of the circle — Jacques would start to move across the laterally also, but he would delay so that the shooter gets to a point where he could see more of the far side; the side to which he was moving. The trick was to not move too quickly and expose himself to a shot against the grain, and to lure the shooter into exposing himself.

Jacques figured all this and was expert at understanding the percentages from a goalie's viewpoint and from the forward's point of view.

It was Plante's belief that a goalie should do more than merely stop shots; he felt that the goalkeeper also should be a part of the ebb-and-flow of the play. He advised his defensemen that, if the occasion was right, he would come out of his net and field the puck for them.

Until then, the only goalie who did any wandering at all was Rayner, who was such an expert skater, he actually was stationed at his own blue line during some Rangers power plays. But not even Rayner ever roamed behind his net to trap the puck. It simply just wasn't done. A goalie's place was in his crease and that was that!

Plante's decision to skate behind the net was startling to say the least — but it worked. He helped control play for his defense and rarely was caught out of position. Soon Jacques added to the repertoire; in addition to going behind his net for the puck, he now began moving way out front and, from time to time, to the sideboards.

That Jacques was an above-average skater — for a goalie — helped him immeasurably. Soon other goalies began aping Plante, with the result that an entirely new dimension of strategy was added to hockey's tapestry.

As important as the phenomenon of the roving goalie was, Plante's decision to be the first netminder to wear a protective face mask was even more revolutionary. He first donned the mask at the old Madison Square Garden in New York, after being hit in the face by a hard wrist shot — not a slap shot as some have suggested — fired by Andy Bathgate of the Rangers.

After getting his face stitched up, Plante told his coach Toe Blake that the only way he would return to the game was if he wore a mask. Since Blake didn't have a back-up goalie handy, he couldn't disagree.

Plante came back and won the game so Blake allowed him to start the next game wearing the mask. Jacques won that game as well and proceeded to go on such a winning tear that Blake no longer could talk him out of wearing it anymore.

Once again, other goalies were reluctant to follow suit. Playing barefaced was considered a "macho" move in a "macho" game and felt that if Plante wanted to break tradition that was his business but the others continued barefaced.

During that era none of the goalies — with the exception of Plante — wore masks in practice. That meant that the shooters had to keep their shots low. After all, goalies wanted to survive, physically as well as mentally.

As the shots began coming in harder and harder, it posed a problem for the maskless goalie. Here's what I mean: nowadays we stress that a goalie should position himself so that he is "square to the puck." That means getting your face right in the middle of that puck.

You can do it now thanks to the mask but a goalie couldn't do it then because he'd get killed. What they did was position themselves so that their face was not square to the puck. Worsley told me that the trick was to create an illusion where you would play off one side or the other. You would give the shooter an area to shoot and you could then just angle your head off a little bit and know that he was not going to shoot where you were standing. The puck would probably go to the other side.

Another method maskless goalies used to avoid getting killed by the puck was the sliding two-pad (stacking them) save where they skim on their side across the crease with one leg atop the other. That wasn't used because goalies necessarily thought it was a more efficient move but because the pads were there to stop the puck, not their face!

There was only one problem; shots were starting to be fired harder and harder as improvements were made in stick manufacture and other players learned to copy the Geoffrion slapshot. Then, Bobby Hull and Stan Mikita of the Chicago Blackhawks introduced the curved stickblade. A slapshot coming off the banana blade looked like a knuckle ball coming at you at anywhere from 85 m.p.h. to 100 m.p.h.

To my mind the most courageous athletes ever to play a sport were the NHL's maskless goalies of the 1960s after the Hull-Mikita hooked sticks were perfected and being used by dozens of shooters.

Prior to the banana-blade, the NHL had mainly been a low-shot league. The thinking in the old days was that a shot about a foot off the ice was the hardest to stop. Hull soon realized that a shot at the goalie's head was just as effective because it psyched him out for the rest of the game.

I remember hearing forwards say, "Let's waste one and shoot it high the first time and then give them the low one later." More and more shots were threatening netminder's heads and they reacted normally. Which is to say other goalies began experimenting with the mask — Sawchuk, Don Simmons, et. al. — although ultra-conservatives like Hall and Gump Worsley adamantly refused to add it to their gear.

Forwards tried to cope with all the new moves by the goalies and, in some ways, they were successful. When Plante began roaming, some attackers took dead aim at him and would try to bodycheck him as they would any other skater.

Red Sullivan of the Rangers was the most ardent Plante-hitter but one night at the old Montreal Forum, Sully tried to nail Jacques along the boards. Plante dropped to his knees and the Ranger went flying right over him and into the wall. Plante got up laughing.

Plante's original mask was a molded piece of plastic that offered more moral protection than physical protection. Once during a playoff game, he reacted slowly to a Freddie Stanfield slapshot which hit him dead on against the mask. Jacques fell to the ice as if he had been killed and it's a sure thing that the mask did help but it also demonstrated that the plain, molded plastic mask was not enough.

That was a scary moment for goalies. It was at that moment we knew that improvements were needed in the safety quality of masks.

As a result different companies began designing variations on the original. Eventually, some were created along the lines of baseball catcher's masks and each time a new one came out it seemed to have added safety features.

Some Europeans came over with the cage-style mask in the late 1970s and the North Americans would study them because we hadn't really thought of that kind of protection. What we saw was that when a European goalie got dinged in the head with a puck, he wasn't as badly shaken as the North American goalie was when he got hit in the molded mask. The European would just shake his head and continue playing. I wore a molded mask and once got hit by a Bobby Nystrom shot in practice. He hit me straight on and broke my nose. The catcher's-type cage began to catch on and, so, another innovation was introduced that enabled the goalie to play with his face in the action.

Hall, who had moved from the Red Wings to the Blackhawks, was responsible for a technique which has had an impact on goaltending to this day. Glenn was the grandfather of the butterfly save. He was the one who got the idea of falling to the ice with his legs spread out into an inverted "V" formation so that the pads covered the ice, post-to-post.

Even though Hall was vulnerable to a point because he was down, he also developed a spring in his legs that allowed him to spring right up as easily as he had gone down. The

important point is that he was able to more effectively cover more net with his maneuver than anybody before him. Once again, the bottom line was that it worked!

After Hall left for the St. Louis Blues when expansion came in 1967, Tony Esposito became the next great Chicago goalie but with a technique that was hard to define other than the fact that he keep most pucks out of his net.

As goalies go, Esposito became renowned as one of the all-time great cheaters. Every goalie likes to do anything possible to get an advantage on a shooter but Tony came up with a new one; he would add pieces to his equipment in the hopes that the additional material would get in the puck's way.

One of his best moves was sewing a tight elastic mesh between his goalie pants. He would have such a huge amount of material there that would hang down so that when he went into his butterfly the webbing would cover the empty space and help him make saves.

Nobody knew about this for some time until an enemy forward shot the puck at Tony and saw the rubber go between his legs. The shooter figured it was a sure goal and put his hands up to celebrate. All of a sudden the puck came right back at him and he said, "Hey, what's going on?" The league checked out Esposito's equipment and found the webbing. An adjustment was made right after that.

Tony was also responsible for the growth in size of the catching glove into what we have come to call the "cheater." The catching glove had evolved from the design of a baseball first baseman's mitt. Hockey trainers began getting more and more creative, adding a cuff to it until Tony finally extended the cuff so that it was the same width as the blocker.

Of course, manufacturers were trying to beat each other out with new innovations in equipment and it was the Cooper company which developed the cheater into what basically is its present form. It not only became as wide as the blocker but extended to the thumb of the glove adding another three inches.

When I first looked at it I said to myself, "That's gotta be illegal!" But we checked the rules and discovered that it was within the rulebook's dimensions. That's how the big catching gloves got to be the way they are today. But I can remember the first time I tried one; the extra weight hanging over my wrist outside the glove threw my hand off-balance. But after a while — like all the other goalies — I got used to it.

Esposito showed that an amorphous style could work although there remained some traditional stand-up goalies who continued to excel. Bernie Parent, who won two Stanley Cups for the Philadelphia Flyers in 1974 and 1975 was one of them.

Parent was a disciple of Plante and mastered what Jacques had taught him. He didn't do anything spectacular except he always was in good position, played the percentages and often got hit with the puck. Bernie employed the same low leg bend that Plante liked and he moved fluidly across the crease. His lateral movements were excellent and I would have to say that he was one of the last, great stand-up goalies, closely followed by Ken Dryden, who came to the Canadiens at the start of the 1970s.

Dryden was much larger than Parent and consequently covered more area. They had one trait in common; they didn't beat themselves much. Dryden was better on straight-on shots and shots he could reach; rebounds he could reach with his legs and arms from that position.

Kenny's weakness was moving laterally. That's why he was exposed by the Europeans who began coming into the NHL during the latter stages of Dryden's career.

He didn't work on his lateral movement because he was more of an angle goalie; a stand-up type who really made sure he stopped the first shot.

In 1978-79 Dryden led Montreal to its fourth straight Stanley Cup and then he retired. Kenny's retirement coincided with the advent of the Wayne Gretzky Era as well as the influx of Europeans who also altered the traditional NHL game plans.

Gretzky had a couple of patent moves. On one he would fake the shot, delay and move across laterally. When he would come outside, he wouldn't just slap it off the wing. He would curl up and look for the late guy coming. He was one of the first and most consistent to attack that way. The Europeans — excellent skaters and stickhandlers — were ardent students of the game.

They would fool goalies by passing up good shots while the goalie had come out to challenge, and while the goalie was out of position, they would pass off to a winger or defensman joining the play late.

Players like Gretzky were the beneficiaries of the high-tech improvements in equipment. Skates, with lighter material, enabled them to skate faster and sticks became lighter and lighter with more power as metals were introduced. To keep pace with the better shots, goaltending students continued to add new dimensions to the mask. It became stronger to the point where goalies knew that even a hard shot couldn't hurt them.

As the butterfly became more widely used in the 1980s, forwards analyzed ways and means of beating it. The opening was the five-hole but, at first, no players really thought of shooting for it because the shooter actually would be firing right AT the goalie.

Mike Bossy, my teammate on the Islanders, changed that. Bossy was a student of shooting and became the first forward to specifically shoot for the five-hole; meaning at the opening directly above the goalie's stick and around the ankles.

Mike once told me, "When I put my head down to shoot, the goalie's legs open up and that's where I would aim the puck." Pretty soon others were planning five-hole shots. Meanwhile, the game was starting to move laterally — because of the Europeans and Gretzky — rather than just up and down the wing with power.

Goalies had to adjust and they realized, for the most part, that the stand-up style was not cutting it. They understood that they could move laterally much better with the butterfly, get down and take away the low net much better than with any other method.

The equipment improvements also meant that goalies could approach practice with less fear and take more high shots. A goalie could take a slapshot in the head and barely even feel it. The blow would momentarily stun but not cause sustained injury. By the time the 1980s had ended the mask had become so effective that the physical fear had gone out of goaltending and goalies actually were making saves with their masks! In fact goalie masks have come so far that nowadays baseball catchers are using them behind the plate.

Some people may wonder how the designs got put on the masks because in the earliest versions they were simply plain pieces of equipment with no markings and no color at all.

Gerry Cheevers, when he was with the Bruins, started the trend of markings by putting stitch marks on the spots of his mask where he got hit by the puck. Cheevers estimated how many stitches he might have needed had he not been wearing a mask and then had the stitches painted on. Pretty soon his mask was covered with stitches.

But Cheesie's mask had no color to it. I'm proud to say that I introduced the colored

mask to the NHL. It happened one day when our clubhouse attendant told me that his girl-friend was an art major at a Long Island high school. "She'd like to paint something on your mask," he said. "It would be the map of Long Island and the NY symbol."

Why not? She did it and I liked the mask so much I began wearing it regularly. It was the first designed mask with some art on it other than stitch marks. And that mask is now in the Hockey Hall of Fame.

The last area on a goalie's body that went without adequate protection was the neck. A few serious injuries — in particular Clint Malarchuk of Buffalo having his neck sliced by a skate — stirred goalies to think about a new device.

Billy Smith of the Islanders got the idea for hanging a bit of a plastic scoop as an extension of his fiberglass mask. It came farther down below the neck and then scooped out so when he put his chin to his chest, it wouldn't restrict him.

That eventually led to other improvements in design so that the neck scoop is an essential part of as goalie's mask equipment. The mask now has it all; it's lightweight comfortable, protects well, and doesn't impede vision.

What this means is that goalies are now more intrepid than ever. They think nothing about putting their face square to the puck. And when they dive across the crease, they know that if their legs are under them, it's much easier to dive face-first than it is to throw out the legs as they did in the old days.

All of these improvements have virtually eliminated the stand-up goalie in the NHL. Here's one example why a butterfly has put the stand-up out of business:

If there's a scramble in tight, a shooter can pretty easily come around for a wrap-in. The stand-up goalie is telling himself, "Stay up, stay up!" But his pads and body are not wide enough to cover the whole lower part of the goal.

With the butterfly, goalies are "cheating" in advance. As soon as they see the puck get within ten or twelve feet of the net, they start going down, spreading the pads and cover-ing the bottom of the net. The butterfly goalie reasons that out of twenty players on the opposition only three would be good, high shooters. He's saying, "I can live with those guys if they have the time to hit the corners. I'll take care of the guys who are average shooters. I'm cheating low; they can't get the puck up."

Some wonder why the butterfly didn't come along sooner than it did and the answer is, the mask. Before the mask was perfected, goalies were reluctant to expose their face as much as they have to when they do the butterfly.

It all comes down to survival. During the stand-up era, when a shot came, the goalie would make the skate save by moving his face back, turning his leg and then kicking out his skate. That way his face was out of the play and his weight was on the back leg.

These improvements, in large part, have been responsible for the drop in goal-scor-ing. Close-in goals simply are not being scored as often as they had been in the past, because goalies get down earlier and that takes many of those potential chances away.

Another reason for the decline in scoring — and why goalies smile more nowadays — is that the slapshot has lost favor. In the 1970s and 1980s everybody was working slap-shots. Then came the European influence which favors wrist shots from the top of the cir-cle and you have the decline of goals. A slapshot can be blown by a goalie; not necessar-ily a wrist shot.

The goalie skate itself has undergone considerable improvement although its configuration is essentially the same as it was in decades past. The earlier skate was covered with a hard piece of protective leather that covered the toe and the side.

A problem was that the leather would get wet from the melted ice and soften up over the course of a game. In time somebody got the idea of replacing the leather with plastic. Where once a goalie couldn't go more than three games without some sort of foot bruise — or worse! — that's not the case anymore.

If there is one vulnerable spot on the goalie's body that hasn't been completely covered it is the area right above the pads and below the goalie's pants. When a goaltender is in a bending position, the pants do not go down far enough to cover the knee. I have seen goalies such as Marty Brodeur take a puck on that spot and *really* feel it.

Since it is the only area that still is exposed you would think some kind of pad might be inserted to cover it but when a goalie straightened his leg after bending, the pad would be restrictive.

Actually, I don't think it's such a bad thing for a goalie to be hit there once in a while. It's good because they should feel some pain once in a while to know that they're still is in the game, that they're still vulnerable.

Which brings us to another area of goaltending evolution and that's the goalie stick. From the pre-World War II era through the 1960s, the stick remained essentially the same. The blade was straight, the wood thick and the overall feel was heavy.

Since netminders for more than three decades stayed in their crease and used their stick in basically one position — with the stick-hand half way down the shaft — there was no reason to change either the style or weight of the goalie stick.

But once Jacques Plante began playing the puck along the boards and other goalies began copying him, the stick now had other uses, including stickhandling. And then — years later — when Ron Hextall proved that goalies could easily clear the puck out of their zone, the stick had multiple uses and, therefore, had to be refined.

Newer materials enabled manufacturers to lighten its weight and also make the blade more flexible. Since forwards learned that a curve could help them release shots quicker, goalies determined that a curve on their stick blade would find it simpler to deliver the puck up ice than with the traditional flat blade.

Another innovation was a curve on the stick shaft — a little bend where the goalie grabs the stick with his glove — which was supposed to enable goalies to have an advantage when they put the paddle down on the ice. The "Curtis Curve" was considered better than the straight stick in the sense that it enabled the paddle to be flat on the ice and thereby closing the gap through which the pucks might have gone. The Curtis Curve takes a little getting used to — a slight adjustment — but I considered it a good idea and was the first to use it. Andy Moog also is a Curtis Curve man but most goalies have stayed with the straight shaft.

We couldn't complete a section on goaltending evolution without mentioning the advent of the goalie coach.

Nowadays many teams employ either a part-time (Buffalo with Mitch Korn) or full-time (Devils with Jacques Caron) goalie's helper. In the old days this was unheard of and it wasn't until after the NHL expanded from six to twelve teams in 1967 that the idea was even considered.

When I was with the Islanders, Bill Torrey brought in Eddie Giacomin as part of the club's broadcast team. Giacomin was a Hall of Fame goalie with the Rangers who Torrey decided also could work with me and Billy Smith when he wasn't doing his broadcast work.

I was fortunate to have Giacomin around to give me advice on improving my game and as a sounding board. This was something brand new for the game and it worked. I later had by boyhood idol, Glenn Hall, as goalie coach when I played in Denver for the Colorado Rockies.

Hall later became goalie coach for the Calgary Flames and to this day, Mike Vernon has said that Hall helped him win two Stanley Cups; the first with Calgary in 1989 and the second with Detroit in 1997.

By the start of the 1990s at least half the teams were considering goalie coaches or already using them. Most of those employed were part-timers such as Mitch Korn, whose full-time job was with a university but who periodically consulted with the Sabres goalies.

One team that hired a full-timer was the Devils, who hired Jacques Caron in August 1993. Ever since the 1993-94 season Caron has been as much a part of the regular coaching staff as Jacques Lemaire and Robbie Ftorek.

He has worked on a day-to-day basis with Martin Brodeur ever since Marty became a number one goalie in 1993-94 and if there's any doubt that a goalie coach can do a top-flight job, all you have to do is look at the maturation of Brodeur to the top level of goaltending in the league.

How goaltending will evolve in the new century is anybody's guess. Certainly, the profession has improved markedly in every way, from the development of the mask to the swing from stand-up to butterfly goaltending.

The proof is in the numbers. Goalies have gotten better; goalscorers are having a more difficult time putting the puck behind them.

In 1996-97 they tried to increase scoring by trimming the goalie pads and policing the netminders on a regular basis.

Guess what? Scoring still stayed down.

The conclusion can only be that on the evolutionary scale, goalies have improved more than any other hockey species.

Style Analysis

STYLE ANALYSIS: JOHN VANBIESBROUCK

Many goalie coaches working with young goalies, and especially with beginners, will tell you that professional goalies are not often the best models for their students. And you know what? Very often, they are right.

The pros play a different game than kids and some professional goalies play a big-guy style, going down early on some plays near the goalmouth. However, a small goalie like John Vanbiesbrouck (five foot eight) has to play like a "little guy," wait longer and play more of a reacting game.

Technically, Vanbiesbrouck is almost perfect. Because his positioning is so good, he is rarely out of position and it seems like he has a chance on every play. His anticipation and recovery are exceptional. In short, he is a great model for 95% of goaltenders.

The next time the Florida Panthers are on TV, get your VCR going and take a close look at Vanbiesbrouck. Replay the situations over and over again, in slow motion as well as in real time. You will be amazed to see what a great technician he is. In the meantime, here are some notes on the player of the month (October '96) in the NHL.

BEFORE A SHOT

Just before a shot from 15- feet or further away, Vanbiesbrouck is almost still. His stick blade is on the ice but a little bit to his left, leaving a hole on the ice between his right foot and the stick blade's heel. Vanbiesbrouck brings back his blade slowly to the middle as the shooter winds up.

In his basic stance, the stick is six to eight inches in front of his feet; his catching hand is on the side and low. There is no hole between the arms and the body. The pads meet at knee height. The feet are wider than shoulder width (see #1 below).

Sometimes, Vanbiesbrouck will crouch real low with his stick blade angled and way up front. He will bring his stick blade back and move back up slowly as the shooter is winding up.

Vanbiesbrouck's V-stance (#6) indicates that he is ready to go down into the butterfly, but he is also ready to push right, left, and even up.

STICK POSITION BEFORE THE SHOT

The heel of the stick blade is slightly to the left of the median line and moves right, slowly. The end of the stick blade is a couple of inches high. The blocker double covers part of the right pad at knee height, but that is necessary in order to cover the hole between the arm and the body. (#1)

VISION

Vanbiesbrouck follows the puck extremely well through traffic and is able to react quickly to deflections (#6). As mentioned before, Vanbiesbrouck turns his body well toward the puck and can stretch his arms behind (#2) to make some big tip-in saves.

Rebound control

Since Vanbiesbrouck's crouch is low, he can scoop many pucks on the ice with his glove. He is good with the stick, too.

BALANCE WHEN REACTING

Beezer has unbelievable balance! Not only can he stretch quickly in any direction but he can also carry his body to his right or to his left when making a save. In other words, he can push left, right, or even upward on some high shots. He can even stop a downward butterfly move and jump for a high shot (#10).

If the puck is shot at him, his body will remain square to the puck. But if it is shot to his left, he will turn his body and his head will lean slightly to his left. His whole body will go left (#9).

You will rarely see John Vanbiesbrouck make a left-pad save and balance his body by extending his right arm to his right. His right arm will go left (#9) or stay there (#2).

On a right-pad save, Vanbiesbrouck's left arm will remain bent and go slightly behind his body, instead of extending to the left (#8). Since his arms are not spread like bird wings, the weight shift is smoother.

BALANCE AFTER A SAVE

No one gets up faster and more smoothly than John Vanbiesbrouck. After most saves he maintains excellent balance because he turns and leans toward the puck and also because his opposite arm does not extend fully to the right for a left-side save, and vice versa.

He just has to bring back his foot under his knee to get up smoothly. The weight transfer toward the skate blade (#3 and #8) is easy because his head and upper body are leaning left for a left side save (#9) and right for a right-side save (#8).

RIGHT KICK SAVE

Vanbiesbrouck's kick save is marvelous. He just stretches his right leg with his toe facing the puck. After the save, his right foot turns to the side, a bit like the old skate save, and he brings it back underneath his body to lean on it and to get back up (#8). His left arm does not stretch way back. It sort of lays there, with no extreme weight transfer.

LEFT KICK OR PAD SAVE

Vanbiesbrouck's left-pad save is like the right. His blocker does not extend way back. His left arm goes slightly back and moves back up.

CHEST SHOTS

On hard shots to the chest, Vanbiesbrouck will try to turn the body to the short side even after starting a downward butterfly move. He can thus avoid giving up difficult rebounds in front of the net.

HIGH SHOTS

Vanbiesbrouck likes to raise his thigh and knee along with his arm for double protection on the blocker side as well as on the catching side.

Because of this, he will make many knee saves on medium-height shots on both sides. Many of his saves involve a "T-push", i.e., he will push with his right foot for a left-side save. He really goes to the puck. If it's high, he might even jump.

Beezer catches the puck on the side (#11) or slightly behind his body (#2).

BLOCKER SAVES

Vanbiesbrouck has excellent control over his blocker and stick. He can do what he wants with his right hand, controlling rebounds exceptionally well.

He can direct the puck where he wants to. On very tough shots, he will direct it to the right corner or straight out if it is the best option.

If he has a little time and the puck is shot close to his body, he can also direct it to the left corner when it is the right play. He can also let it die in front of him for a defenseman or for himself.

On medium-height shots, his right knee will very often follow the blocker after a push from his left foot (#8).

LATERAL MOTION

Since Vanbiesbrouck is a small-sized goaltender who does not come way out, he is rarely out of the play against a pass (#4). He also has good speed and remains compact.

REGAINING HIS STANCE

Vanbiesbrouck has the uncanny ability to make a kick save and bring his foot right back underneath his body to get back up (#8). That is because he bring his left arm back a little bit instead of sideways on a right leg save. Furthermore, his stick comes back behind his left after the kick while his body turns to the right. No one gets back up in position better than John Vanbiesbrouck. His thigh, right or left, depending on the situation, goes right back up.

BUTTERFLY

Vanbiesbrouck has an excellent butterfly and although he does not employ a butterfly block as often as Patrick Roy, he uses it effectively.

Whenever he goes down, he bring his catching hand close to his body (#5).

Vanbiesbrouck has the uncanny ability to start a downward butterfly move and to stop the moment the shot is taken if he sees the puck is going high. He will straighten up the body or stretch his glove hand. That is great, great balance.

Vanbiesbrouck makes good transitions from moving laterally to the butterfly block.

BUTTERFLY AND REBOUNDS

On long shots, Vanbiesbrouck can direct the puck to either corner. In the butterfly position, he can direct the puck to his right with his stick even if it has been shot on the ice slightly to his left (#5).

BREAKAWAYS

On breakaways, Vanbiesbrouck stays square to the shooter with his catching hand really low in a compact position. The 5-hole is small (#1) but he is still able to go down in the butterfly while moving backward.

He does not go that far out, perhaps two feet ahead of his crease line (#4) and backs in slowly. He never makes the first move and he makes it tough for the shooter to make the ultimate decision of shooting or deking. And the more the shooter waits, the happier Vanbiesbrouck is.

The 5-hole on Vanbiesbrouck does not look like a good option to the shooter on breakaways because it is not big. If the player shoots low, he has to go right or left and the veteran netminder has an excellent butterfly. Shooting low on the breakaway against Vanbiesbrouck is tough.

Going high is the other shooting option, but Vanbiesbrouck has great hands and reads the stick well from in tight. The shot has to be perfectly roofed. If the player succeeds, Vanbiesbrouck will tip his hat off to him but he won't start to open up and change his style.

Deking on Vanbiesbrouck is also tough. He is small but can stretch, and he won't be caught out of position. His extended leg will go to the post and remain square, toes down. He can be deked through the five-hole like most goalies, but it will take a perfect move to beat him.

PARTIAL BREAKAWAY

If a player gets a pass in front and skates in all alone in a semi-breakaway situation, Vanbiesbrouck will back up slowly to the middle of the crease and stand still, forcing the player to shoot. Surprisingly, players will often shoot wide on Beezer in these situations just because he remains square and patient.

If a player dekes, Vanbiesbrouck will be able to get to the post with his pad.

PLAYER CUTTING IN FRONT

Vanbiesbrouck moves out slowly, one or two feet outside his crease line. He follows the player, square, ending up near the goal post if the player keeps on skating all the way around.

On such a play to the left, his stick is on the ice, catching glove on the side and behind, leaning on the left pad. There is no room between the arm and the body.

If the player skates really fast, he will leave the shuffle and use a T-push, raising his left thigh and dragging his right foot after the push.

If he has to, he will finish the play with a butterfly slide.

PENETRATION PLAYS

When there is no pass option, Vanbiesbrouck likes to be one or two feet ahead of his crease in his wide stance (#6), leaving only the 5-hole and the upper corners open. He stands still and waits for the shot.

TWO -ON-ONES

Vanbiesbrouck plays the two on one situation like a breakaway. He comes out about two feet ahead of his crease, faces the shooter and backs in slowly.

REBOUNDS

On rebounds, Vanbiesbrouck likes to put the shaft down even after a butterfly save (#7).

SCREEN SHOTS

On screen shots, Vanbiesbrouck likes to spread wide, ready to butterfly (#4 and #6). He is tough to beat low to the corners since the only space left is between the legs. He focuses on one move or closing down the five-hole or stretching high.

WRAPAROUND PLAYS

When the puck is behind the net, Vanbiesbrouck likes to stay low with his feet wider apart than usual. Moving from post to post, he will stand up and place his stick blade in position to cut a pass. If the pass connects, he finds himself in a wider basic stance, ready to go down in the butterfly. If he is behind the play or if there is traffic in front, he will go down with his stick in a horizontal position.

On a wraparound shot just outside the goal line, to his right (often a soft backhand), he will bring back his stick blade in a normal basic stance position and he will place his glove just above it to cover the wide 5-hole so the puck does not carom off his left leg into the net.

PLAYS FROM BEHIND THE NET

Sometimes Vanbiesbrouck likes to take a whack at players trying the wraparound. He will take a full swing so if he does not get the puck, he will get the player. He has learned this from his goalie coach, "Battling" Billy Smith, who was a master of the sword but also quite a goaltender.

On a play from behind the net to his right, Vanbiesbrouck will keep his hand on the shoulder of his stick and attempt to cut a pass, but he won't put himself out of position to intercept it. If he misses, he will bring his stick back into a standard position.

HANDLING THE PUCK

Vanbiesbrouck is not the most spectacular puckhandler but he gets the job done with simple plays. He is good at clearing the puck from his crease and directing it to a teammate. He reads situations very well. After a save, he will often shoot the puck quickly through the middle and into the neutral zone to relieve the pressure, especially when the Panthers are playing shorthanded.

Vanbiesbrouck is smart with the puck and sometimes when he does not have a play, he will just flip the puck high and off the glass. This buys time for his defensemen, who will be able to check the opponent struggling to get control of a high puck.

FREEZING THE PUCK

Vanbiesbrouck likes to freeze the puck, standing on one foot, ready to get back up quickly if he has to. Bernie Parent used to do that.

TWO-PAD SLIDE

Occasionally, Vanbiesbrouck will do a two-pad slide but it is very controlled and when he does, it is often mixed with a poke check attempt, especially when he slides to his glove side.

When he goes left, on a pass to a right winger coming in for example, Vanbiesbrouck starts with a butterfly to the left and halfway, he brings the right leg underneath to make a two-pad slide, blocking most of the net on a goal mouth play.

Seeing the big pads coming, the right winger might decide to deke but when he tries to go around Vanbiesbrouck's body, his big goalie stick sweeps the puck away.

#1: Basic Stance: In his basic stance, Vanbiesbrouck's stick is six to eight inches in front of his feet; his catching hand is on the side and low. There is no hole between the arms and the body. The pads meet at knee height. The feet are wider than shoulder width. He is very tough to beat low (corners and five-hole).

#2: Great Glove: and great balance because the body is turned to the puck. After a move to his left, he quickly raises his left thigh, leans on his skate and gets back up.

#3: Fast and Smooth Recovery: No one gets back up faster than John Vanbiesbrouck.

#4: One to two feet out, max!: Here is where Vanbiesbrouck likes to be when facing a shot. He rarely moves further out. That way he is also ready to move laterally on a pass.

#5: Quick Butterfly: Even in the butterfly, Vanbiesbrouck has good control over his stick. He can even direct a puck close to his left knee to the right corner.

#6: Wide Stance on Screens: On screen shots, Vanbiesbrouck takes a wide stance, taking away the low corners. He focuses on closing the five-hole with a butterfly move.

#7: Shaft Down on Rebounds: Vanbiesbrouck likes to use the "shaft down" technique on close rebounds after a butterfly save. He will also use it on some wraparound plays.

#8: Balance: After a pad save, he turns his foot and brings it quickly under his knee to get back up smoothly. Left arm behind, and not fully extended, helps recovery.

#9: Weight Shift to Left: Vanbiesbrouck's weight is all going left on this glove save. To get back up quickly and smoothly, he just has to bring his left foot under his knee.

#10: High Shot Jump: Only five foot eight, Vanbiesbrouck is strong on high shots. He has a great glove, but he also uses his body with a jump on chest/shoulder shots. He can also push left or right to reach wide shots. He goes to the puck.

STYLE ANALYSIS: ED BELFOUR

Like two other great Chicago Blackhawk goalies, Glenn Hall and Tony Esposito, Eddie "The Eagle" Belfour was an immediate hit when he arrived in the NHL in 1990-91.

Since his first NHL season when he earned both the Calder and Vezina trophies as best rookie and best goalie, Belfour has been one of the most consistent goaltenders in the NHL. He has accomplished this despite the fact that many thought of him as a "flopper," lucky to be playing for a good defensive team.

Belfour is very aggressive and yet, his style is admirably simple.

BASIC STANCE: THE BELFOUR TRAP

Belfour uses a very wide stance (#1) with a big five-hole and with his hands high. It looks like there is nowhere else to shoot than at that big five-hole but he closes it so quickly that players just don't know where to shoot. His stick is very close to the feet. His blocker is angled not sideways, but inward. This helps him to go down very quickly in his "shaft down" position. On very tight situations, this also helps him to keep rebounds to his glove side, where they are easier to stop. If the rebound goes right, he pushes explosively with his left leg for a right-side dive and, with his shaft down, covers the low net.

POSITIONING

Belfour's philosophy is to cover as much net as possible. If a player has no pass option, you can bet that Belfour will be out two or three feet outside his crease and even more sometimes. On point shots, he will be just outside of his crease. On penetration plays, Belfour likes to come way out and back in using his wide stance (#1), ready to butterfly.

VISION

Because he crouches low, Belfour sees the puck very well through traffic.

TWO ON ONES

On two-on-ones with the puckcarrier to the side, Belfour will come way out, confident that his defenseman will take the pass away. He will start backing in a bit before the puckcarrier reaches the face-off dot. If he chooses to shoot, the puckcarrier has only the 5-hole to go to (#1).

LOW SHOTS

On low shots, Belfour invariably goes down in the butterfly. If the puck is to the left corner, he will do a half-butterfly, stretching the leg square (#8), giving rebounds off the pad. Belfour is so agile in his stick-down position that he can even deflect a puck high in the stands with the heel of his stick. He uses that move on long shots.

MEDIUM-HIGH SHOTS

On medium-high shots, Belfour goes down in the butterfly and uses his catching glove or his blocker while stretching the leg.
Screen Shots

On screens, Belfour goes down in the butterfly. If he doesn't see anything at all, he will use the shaft down-technique, and he is an expert at it (#3).

LONG SHOTS

On long shots, Belfour is very aggressive. If the puck is shot wide, he will go after it using the T-push. (#5).

AROUND THE DEFENSEMEN

When a player is trying to go around a defenseman on his left, Belfour puts his shaft down on the ice, ready to move across without giving a single inch of the ice.

SCRAMBLES

If a pass is made through a bunch of players, Belfour will put his shaft down, ready to move toward the "lucky" receiver. (#3)

ONE-TIMER LW TO CENTER

On a pass from the left wing to a left-handed centerman ready for a slap shot, Belfour will move across but will not completely face the shooter. His blocker will be turned inward but his left leg will be slightly ahead (#1), as if he were ready to explode left. And ready to explode, he is.

GOING DOWN FAST

Because of his blocker position, Belfour is probably the fastest goaltender to go from a stand-up basic stance to a shaft-down blocking position. That's why Belfour does not hesitate to "dive" on breakaways, especially when a player is trying to deke around his blocker side.

BREAKAWAYS

Belfour will move out on breakaways and back in. He will go "shaft down" just when a player is deking, and he will do so at the very split second when the player can't shoot, so he does not get beat when his shaft is going down.

PUCK BEHIND THE NET

When the puck is behind the goal line to his right, most of the time, Belfour will stand up in a classic position with just the stick blade turned. This is a little surprising considering the fact that he is a master at the shaft-down position. On his left side, though, he will go down in the shaft-down position much more often.

CUTTING PASSES

Because his right hand is turned inward, Belfour won't be able to cut some passes from

his left within easy reach of his crease. If he succeeds in putting some wood on it, that will be the front of his blade and he will just deflect the puck to the slot area to his right. In fact, this is not much different than using the back of the blade. The only difference is by going backhand, it is easier to deflect the puck high through the slot instead of seeing it flat on the ice.

On a centering pass from a right wing to the center, Belfour, who goes down quickly in the shaft-down position, will sometimes cut a pass with the knob of his stick.

TWO-PAD STACK

If a player is cutting to his blocker side, Belfour will go down in the shaft-down position, but if the player stops his deke and looks as if he is going to shoot, Belfour will stack the pads to get as much space covered to his left.

REGAINING STANCE

To get back up, Belfour is not as smooth as John Vanbiesbrouck but for that matter, nobody really is. Belfour is still very quick at getting back up and at moving laterally from a down position. Because of his rough weight shifts and his hurry to get back on his feet, Belfour often falls backward or forward and uses his hand to get back up (#2).

PUCKHANDLING

Belfour is a good puckhandler. He gets to the puck fast, but sometimes he forwards it too hard instead of going for the soft pass.

#1: The Belfour Trap: It looks like there is nowhere else to shoot than at the five-hole but Belfour goes down in the butterfly so fast that it is almost hopeless for a player to shoot there. Shooters may try the top of the net which is the toughest shot.

#2: Getting the Job Done: Belfour is one of the toughest goalies to beat on the first shot as well as on the second. On almost every shot, he puts at least one knee down even on high ones, he will often use his glove to help him get back up. Not pretty, but Belfour gets the job done and that's what matters.

#3: "Shaft Down" Position: Even in his "shaft-down" position, Belfour can move laterally very quickly.

#4: Low Butterfly: Because he stands very wide, hands high, in a "sit" position with his weight on the balls of his feet. Belfour will often end up in a "sit" butterfly, weight on his butt.

#5: Going after Wide Shots: Ed Belfour is very aggressive. He pushes with his right foot to go after long, high and wide shots. This is about the only time Belfour won't put a knee down on a shot.

#6: Ready to Dive Right: Belfour, the master of the "shaft-down" technique is ready to dive to his right from a left-foot push. His stick will stay down. He will block a high shot with his chest or his arm.

#7: Right Pad Save: Belfour goes full stretch on low shots because he has a tendency to "sit." His crotch is very low, leading to a full leg extension which makes the recovery more difficult.

#8: Left Pad Save: Again, he uses full leg extension on a low shot. "Pretty" goalies like John Vanbiesbrouck do not extend as much because their crotch is higher. What matters is the result.

#9: Ready for the Rebound: Perfect shaft-down position, ready to dive right (with the blocker leading), Belfour is also ready for a rebound on the glove side with the left leg extended.

#10: Stick Perpendicular: In his basic stance, Belfour's stick is perpendicular. Sometimes, his stick blade is very close to his feet. That's why he can go down so fast in the "shaft-down" position.

#11: Low on Scrambles: When Belfour is down on a scramble, he stays down until he knows he can get back up safely without being scored on low while trying to return on his feet.

#12: Ready for High Ones!: High shots from in tight are rare, but Belfour is ready for them. Very aggressive, Belfour also tries to clear pucks away with his stick when he has a chance.

Style Analysis:
Martin Brodeur

Martin Brodeur is a big-sized goaltender and unlike most Quebec goalies, he does not use a classic butterfly style. He will stand up more on low shots than his fellow Frenchmen. He has lightning quick reflexes and he knows how to square his big frame in front of the puck, leaving little room for the shooter.

Brodeur's body is intimidating to the shooters, he seems to get larger as his reputation is growing. In today's hockey, goalies tend to move out and back in with the play, but Brodeur, playing on the best defensive team in the league, likes to move out to the shooter, pressing him to make a quick play. The chemistry between Brodeur and his defensemen is superb; it is strong in the defensive phase as well as in the breakout phase (see #1).

The New Jersey Devils have perhaps the brightest coach in hockey in Jacques Lemaire and they play a very organized system which also involves Brodeur. When he takes control of the puck, his defensemen immediately go to specific spots. Brodeur is an excellent puckhandler and Lemaire takes advantage of that skill and incorporates it into his system.

Brodeur also has confidence in his long reach and uses the poke check better that any other goalie in the league.

PHYSICAL SKILLS

Physically and technically, Brodeur is very strong, but his best assets are on the mental side. Brodeur is perhaps the best puckhandler in the game and also the best poke-checker, a lost art nowadays.

STANCE

Brodeur likes to keep his hands high and way up front. Since he usually stands a foot or two in front of his crease, there is virtually no room to shoot at in the upper part of the net. His crouch is medium deep and his upper body is straight up. His stance is fairly wide, except on bad angle plays when he takes a compact stand-up stance. At 6'1" and 205 pounds, Brodeur is no dwarf, but he looks more like a 6'4"-220 pound goaltender because of his stance. On plays in tight, Brodeur will often choose the paddle-down position over the butterfly. Sometimes though, he will keep his left skate blade flat on the ice ready to kick.

RECOVERY TO STANCE

Brodeur is a big guy and his ability to get back up after a save is just a bit better than average. On a team like the Devils, this "weakness" doesn't matter very much. When he sees a second or third shot, Brodeur often bails himself out with his long reach. In scrambles, he gets back up as soon as he gets a chance, whereas many goalies stay down longer in the paddle-down position.

SKATING

Brodeur has a big frame to carry and it's normal that he doesn't take off as fast as a smaller goalie. However, this is a part of his game he has to improve. He has to work on his legs and on his lateral play because he is average on odd-man situations. Even if some people consider him as good as Hasek, it is unlikely he could match Hasek on a weak team like Buffalo. In other words, Hasek would be as efficient if he played for the Devils, but Brodeur, right now, couldn't do what Hasek does with the Sabres. He would be good but not as efficient as Hasek.

BASIC MOVES

Brodeur focuses well on the puck. On very low shots he uses the half-butterfly, but on medium-high shot, he often kicks the puck (#3). You won't see Brodeur do the dazzling split glove save very often on knee-high shots. He prefers using his legs and at that height, he kicks like the old stand-up goalies, especially on the glove side where he likes to turn the skate (#2).

ABILITY TO CLOSE FIVE-HOLE

Brodeur's butterfly is not as wide as it could be for a goalie of his stature but he closes the five-hole very quickly. Because he doesn't use the butterfly on a consistent basis, he gets off balance sometimes after a five-hole save and tends to fall sideways a little bit, especially on a lateral play (#3).

ABILITY TO FILL SPACE

Brodeur fills a lot of the net and when he is in trouble, he usually finds a way to get a part of his body close to the puck to take away the angle. To accomplish this, he will dive, slide, move an arm, a leg, or his stick forward.

LOW SHOTS

Brodeur is very strong on low shots, using the butterfly sometimes but mostly the half-butterfly. He stretches those legs very quickly.

REBOUND CONTROL

Brodeur is excellent with his stick and with his hands, but since he uses his pads a lot on medium-high shots, he has a tendency to leave some rebounds, especially on the glove side. With a defensive team like the Devils, and given his aggressiveness, rebounds don't hurt him very much.

POSITIONING

This may be Brodeur's strongest point. He is very aggressive and likes to be on top of his crease. Since he squares his big body so well, he doesn't leave much room in the upper corners.

TWO-PAD SLIDE

Because he is not that quick laterally, Brodeur will use the two-pad slide more often than

most goalies today who tend to rely on the butterfly slide. On his blocker side, Brodeur likes to dive with the paddle-down. Brodeur can combine the two-pad stack with the poke check. He often finds himself on his side to play a rebound (#2).

MOVEMENT TIME

For a big guy, Brodeur moves himself pretty quickly in every direction. Because of his size, he doesn't take off as fast as he could on lateral plays, but on the other hand, he reads the play well.

USE OF STICK

Brodeur is one of the best with his stick defensively as well as offensively. Because of his long reach and his strength, he has a great quick-release wrist shot, both on the forehand and on the backhand. The goal he scored on April 17, 1997 is a great example of that quick release. Defensively, he bails himself out very often with his stick by bringing it close to the shooter. Aggressive, he likes to poke check on plays from behind.

MENTAL SKILLS

As one of the top five most efficient goalies through the last four seasons, Brodeur has proved he comes to play every night. He has also proved he can win the big game in the playoffs. His determination, work ethic and intelligent play have made him one of the best in the business.

POSITIONING

Martin Brodeur is one of the toughest goalies to beat on the first shot. On penetration plays, he is always a foot or two atop his crease (#1), and since the New Jersey Devils forwards are very dedicated at backchecking, shooters have to decide quickly whether to shoot or pass.

Brodeur doesn't give them anything and his defensemen usually cover their men pretty well. As a result, the puckcarrier often hesitates and Brodeur is laughing. Brodeur has so much confidence in his defensemen that he plays the odd situation like an even situation, forcing the pass (#1). When his opponents connect, which doesn't happen very often, he is behind the play relying on his reach and aggressiveness.

READING THE PLAY

Brodeur has above-average anticipation and he is even better at forcing the play, just like his teammates. In tight, Brodeur likes to go at the puck carrier who is usually pressed by the defensemen too. Going around Brodeur is very tough.

PUCK FOCUS

This is perhaps the most important asset a goaltender can possess and Brodeur's focus is excellent. He sees the puck well and reacts promptly when it bounces off his body or someone's skate. He also follows the play well on tough scrambles from in tight.

BREAKAWAYS

"On breakaways, move out and back in with the player," say 99.9% of goalie coaches. They also say, "Don't poke check on a breakaway from the middle." Brodeur loves to challenge these axioms. He will often stay at the top of his crease, move out slowly, and then charge the player combining his action with his great poke check. He likes to dive with the paddle down on a deke to his right.

GENERAL

Big save ability, big game ability, coachability, concentration, consistency, desire, work ethic, great reflexes, confidence... Martin Brodeur has the whole package. His career is still young, but he seems on his way to a niche in the Hall of Fame. There can be no doubt that he is the best goaltender in the world under the age of 25. Dominik Hasek is in a class of his own and Brodeur is at the next level with a few 30 year old goaltenders like Roy, Hebert, Joseph, Richter, and Vanbiesbrouck.

INSTINCT

Brodeur can read the play, read the puck early and make desperate instinctive saves like few goalies can. He's got the whole package.

#1:   Third Defenseman: Martin Brodeur works in sync with his defense. Since he has good defensive support, he is not afraid to move out and play the shot. He loves to be on top of his crease to challenge the puckcarrier, leaving his defensemen the task of cutting off the pass.

#2:   Brodeur Kicks on Many Knee-High Shots: On medium-high shots, Martin Brodeur not only stretches the leg, he also gives a little kick forward or sideways with the toes facing up. Rebounds on this type of save tend to bounce further out, giving Brodeur an extra second to get set.

#3:   Five-Hole Shots: Unlike most Quebec goalies, Martin Brodeur doesn't go down systematically into the butterfly on every low shot. Sometimes, on a five-hole shot, he will get caught off balance and he will bring one leg in. As a result, he will end up leaning slightly to the side which hinders his ability to get back up quickly. On lateral slides, Brodeur often ends up in this position and has to play the rebound aggressively.

Style Analysis:
Dominik Hasek

There is only a Stanley Cup missing before two-time Vezina Trophy winner Dominik Hasek will get the recognition he truly deserves, which is "the best puckstopper in the world." He's earned that label by being the most efficient NHL goaltender over the last four seasons. His problem is that the Sabres are no good. In fact, Hasek is 80% of the Buffalo Sabres, who don't even have one player among the top 50 scorers. Worse, they are outshot 9 out of 10 games. With the Sabres finishing second in the Eastern Conference, Hasek should get the Hart Trophy as the NHL's most valuable player. He is a marvelous goaltender, with the best reflexes in the game. No one sees the puck better than he does. He looks bizarre sometimes, falling on his belly or on his back, dropping his stick, or looking like the Statue of Liberty with his catching hand straight up while he is down on his knees. Don't be fooled though. Hasek knows what he's doing, and what he does, he does consistently. No one is even close to his incredible four-season 92.5% save percentage.

OVERALL STYLE

"Dominik Hasek's style is 'no style.' How many times have you heard that? People even laugh at Hasek, saying he is just plain lucky. Well, he's been the luckiest goalie in the world for the past four seasons. He's been head and shoulders above the rest and by a huge one percent (in save percentage).

"Dom is consistent in the way he responds to situations" says his goalie coach Mitch Korn. "In that sense, he has style even if it isn't always pretty." Hasek has all the tools. Great reflexes, flexibility, great hand-eye/foot-eye coordination (see #1below), excellent puckhandling skills, puck sense, ability to read the play and most of all, he is a fighter.

He wants the puck so bad and he will do anything to stop it (#8). Hasek never, ever gives up on a shot, and he keeps his focus game after game. He rarely goes into a slump and when he gets on the roll, he's just unbelievable. He keeps on going for games with the type of performance he showed at the 1997 All-Star Game when he made 20 saves on 21 shots.

GREATNESS POTENTIAL

Hasek is blessed with immense talent but he hasn't been blessed with good teams. He has the potential to steal a Stanley Cup the way Patrick Roy did in 1986 and 1993, but he does not have the leadership of a Patrick Roy for three reasons: His English, while improving, is still limited in scope, his personality is more low profile than Roy's, and he's never won a Stanley Cup. Very few goalies have strong leadership in the locker room and Roy stands out in that department. Hasek will never be that way, but Grant Fuhr has never been like that either and he's won five Stanley Cups. It looks like Hasek is too good not to win the Cup one day, but he's already 32 years old.

BASIC STANCE AND MOVEMENTS

Hasek likes to keep his hands up front (#11). He is so confident and sees the puck so well that he wants to use his hands on every save (#4 and #9). His glove hand is right above the top of his left pad and his elbow is tight to the body. You will rarely see a puck go through Hasek's body. His stick is perpendicular and his legs are pretty much spread apart. The five-hole is low. Hands are in front. Hasek likes to stand still on a straight shot when a player is releasing. He wants to catch the puck or deflect it to a corner.

STRAIGHT SHOTS

Hasek will put a knee down (or both knees) on most shots, even high ones. His upper body stays upright when he feels the puck will go up (#1) and folds when the puck is low to the crotch (#2). Hasek is also very flexible and will raise his blocker or catching glove way above his shoulders (#1) and with incredible speed. Down on his knees, he can make a point blank save with his hands on a shot going just under the crossbar. Hasek has a good butterfly (#7), and a good half-butterfly on either side. When Hasek is off his game, which doesn't happen very often, he has a tendency to stand up a little too much on medium-high shots. He is most efficient when he does a half-butterfly on shots to the lower corners. Most of the time, he will make the save with his blocker or with his glove hand.

REBOUND CONTROL

Hasek may not be pretty but he is not sloppy. He is perhaps the best goaltender at controlling rebounds either by deflecting them to the corners, smothering them into his body or jumping on loose pucks at great speed (#10). Sometimes it's hard to freeze a loose puck on the blocker side, but Hasek is so intense that he can get rid of his stick and freeze the puck with his right hand in one move (#10). This is very hard to do in scrambles when you have to jump on the puck like a cat on a mouse.

PLAYING THE REBOUND

This is one part where Hasek is a master and paradoxically, this is also where he may look "funny." Hasek follows that puck like no one else does. He sees it bouncing off his pad or off his chest and when there is danger on the rebound, he leads all of his movements with his head (#8).

He wants his head and his body close to the puck. If it's in front, he may fall forward on his belly (#6z). If it's behind him or to the side, he may fall backward or to the side. He may also use the shaft-down technique, the butterfly (#7), the dive, the two-pad stack (#5), the half-butterfly, or the Hasek "special sprawl." If he is on his knees, weight forward, and the puck is far to the side, he won't go headfirst to the puck like he often does. He will fall forward on his belly (#6) and stretch the leg all the way behind him to the post or even forward toward the shooter's stick blade. By doing this "ugly" move, Hasek achieves one thing, he reaches out further and faster. A smart play.

SCREEN SHOTS

As mentioned before, Hasek is a fighter. He will do anything to see that puck but if by some chance he does not see a point shot take off, he has the ability to scan through the

screen and see that puck coming out of nowhere and to make a reflex save with whatever part of his body is closest to the puck.

PUCK BEHIND THE NET

Hasek plays pretty much a classical game there. He stands up and does not try very much to cut the pass. His body faces the front of the net and just the head is turned. He moves well toward the shooter, charging standing up or in the butterfly.

THE TWO-PAD STACK

Hasek will use the two-pad stack on a third shot after a butterfly save or on a breakaway, combining the stack with a poke check attempt. He may also use it on a passing play and sometimes on a screen (#5).

PUCKHANDLING

Hasek likes to chase loose pucks. He wants that puck and really goes after it. He is an excellent puckhandler with good vision of the play. He always makes the right play. He is also always looking to make a pass when he is in control of the puck after a save. This is another part of his game that is underestimated because he makes it look so simple. Hasek really helps out his defensemen.

BREAKAWAYS

Hasek likes to come way out, giving the player little to shoot at and forcing him to deke. He backs in with good speed. He is very flexible (#12), so he is very difficult to deke. He keeps very good control over his arm when going down for the stretch so if his leg does not reach far enough, he can stretch out his arm to make another "impossible" Hasek save.

TWO-ON-ONES

When the puckhandler is on an angle, Hasek will move out and back in just like he does on a breakaway. The backward speed he gets helps him to move across the crease on the backdoor option when a pass is made across.

CENTERING PASS THROUGH TRAFFIC

Hasek likes to move laterally in the butterfly and can get back up on his feet very quickly after that slide. He can move and keep control of his hands.

POKE CHECK

Hasek will use the poke (sweep) check on a bad-angle cut, especially from the right wing and even against a left-hander.

HE HAS ALL THE TOOLS

Dominik Hasek really has all the tools. He can stand up, follow a player with the T-push, play the butterfly blocking game, control rebounds exceptionally well and his coach, Mitch Korn, adds that Hasek is a fast learner. "He never makes the same mistake twice" he says. "You tell him something once and he remembers it forever."

A GREAT RECORD

Just to get an idea how great Hasek is, look at his overall record in the past 4 seasons as well as the honors he has collected, both in the Czech Republic and North America.

People most remember Hasek for his famous 1993-94 season where he recorded a 1.95 goals-against-average, the first sub-2.00 season in over 20 years.

However his 93% save percentage was much more impressive. Goalies should be remembered for their saves not for their goals-against.

#1: Vision: Hasek's vision of the puck is the best in the NHL. Dominik Hasek's greatest strength is his focus. He sees the puck like nobody else does. His eyes are glued to the puck. On screen shots, if he doesn't see the release, he has the uncanny ability to pick up the puck when it comes out of the screen and to make a pure reflexive save.

#2: Following the Puck: Hasek follows the puck all the way to his body, leaning his head, a good sign of a hot goalie. That way, he controls the rebounds better and if he can't he's ready to jump like a cat in the direction where the puck is going.

#3: No Sloppy Hands: Even when moving laterally on a centering pass, Hasek keeps control of his hands and is ready to react with both his blocker and catcher.

#4: Picks Up a Puck Out of the Screen: No one reacts quicker to a puck coming out of a screen than Hasek. He will do any move, including ones used by Ken Dryden 20 years ago.

#5: Two-Pad Stack: Hasek uses the two-pad stack on second and third rebounds, breakaways (combined with the poke check), and some screen shots.

#6: The Belly Trick! When out of position in a scramble, Hasek will often fall forward on his belly. This allows him to extend his legs further backward to the post or forward to the shooter's blade.

#7: Great Positioning: One of Hasek's strengths is positioning. He can move way out very fast, stand still on top of his crease or play deep if necessary. Good butterfly, also.

#8: Whatever It Takes: If Hasek gets caught out of position, he will improvise a way to get back in the shooter's line. He does it so fast that he seems to have a chance on any kind of play. Tough guy to beat.

#9: Hands First: Hasek is so focused on the puck and he is so quick that he can use his hands on more shots than most goalies.

#10: Few Garbage Goals: Garbage scorers don't get many rebounds with Hasek. He jumps on loose pucks so fast. He is the only one who can get rid of his stick quick and freeze a puck with his blocker hand.

#11: Hands Up Front: One of the reasons Hasek is so good with his hands is that he keeps them in front of his body in his basic stance. Hasek is a getter. He can block the puck but he wants to get it badly.

Goalies' World
Magazine

Goalies' World

Over the years, the art of goaltending has been the subject of considerable scrutiny both on film and at hockey schools.

But never in the history of puckstopping has there been a monthly magazine devoted exclusively to the netminding profession.

This literary milestone was achieved when Quebec City-native Gilles Moffet published the first issue of *Goalies' World* magazine in February 1996.

"I wanted to create a publication that would make the goaltending position better known, not only to aficionados but to the general public as well." Moffet explains.

As part of its scientific look at the profession, *Goalies' World* designed a new formula to rate goaltenders. According to Moffet, the traditional goals against average is very limited and flawed in evaluating goalies, and although save percentage is an improvement in rating netminders, it doesn't tell the whole story either.

Goalies' World's special formula compares the number of games played, save percentage, and the number of shots faced per game. In addition, the system considers wins and shutouts, although they are less valued.

"The primary reason for the formula is that it enables us to examine the goalies individually," Moffet continues. "It separates their talent from the quality of the team for whom they play. We are able to see how a last-place team could have the best goalie in the league. It is unfair to penalize a goalie if his team is unsuccessful."

On the theory that it takes one to know one, *Goalie's World* is well endowed. Moffet is a goalie himself and has played for much of his life.

"Being a goalie, I can understand how it feels to be misunderstood. I played at the college level for Merrimack in Massachusetts, minor-pro for the East Coast League in Virginia, and I wanted to play pro, but I was late in my development. I thought to myself, `Is there a better way to stay involved in the game and my position?' That's how Goalies' World was born."

Since its debut, *Goalies' World* has drawn critical acclaim from the netminding fraternity, especially since it runs regular instruction pieces by NHL goalie coaches such as Francois Allaire of the Mighty Ducks and Mitch Korn of the Sabres.

"We have the potential of reaching, 40,000 or 50,000 circulation," says Moffet. "We will find a good balance between the serious fan, the media and the goalie."

For those interested in subscriptions to *Goalie's World*, phone (418) 847-0861.

Goalies' World Magazine's
1996-97 Seasonal Awards

BEST-RANKED ROOKIE — **TOMMY SALO**

Patrick Lalime made a theatrical entrance halfway through the season and faded out, but Tommy Salo, who had split time evenly with Eric Fichaud halfway through the season, started to play every game in the playoff drive and had a strong finish. Lalime was more efficient, but Salo played in 58 games compared to only 39 for Lalime.

BEST RETURN OF THE YEAR — **CURTIS JOSEPH**

After a tough 1995-96 season in which he was a contract holdout, Edmonton's Curtis Joseph moved back to the upper class where he belongs. (*Runner-up: Ron Tugnutt*)

SURPRISE OF THE YEAR — **PATRICK LALIME**

No one, including the Pittsburgh Penguins, expected Patrick Lalime to move up in the NHL and to become a hot item like he did this year. (*Runner-up: Ron Tugnutt*)

BEST TRANSITION FROM NO. 2 TO NO. 1 — **JEFF HACKETT**

Ed Belfour's health problems over the last two seasons in Chicago allowed Jeff Hackett to prove his value. He has done so well that he made the legendary Belfour expendable.

MOST OUTSTANDING FEAT — **DOMINIK HASEK**

For a third time in four years, Dominik Hasek recorded an incredible 93% save percentage. Doing this once is phenomenal. Doing it three times is unreal. (*Runner-up: Patrick Lalime*)

MOST REMARKABLE SEQUENCE — **GARTH SNOW...RON HEXTALL**

Four shutouts in a row is something to remember. Garth Snow and Ron Hextall will cherish forever this feat they realized in December 1996, signing two shutouts each. Patrick Lalime's 15-game winning streak is also an NHL record for a newcomer in the league. (*Runner-up: Patrick Lalime*)

BEST DUO — **VANBIESBROUCK...FITZPATRICK**

John Vanbiesbrouck and Mark Fitzpatrick are the only pair of goaltenders the Florida Panthers have had since their first season in 1993-94, and they are doing quite a job. The Beezer is one of the best No. 1 goalies, and Fitzpatrick, one of the top backups. (*Runner-up: Ken Wregget...Patrick Lalime*)

IS HE FOR REAL? — **PATRICK LALIME**

After fantastic results following his midseason promotion from the IHL, Patrick Lalime

went cold. Is he a superstar in the making? Is he backup material? Is he just a minor-leaguer? The answer could be yes to any of the above questions. He has all the tools though. (*Runner-up: Tommy Salo*)

BEST QUOTE OF THE YEAR — **ANDY MOOG**
"The NHL is going to find out that the best players in hockey are the goalies."
- Andy Moog, November 1996, a few days before the installment of the new rule on 12-inch pads. Scoring did not increase since Nov. 15.

SAVED HIS CAREER — **RON TUGNUTT**
In one year, 30 year old Ron Tugnutt went from a minor-league goalie in 1995-96 to a backup NHL goalie, to a season savior with Ottawa. (*Runner-up: Byron Dafoe*)

MOST OVERRATED — **BILL RANFORD**
Bill Ranford isn't the same goalie he once was. The Capitals thought he would carry them into the playoffs, but he didn't. (*Runner-up: Jim Carey*)

MOST DISAPPOINTING GOALIE — **JIM CAREY**
A Vezina Trophy winner falling flat on his back like Jim Carey did this year is certainly a huge disappointment. Kirk McLean's 88.9 save percentage is also quite short of his talent.

MOST TAKEN FOR GRANTED — **FELIX POTVIN**
Felix Potvin struggled at times but he is still one of the few bright spots in Toronto. (*Runner-up: Jocelyn Thibault*)

MOST FRAGILE GOALIE — **TOM BARRASSO**
Big goalies are not necessarily the most durable as the last season proved. (*Runner-up: Darren Puppa*)

WORST DUO — **KIRK MCLEAN...CORY HIRSCH**
In Vancouver, Cory Hirsch has not established himself as a No.1 goalie and Kirk McLean is not what he once was. (*Runner-up: Damian Rhodes...Ron Tugnutt*)

BEST SINGLE-GAME PERFORMANCE — **CURTIS JOSEPH**
Edmonton Oiler Curtis Joseph made 52 saves in a 0-0 deadlock on December 10, 1996, at Detroit. On March 2, 1997, Patrick Roy stopped 46 Whalers shots in a 4-0 Colorado win.

A GAME TO FORGET — **PATRICK LALIME**
Pittsburgh Penguins rookie sensation Patrick Lalime gave up four goals on five shots and was pulled after eight minutes of play on March 26, 1997, in Montreal. On February 1, 1997, in Hartford, young Whalers prospect Jean-Sebastien Giguere got the hook even faster, after only 5 minutes of play. He had given up three goals on five shots.

WORST MANAGEMENT DECISION — **MONTREAL CANADIENS**

When the Montreal Canadiens fired veteran backup Pat Jablonski in February and called up a young tiger in Jose Theodore, they added incredible pressure on to the shoulders of their 22 year old No. 1 goalie, Jocelyn Thibault, and it affected his play.

MINOR LEAGUE GOALIE DESERVING AN NHL CHANCE — **FREDERICK CHABOT**

Any NHL team in need of a backup goalie ought to look seriously at the best minor league veterans such as Frederic Chabot, Geoff Sargeant, Stephane Beauregard, Jean-Francois Labbe, and a few others. Just look at what recent minor-league graduates Patrick Lalime, Steve Shields, Ron Tugnutt, Tommy Salo, Marcel Cousineau, and Dwayne Roloson have all accomplished this season.

Goalies' World
Top 26 Ratings

1. Dominik Hasek
2. Martin Brodeur
3. Guy Hebert
4. Patrick Roy
5. Felix Potvin
6. Mike Richter
7. Nikolai Khabibulin
8. Curtis Joseph
9. John Vanbiesbrouck
10. Grant Fuhr
11. Jeff Hackett
12. Jocelyn Thibault
13. Sean Burke
14. Tommy Salo
15. Rick Tabaracci
16. Andy Moog
17. Chris Osgood
18. Stephane Fiset
19. Patrick Lalime
20. Trevor Kidd
21. Ken Wregget
22. Ron Hextall
23. Ed Belfour
24. Byron Dafoe
25. Mark Fitzpatrick
26. Bill Ranford